War and Peace

War and Peace

The Life and Times of General Sir Richard Barrons

Richard Barrons

To Duncan,

With best wishes

Richard Barrons

Pen & Sword
MILITARY

First published in Great Britain in 2024 by
Pen & Sword Military
An imprint of Pen & Sword Books Limited
Yorkshire – Philadelphia

Copyright © Richard Barrons 2024

ISBN 978 1 39905 498 0

The right of Richard Barrons to be identified as
Author of this Work has been asserted by him in accordance
with the Copyright, Designs and Patents Act 1988.

A CIP catalogue record for this book is
available from the British Library

All rights reserved. No part of this book may be reproduced or
transmitted in any form or by any means, electronic or mechanical
including photocopying, recording or by any information storage and
retrieval system, without permission from the Publisher in writing.

Typeset by Mac Style
Printed in the UK by CPI Group (UK) Ltd, Croydon, CR0 4YY.

Pen & Sword Books Limited incorporates the imprints of After
the Battle, Atlas, Archaeology, Aviation, Discovery, Family History,
Fiction, History, Maritime, Military, Military Classics, Politics,
Select, Transport, True Crime, Air World, Frontline Publishing, Leo
Cooper, Remember When, Seaforth Publishing, The Praetorian Press,
Wharncliffe Local History, Wharncliffe Transport, Wharncliffe True
Crime and White Owl.

For a complete list of Pen & Sword titles please contact:

PEN & SWORD BOOKS LIMITED
47 Church Street, Barnsley, South Yorkshire, S70 2AS, England
E-mail: enquiries@pen-and-sword.co.uk
Website: www.pen-and-sword.co.uk
or
PEN AND SWORD BOOKS
1950 Lawrence Road, Havertown, PA 19083, USA
E-mail: uspen-and-sword@casematepublishers.com
Website: www.penandswordbooks.com

Contents

Introduction		vi
Chapter 1	Cold War Germany	1
Chapter 2	Surprise	17
Chapter 3	Bosnia 1992	32
Chapter 4	Travel	53
Chapter 5	Afghanistan 2002	64
Chapter 6	Work	89
Chapter 7	Iraq 2003	104
Chapter 8	Technology and War	123
Chapter 9	On Nearly Being a General 2004–8	141
Chapter 10	Leadership	156
Chapter 11	On Being a Major General	173
Chapter 12	Senior Generalship	196
Index		214

Introduction

My Dear M,

So here – finally – is the bundle of recollections, ramblings, observations and recommendations that has filled quite a lot of correspondence between us one way or another for the past few years. Mostly from me to you, with you doing a lot of 'uhuh', I realize. I agree (now) that it is neater to have them bundled in one place, but I am still pressed to explain if or how they are worthwhile in any way? Is there anything here that will add a single jot to the sum of mankind's wisdom and behaviour, even if there bloody well should be after all this effort? But then, as you know well, the point may have passed some time ago in my little life when the giving of a fuck of any shade ceased to have any great utility.

Nonetheless, in unburdening myself of all this I feel better. These letters lay before you whatever has most forcefully struck me about my meander through life. They are mostly about 'a career' in the British Army (for want of a better explanation for expending the central portion of an entire adult life on the subject of duffing up the enemies of the Queen (now King) when invited). And now I dwell in the Afterlife, out of uniform and operating in alien country – business mostly, but some other cobblers too. The army was a universe I understood well, enjoyed mostly, and generally tolerated its many madnesses and idiocies with something approaching good humour.

Latterly, with uniform off and suit on (yes, a suit, not and never sportswear in the workplace I suggest) there is an entirely new universe to come to terms with. I am navigating the wobbly transition from general steely-eyed killer, to captain, of industry. On some days I would think that having my genitals whipped off in a forcible exchange of Mr for Miss (or the other pronoun in the middle that I can't recall but is suddenly really popular and – I concur – important) would be an easier and more explicable transition. For sure, a running comparison of how my life was then with how it is now is a constant source of wonder to me. As you know to your cost in periodic lost evenings at dodgy restaurants, the change provokes some observations about what I used to do and sprouts talk of where life/afterlife have themes in common or diverge.

What both lives have in common is that the failure to do what is known to be the best or right thing to do is not only daft but also courts certain disaster. And yet our lives are beset by so many 'errors of drill', by accident or design. Whether it is loading an artillery gun with the shell back to front (don't try this at home), or failing to keep an eye on the cash flow in my business like, these basic drills do matter – and the same applies in matters of state and strategy, with even more spectacular consequences for trying to wing it despite knowing better.

To some extent these letters to you are nakedly autobiographical, because they draw quite heavily on the things I did or the prominent features of what turned out to be almost for forty years on the payroll of the British Army. But this collection is still not meant as autobiography because I see no need to dredge up anything dull or disappointing (as these would fill at least two more volumes, and you don't have that much trouble sleeping). I stick to just some bits of a life that strike me as more interesting or relatable. Some of these are about the lessons I took rather than the history of what happened in detail. Loads of others do that better. I don't think I have made a whole lot up.

You have often asked me why I joined the British Army in the first place and why it turned into such a relatively long stay, and I still don't think I have an answer that can explain it adequately. If you ask me now if I would do it all over again the answer is … 'obviously not' – it was way too much like serious hard work some of the time and the pay is nothing to shout about.

Next time I'm going to be Bruce Springsteen, apart from the bit which involves me driving across America in the dark, with no money for gas and half starving. There must have been more to me taking the Queen's shilling than just being army-barmy as a youngster, though I certainly was enthusiastic about marching my siblings and peers up and down the road by around 9 years old, whether they were keen on this or not. Probably good that I was not born in time for some of the Big Marching aspects of the 1930s. Still, it was always clear to me then that my juvenile troop needed as they still need today, to put much more work into their foot drill and saluting. My mother thinks I've always had a bit of a thing for a smart hat. I ever really thought I understood myself well enough to explain why I started as a soldier, I now hide behind too many years to look back on it with enough wisdom and objectivity. I will commit only to set down for you what looks groovy enough for posterity. Probably not unique in adopting this stratagem.

So it was all long ago enough that I just don't recall well what got me to the gates of the Royal Military Academy Sandhurst to start (on 2 September 1977) what was then called a University Cadetship. I am going with the explanation that there was more to it than a solid conviction that a splendid uniform would be a lady-magnet. If I did think that, experience clearly establishes that the pulling power of the magnificent Royal Regiment of Artillery mess dress, notably the taut buttock-hugging trousers with a hot red stripe worn over knee-length leather riding boots and spurs, is an ensemble that scores highly on attraction and very poorly on execution.

Basically, by the time one has secured (lawfully) a lady (in my case) in one's quarters and successfully extracted oneself from the tight grip of Victorian trousers by lengthy and sweaty rolling about on the floor, the lady in question has usually either gone off the boil and is now being disparaging about my failures in baking and knitting. There might have been serious career alternatives, being a lawyer for example, but this looked too much to me like a life sentence of permanent detention indoors stuck dealing with a lot of whingers, with hardly any scope for shooting even the most annoying tosspots. Soldiering at least meant that some bumping off would be allowed in the name of Her Majesty.

All the memory capacity available at the time I joined up was immediately filled by a state of constant exhaustion, alarm, bewilderment, and occasional joy, tightly woven with obsessive ironing and advanced shoe polishing. This is the traditional entrée to La Vie Militaire, a process of calibrated personal reduction through constant superfluous shouting, whilst absorbing a tonne of new stuff like shooting and all that synchronized brisk walking in threes. The latter, as noted, I already had good form in. This reduction to a state of military malleability is still the essential rite of passage before one eventually rises to the required glittering status of a young officer, like a brilliantly executed soufflé.

There is some joy in the Afterlife now, and a whole lot less exhaustion, alarm, and bewilderment, but my trousers will bear creases sharp enough to cut toast and my shoes will exist in a state of ecstatic burnish for as long as there is breath in my body. I automatically recognize the importance of being five minutes early for everything (which cumulatively across a lifetime must be at least a year's worth of premature). I also retain the imperative of avoiding at all costs being lost in the dark in a wood as an alternative to sleep, and I accept still that a compass in the hands of a muppet like me is an aid to navigation that pretty much ensures being lost and sleep deprived.

Perhaps more usefully, the career-long debate started at Sandhurst about the lunacy of trying to compel me, the one only able to shoot with my left eye as the other one likes to do its own thing, to shoot from the right shoulder because it is 'neater' (and since about 1984, this does also avoid being burned and bruised by spent cartridge cases). Perhaps this is why I was drawn to the Royal Regiment of Artillery, with guns so large that the choice of eyeball was irrelevant? Maybe that is why I am a Gunner.

My military initiation at Sandhurst lasted only three weeks before I also started as a student at Oxford, where I could develop at my own pace into one of the very worst Philosophy, Politics, and Economics undergraduates that The Queen's College has ever sponsored. I am certainly their only Honorary Fellow appointed to celebrate that the College has a sense of humour. I'm still hopeful that my lack of studiousness was not only because I was relatively thick for the population of the Dreaming Spires, but mostly because there were really quite a lot of other things to fit into an eight-week term.

This did include more army stuff than was really necessary or useful, and of course deep theoretical commitment to polishing up the genitals-based skills and drills that were a massive priority of the day. When my three years as a student paramilitary were up, I would undoubtedly have headed to the city like everybody else at the time, but the five-year commitment I contractually had still to deliver to the army meant otherwise – the door to riches clanging – eternally it now seems – firmly shut behind me on the day I left Oxford. In fact, the deal in 1980 was I could stay in army boots until I was 55, the kind of job security that only nuns and BA cabin crew get now.

Why did it really still take so long to leave? Even with the benefit of well-researched hindsight I struggle to articulate a cogent answer. There is definitely something about military service being a vocation and I recall in the early years regarding any dark thoughts of bailing out as essentially heretical. This was a pity as those dark thoughts came free and full on almost every occasion when I was passing my evening in a cold, wet wood somewhere in Germany without realistic hope of sleep. Bailing out, in the mid-1980s, obviously still meant heading to the City, where it seemed to me my peers were doing an excellent job of trousering huge bundles of cash, the fruits of bounteous de-regulation of the financial services sector. They were not *all* doing things like buying mews houses in Knightsbridge and spanking-new Ferraris to park outside, but most bloody well were.

I yearned then, as I yearn now, for cars that start every morning and come with generous manufacturer guarantees – and in 1983 I also yearned for the sweet magic of a stereo cassette player with tiny coloured lights flashing in utterly incomprehensible and irrelevant ways, roughly accompanying the banging-most tunes of the day. In addition to taste-free automotive HiFi, my civilian peers were also all squiring their way through well-executed sequences of lady-friends (remember that at this time being homosexual was wholly unfashionable due to the beatings that inevitably accrued). My only constant night-time companion at this time in Germany was the British Forces Broadcasting Service, which back then basically took the very best of BBC and ITV, put it all straight in the bin and broadcast the rest with huge pauses for preachy bits like 'be nice to the Hun, they mean well now'.

The ladies being squired by my London friends were, of course, also the beneficiaries of the city cash fountain. This largesse underpinned the dedication with which I observed (only from afar) how they honed their loveliness with fabulous, pheromone-infused unctions, and regular elimination of any hint of unwanted beard or claw. As I saw it from my unrelenting BFBS-accompanied isolation in a shithole garrison somewhere in a part of Germany that even the Russians didn't really want, the advantages of buying my own roof and using it to bring great joy to the fragrant ladies of the town was a stronger pitch for my life's energies than shelling stuff to bits. If the alternative in 1984 really was spending weeks, turning to months, turning to years in wet pine forests whilst I rose slowly from junior to slightly less junior officer, all just in case the Warsaw Pact arrived on a big tank-based excursion to the West, I realized I was going to crack quite quickly. There might have been some nobility of purpose in stagging-on, but not one I could swing with forever. And yet.

And yet, stay I did. About ten years of regimental duty were focused on being ever readier for heroic annihilation in the early stages of the Cold War as 'I popped in and out of stints in West Germany, leavened by the courses that festoon a junior officer's life. There was the occasional dangling of a chance to serve in the latter stages of an extraordinarily long and lumpy campaign in Northern Ireland. On reflection, in an era well before even Mark Zuckerberg was invented, I now realize that there was an analogue algorithm at work that meant there was always a hurdle approaching in the steeplechase of military life that would be sufficiently compelling to see if I cleared in competition with my peers.

There were exams to pass and recommendations to earn, as well as generally very stimulating passages of time learning to lead, understand, and more than occasionally laugh with soldiers – and they at me. In what other profession can one ask one's subordinates about their aspiration for immediate relaxation, once the tedious horror of yet another week rehearsing our certain destruction in a cold wet wood had passed, to be informed in the broadest Yorkshire of the earnest intent to:

'Fookin gerrome, gerrold of the missus, get fookin shitfaced'.

You don't see much of that on Twitter.

When the Cold War inevitably and inconveniently ended itself in 1990, there was another moment when ducking out for a different career looked sensible. If the entire edifice of the British Army of the Rhine was about to crumble without the Soviet Union around to abhor, how might one find fulfilment in the shape of new and bigger badges and a properly menacing foe to tackle? Happily, Saddam Hussein promptly helped out a bit by invading Kuwait, although I was by then entrenched in my stint at the Army Staff College and thereby rendered unavailable for giving him and his agents the kicking that they had so usefully brought upon themselves. It is hard to underestimate, even at this distance, what a shock it was in 1991 for the army to have to take most of itself to a desert and actually expend tonnes of ammunition in earnest; it is even harder to articulate the misery of those of us who were left out and kept in school.

Worse, possibly, was accepting the reality that the price of a place at Staff College was tantamount to a commitment to stay in uniform for at least another decade or so. This dawned even as the serious limits of an army captain's pay to render unto a wife and what would shortly manifest as a brace of daughters all the essential trappings of middle-class life hit home hard. The British Army clung to the Edwardian sense of social order rather longer than the Edwardians, but even so the imperative to convert a smallish married quarter with 1950s plumbing into Downton Abbey was never to be matched by the cash from the Queen that this mission demanded. All my Staff College contemporaries were in the same boat, apart from the students from the Gulf, who seemed to have tonnes of moolah. The obvious answer for us was to plough all available spare cash into a Labrador, as walking and clearing up dog sick is free.

Moving still further out of reach at this time (and indeed now) were the loft apartments and increasingly shiny and menacing BMWs of the civvy contemporaries who were beginning to rejoice in their standing as a deputy this or associate that in the civilian profession or larceny of their choice. On the other hand, the time bar on leaving that came with Staff College was tantalisingly amplified by the prospect that just after it expired I would be sort of pensionable and I might make the cut for promotion to lieutenant colonel and the absolute gold plated and velvet lined prize of command of a regiment. I thought then, as I think now, that command would be a life led to the full. I may be a duffer in so many ways, but I was still the commanding officer of 3 Regiment Royal Horse Artillery and fewer than twenty-five living souls can say that at any one time.

On the other side of the equation just as I felt the sugar-rush of command, I now detected that just perhaps some of the light was beginning to go out behind the eyes of my civvy counterparts. Maybe the joy they found in posh metal and decorous housing was diminished by the seeping realization that the things they flogged over in their well-padded offices, with free frothy coffee for so many hours each day, would be the very same things they had to flog for the rest of their working lives. I, in contrast, could still devote myself to understanding how to visit violence ranging from industrial-scale slaughter to a bijou killingette upon all and any enemies of my country – which by happy circumstance were increasingly becoming the enemies of the United States. That seemed to bring more and bigger work. I may have only owned one working suit, but I did not have to contemplate the cruelty and misery of a packed commuter train five days a week, and I resolved to make it a lifelong objective never to do so. That bit hasn't entirely worked out.

What actually followed was broadly a decade spent on the Balkans. The first encounter as a major when newly installed as the chief of staff of an armoured brigade in Germany I found myself in late 1992 setting up the initial British deployment to Bosnia at a week's notice. Then came a six-month stint as a Balkan 'expert' in MoD; then training and deploying for another six-month Balkan tour as Battery Commander of B Battery RHA (boss of about 100 men and women working very large artillery guns). This actually lasted only a week before morphing into a lively year as a spanking-new lieutenant colonel working for the Office of the High Representative in Sarajevo and Brussels. Finally, in 2001 I took my regiment, the fighting 3rd Regiment Royal Horse Artillery (550 soldiers), on another six-month deployment to both Bosnia and Kosovo concurrently. So the Balkans became a big deal for me, and it is gratifying to see how very settled, prosperous, and cordial the whole place is now.

This decade was so different to the Cold War and so unscripted at the start that it constituted a personal and professional voyage of discovery. There were many cock ups, some genuine disasters, some actual successes, and enough adrenaline to feel like life on the edge from time to time. Having been sent in 1992 on the strict understanding that for the UK this would be, without a shadow of a doubt, at most a six-month job I could be forgiven a hint of an ironic smirk when as a brigadier in around 2007 (just the fourteen years later) I finally went to a place called Banja Luka to check how it was being shut down. Nor does that mean it's actually over, there are still British soldiers working in Bosnia as I write. Some of the learnings from all this appear later in our correspondence.

The experience of working in a broken, rundown, deeply factionalized and occasionally bizarre environment was pretty faithfully replicated by my stints in the Ministry of Defence in London. The first of these occurred in the mid-1980s, when as a twenty-something captain I was catapulted into Fulham from a lengthy rural confinement on a former Second World War air station in the middle of Warwickshire. I had been well occupied there, mostly cultivating being stentorian, as the Adjutant of the Royal Artillery's Junior Leaders' Regiment. This regiment took in 16-year-old school leavers and gave them such an excellent year of education, development, and training that it produced some of the finest soldiers in the army, many of them serving for twenty years or more. The cost of that year per head was more than Eton, but the return to the taxpayer was worth way more and didn't involve quite so much overdressing or crumpeting. Though since resurrected in apprentice form, this particular regiment was such a good scheme – transformative for the young men who found a place there – that somebody very wise felt it needed to be closed down in the 1990s.

In Warwickshire, I had noted with bitter regret in between mandatory church parades that the army's idea of amusement was to post me from a German wilderness to an English one, just at that time in one's life when considerations of founding domestic bliss and a spot of breeding had begun to impinge upon the hitherto unquestioned dominance of reckless driving and serial rumpy-pumpy with ladies of few questions (or, generally, any names that I can now recall). Forgiveness came easily on the day when a large army truck dumped me and all my worldly goods outside a one-bedroom flat just off the Wandsworth Bridge Road to start a two-year posting in Whitehall. This was like being born again: no more wilderness, or cold dark woods, or PT before breakfast unless I really wanted to, or the highs and lows of life in an officers' mess committed to theme-parking a period costume drama.

Instead, there would now be bright lights, central heating that worked, restaurants which offered more than very very long-dead fish accompanied by soggy chips, and cinemas that were not full of 17-year-old boy soldiers noisily fuelling their skin dramas with dollops of fat, sugar and carbon dioxide. There would also be, let's not forget, the need to embrace with joy public transport – a need considerably expedited by the early theft of my beloved bicycle from outside the flat.

There would, for the first time, also be the need to go to work dressed in a suit and tie, something of a shock after several years of combat pyjamas and boots. My need to get a grip of my wardrobe became apparent when quite early on in the tour the arse of my trousers rent asunder in the office, resulting in a long day with the remnants held together through prodigious and discomfiting use of the office stapler. Far more egregious, however, was that for the first time since leaving Oxford I now fell back on my almost totally absent skills in catering. This has never been a strong hand, still almost no progress from student days to now, and I was as grateful then as I am now to whomsoever provided mankind with the miracle of the microwave oven and the artfully constructed dishes of comprehensively processed pap that become nourishment in four minutes. Followed by chocolate anything.

This – in 1986 – was the old Ministry of Defence, broadly speaking wheezing along exactly as it was built in the late 1930s. It is possible that it had been dusted once or twice in between. The layout reflected the preference of an age when it was normal for a human to want their own space, so there were corridors of corridors, each hundreds of yards long, sprouting an immense and probably uncountable number of small offices containing somewhere between one-to-four servants of the State. The colour scheme was Resolutely Brown. In order to keep Russia out of meddling in the supply of socks and biros to the armed forces, each door had to be secured with the key provided whenever a room was vacated. A lock with the breaking-strain of a Mars Bar stood between the secrets and the foreign spies patrolling the corridor twenty-four hours a day. Civil servants were still provided with soap and a towel, which obviously had to be handed back when they took holiday. Military had to provide their own. No, me neither.

As an Army captain in this 'strategic environment' I was positioned somewhere between an amoeba and deeply insignificant bacteria on that long scale of life that peoples the ministry. There were so few of us children that we attracted a certain casual curiosity, performing like super magnets to attract any truly rubbish work that nobody else ever wanted to do. My role was to programme every waking minute of the life of a very senior general, reducing the number of occasions on which he stepped out on vital business either wearing the wrong attire (from a choice of at least sixteen different forms of dress), or without a written note telling him where he was going, why, a couple of lines to make it look like he cared, and a note of his name and home address. I felt I was busy enough anyway.

I quickly established that the key to a happy life was to encourage the Military Assistant to the Master General of the Ordnance, in my capacity as the Assistant Military Assistant to the Master General of the Ordnance, to agree with the Master General of the Ordnance himself where in the world they most needed to go for at least a fortnight. The purpose of this visit would be to study something crashingly dull in foreign lands about how military procurement fails as spectacularly there as it does in the UK, and report back in writing.

These trips were especially useful if they included the US or Australia, the former accessed via Concord if enough of a sense of urgent crisis could be conjured up. As I could always find enough of the crushingly dull things my master liked to goggle at somewhere warm and exotic, the pain of the journey was easily ameliorated anyway. This was the day before computers took everything over, so as long as I could find my way through the giant book in tiny print that recorded every single flight everywhere in the world, I could stitch up something reliably interesting and with decent business class flights. All would be well. Whilst the party travelled, I stayed in London to keep a vague and untutored eye on what was going on back in the shop, otherwise at liberty to explore the capital without all the distractions that having a demanding employer around conferred.

When I later went back to the MoD as a lieutenant colonel in 1997, for two more years of weekly-boarding as the Military Assistant (i.e. a private secretary with shinier shoes and a decent haircut) to the Chief of the General Staff (the general who ran the army), nothing about the building had changed a jot. I was by then no longer primordial, having risen up the chain of life to settle somewhere around homo sapiens, but definitely below the level of celestial. Only a key to one of the private lavvies reserved for the most senior and ancient could unlock that.

By this time (1997), I understood the MoD well enough to know that it was the place that politicians, civil servants, and the leadership of the armed forces came together to throttle each other – pausing only occasionally and with impatient exasperation to fend off nuclear holocaust or the threat of invasion to congeal into enough of a tissue of cooperation. Some of this is historic, the antipathy a navy, army, and air force feel for each other is deeply rooted in the conviction that their sibling services are gobblers of money, attention and enemies that should rightly be left in the safe hands of (insert preferred service here). Thus, the navy would thrust itself forward as the vital act in the campaign in Afghanistan even though this blighted country is 1,000 miles from the nearest sea; the RAF could not imagine why the navy needed any flying machines when they could be so superbly provided in a lighter shade of blue; and the army asserted that as all wars are about duffing up loads of humans who inhabit neither the seas nor the skies so the role of the other two services was just to organize the transport.

Whilst these three cats sought out as many sacks in which to scrap with each other as possible, the MoD Civil Service sat around them making it massively complicated to know how all the money had mysteriously ended up in the hands of the defence industry. This was done without much new kit turning up or the old stuff kept in working order – and certainly without end in sight of soldiers' bedrooms ever becoming the beneficiaries of more hot water and less mould. And above everybody a conveyor belt of politicians of all shapes and sizes was passing through in the various flavours of defence minister. Some came as excited as a young man given a free season ticket to a brothel, others in deep despair that they didn't get 'health' or 'education' (though of course hugely relieved to avoid the Home Office), and many were just struggling to know what day of the week it was and where the next biscuit was coming from. The constitutional subordination of the armed forces to ministers supported by a neutral civil service is a good and important thing. How it is made to work, however, is largely an accident of talent occasionally bumping into opportunity whilst most of the edifice is just too distracted clawing at itself to notice and prevent it.

One way, of course, of making the 1990s MoD 'fit for purpose' was to empty it completely for several years – in much the same way that soil infested with Ground Elder can be covered in black plastic for sufficiently long enough to wipe out all traces. The 'decant' executed somewhere around the early noughties was, however, not about extinction but transformation. The building had got to the stage where it was more dangerous to its occupants than Russia, and the ways of working were based on stiff collars and bowler hats rather than anything that needed electricity. Time to change it all by shipping out and coming back to something that would no longer embarrass the twentieth century. This transformation began by establishing how the supply of water and electricity throughout the new building could be done in ways that kept them deliberately separate, removing the hazard of the old establishment of 'death by electricity in bath'. But in particular this transformation meant an end to the corridors of little burrows in favour of the mass open-plan fetish.

In accordance with the very best management bobbins of the day, it was thought to be much better to sit all these people conditioned to a state of deep and mutual loathing elbow to elbow, liberating them from the constraint of locked doors and partition walls that might have inhibited the free-flow of boiling distrust and hatred. It also meant that the most senior people, some carrying genuinely immense responsibility for operations and money, could be ousted from any vestige of a private space they might have desired to think deep thoughts and take hard decisions without the useful backdrop of unavoidably overhearing their supporting cast's latest professional disaster, marital apocalypse, or romantic triumph. This whole thing was enabled by brand, spanking-new government information technology, artfully managing the challenge of satisfying different levels of classified information by refusing to transmit or receive any at all. Logging on was initially impossible without first appeasing an institution somewhere near Swindon with human sacrifice. There is more about leadership, life, and the MoD later in our exchange. Hard to decide what to leave out.

Actually, I avoided the new MoD for much longer than I dared hope as the noughties were swept up by all the tumult that followed 9/11. My 2001 Christmas and skiing holiday prospects were torpedoed by being ordered to

Kabul in December at four days' notice, appearing as a brand new colonel in a brand new job with a brand new team, knowing only that it was viciously cold and I was somewhere on the world map above Pakistan and below what used to be the Soviet Union. Another of those 'you'll definitely be back in ninety days' missions that turned into 186. We come back to that too. Then Iraq in mid-2003 filled a summer with as much Basra heat and sweat as a man could ever desire, preceded by four contented months on the Jedi Knight programme (the Higher Command and Staff Course) having my elbows fitted with titanium for career manoeuvres in confined spaces and my arse concreted over for endurance sitting. Before that, and after coming back from Afghanistan for the first time (with waterworks spectacularly ablaze until Kabul's lack of a sewage system had finally played out in my colon), there was a Fire Service strike to bail out. The strike meant squeezing 'How to Invade Iraq' into hobby status for those manning the stirrup pumps until it was almost time for them to fly to the Gulf.

In fact this decade (the 2000s) was nearly all about Afghanistan and Iraq, less for the two years as a brigadier in Northern Ireland 'supporting the Police Service of Northern Ireland' in Belfast and South Armagh. This was quite a different turn after Basra, and Basra would have been a doddle to secure if it received even half the drizzle Belfast wallows in. Nobody is going out fighting in that. By the end of the noughties I had been in and out of Iraq in various roles, latterly in 2008-9 as a major general – a 'Deputy Commanding General' in what was officially labelled 'Multi-National Corps Iraq' but was in fact the US XVIII Airborne Corps in all its massive warrior glory. A happy tour ensued running relationship counselling between the US Army and the Iraqi Army during some interesting times: two partners equally convinced the other never listened and could not be trusted to be in charge.

Arriving back in Germany in April 2009 (I had to pack the day after I got back from Iraq, which is mutiny territory), I thought I was safely billeted as the chief of staff of HQ Allied Rapid Reaction Corps, a polyglot NATO facing piece of army, and anticipating two years or more of solid, satisfying, not at all dangerous soldiering focused on keeping a newly-lumpy Russia congenially at bay. It required keeping the officers and men of some fourteen other nations amused daily until bang on 16:00 hours when they must by NATO custom resume their business of socially ravaging Germany. It also required deterring the UK MoD from whining too much about how much this all cost, a mission which is the definition of futile.

I was wrong again. About four months in the Allied Rapid Reaction Corps (ARRC) tour I was rather rudely (I thought) shoved aside and heading back to Afghanistan – in the middle of winter again. I went back to the same spot in Kabul, to the camp I had established in 2002 for a maximum of about 350 souls in spartan conditions, which had since flourished at the hands of US and NATO largesse to become home to about 2,000 soldiers stout and true – mainly stout as the cookhouse was the principal source of nourishment, entertainment, and morale in three hefty doses a day.

My job this time was to figure out with some very honourable and highly motivated Afghans how to build a scheme that would encourage their countrymen, particularly the youth who had joined the Taliban to put down their weapons, return home (if they had actually ever left) and take up a noble occupation – ideally not involving processing opium either personally or professionally. For every one supportive person I encountered in the six months or so that I laboured on this, there were about ten others, mostly Americans or Taliban, who remained unhelpfully sceptical. This whole Afghanistan, Iraq, Northern Ireland decade is something we come back to, and this job in particular had some wrinkles.

I have never been clear about the age at which military puberty sets in, that is the point at which in military circles one is a fully fledged actor – a grown-up in any setting. It has generally been the rank which I have just reached, accompanied by a great deal of scoffing at myself that I could possibly have thought I knew what I was doing at any point beforehand. According to the tabloid press an army officer becomes 'senior' on becoming a major, at which point we begin to lose the charm of the honest Tommy toiling in the trenches to ascend to the ranks of the callously weak and indifferent Top Brass. Top Brass status has fully kicked in by the rank of colonel, a title that is paired with 'blimp' almost as a matter of law. So, by the time I reached major general I presumably had had a lobotomy, and by promotion to lieutenant general and finally to general I was well beyond hope or redemption and a risk to humanity?

Lieutenant general found me back in the Ministry of Defence with the catchy title of 'Deputy Chief of the Defence Staff for Military Strategy and Operations' (DCSD(MSO)). This meant I could sit in the still annoyingly loud open-plan MoD for around fourteen hours a day as the UK's military operations director, home and away. This included the opportunity to spend a great deal of time elsewhere in Whitehall as the military voice in the deliberations of the mighty. More usually, I was just the military voice parked at the far end of the table populated by the cabal of senior civil servants passing briefly through top jobs in defence and security, many culturally ill at ease with the idea of killing people and smashing their stuff up. This is actually not a bad thing, but it would be better if they tried harder to conceal their surprise and often (but not always) unconscious disdain that anyone would seriously commit their adult life to being good at it.

It also afforded plenty of opportunity to work closely with the ladies and gentlemen who make up Britain's first-rate spying services, where I was delighted to affirm my understanding that they are as inclined to stick their corporate elbows in each other's face as any navy, army, air force when brought into unhappy proximity. This particular chapter included pursuing Mr Cameron's requirement to finish fighting in Afghanistan regardless of whether the fight was actually finished, a slightly bizarre dose of bringing the prospect of freedom and prosperity closer to the citizens of Libya through bombing and regime decapitation, and the rare opportunity to provide 18,000 service men and women at broadly the last minute to inspect the nation's handbags at the London 2012 Olympics. Leadership and life in Whitehall is a rich seam.

The year 2013 found me perched as a general in the very uppermost branches of the tree I so inexplicably started up in 1977. As Commander Joint Forces Command, I was the proponent of all the stuff that sits between, underneath and around the Royal Navy, Army, and Royal Air Force. This is something of a grand military buffet, spanning as it did intelligence, operational command and control; defence education; training; Special Forces; all manner of information technology and intelligence collection systems, Defence Medical Services, and even vicars and other spiritual guides. It gave me a place at the table as one of the UK Chiefs of Staff (there is no bigger Top Brass to have a go at) and an account worth £4.3 billion a year – which of course was nowhere near enough for all the stuff I was meant to do. Grande Fromage territory though this all is, it also meant being the object of quite a lot of competitive suspicion from the three services and some difficult dating experience with the MoD, which is often keener on the theory of parcelling out jobs and responsibility to others than it is to actually let go of the purse or any other strings. The leadership and other lessons that accrued during these three years feature later in this correspondence, not least where they stand in comparison with the Afterlife.

And then it all ended. After almost forty years of accidental but nonetheless generally fulfilling work, the day came when I was dropped off at the house I shared eternal ownership of with a Building Society and took off my army boots. This wasn't actually the last time as I would need them for various occasions that do still crop up when a uniform is de rigueur, but it was the last time these boots were connected to an actual military *job*. It immediately presented some stiff questions, to which I'd basically never given a moment's thought until the prospect became imminent and then real, summed up as the 'just what the fuck am I meant to do now' that filled my mind as I stood in the drive with my bags.

It soon seemed pretty clear that the after-market for actual hands-on laying waste and slaughter would be quite small and quite possibly in dodgy legal territory. So the thing I am best at was and is the thing I am least likely to do now. When I was eighteen, if I ever thought about this moment at all, the idea of being as ancient as fifty-six and unemployed would have led to the conclusion that all that was required anyway was to sit down comfortably a lot and try not to dribble. At the other end of the tube, however, it felt like at least another fifteen years in the saddle was required, dribbling not helpful, prompted by the quite sharp necessity of refilling the coffers that had not survived contact well with educating two daughters and trying to buy a house big enough to stuff with a lifetime's paraphernalia.

As you know well, the journey of discovery that has ensued from the taking off of my boots to date has been a rich and varied expedition. Quite a lot of it has been a total bitch. Almost everything I thought I knew about the Afterlife was wrong and almost everything I thought I would do never happened. The Utter Shits quotient in my life has risen considerably, something to do with having some wisdom still to offer but now bugger-all authority or money. Four years down the track I think I have enough experience of this new order to make some comparisons between military service and what follows, even if these comparisons reflect what is clearly unfinished business. Some of the letters between us have acquired a thematic edge as a result.

I harbour the thought that – with practice – being a captain of industry will come more naturally than it has at first. I also want to believe that the degree of shiteness that comes with changing lives diminishes too, or at least greater immunity from it accrues. The tribulations (and some joys) of becoming a portfolio monkey, juggling a set of balls of varying size, weight and colour in a blend of advisory stuff, setting up new businesses, some pseudo-academic stabs, a spot of media-tartery and a tonne of speaking events may amount to some sort of accidental hill of beans. Not the hill of beans I would call finished or find great fulfilment from yet, but still some beans.

Then there are all the other aspects of having to think and behave more like a civvy than a soldier to come to terms with. Quite a lot of correspondence dwells on what it means for me to be commuting and working in the strange new world, the world I pretty much swore I would avoid for so many years. Some of this is limited to observations of fact about the legion differences, but in some instances I feel drawn to point out to you where there clearly is a room for improvement in how this non-military life could be conducted. I am really trying not to be judgemental, because I know this is right out of fashion, but I do wonder whether, with a bit of a nudge, there could not still be some appropriate raising of the bar to the greater benefit of us all? Our exchanges sometimes go beyond considering themes to making actual recommendations, which you and I know is a fool's errand – but it is an errand this fool feels better for taking on. I hope you will take all this in the spirit in which it is offered, knowing with some confidence that unless I do really ascend to being World President you are quite safe from anything more authoritative than my random jottings and opinion.

Chapter 1

Cold War Germany

My Dear M,

I went to Germany today, there and back, for a two-hour meeting which was stimulating in a way, though didn't buy me a yacht. Another of those opportunities to do some agreeable technology tub-thumping about what could be made to happen, liberated by the certainty that the chances of it actually happening are equal, to quote my prep-school maths teacher, to the 'square root of fuck-all'. Teaching had different boundaries in the 1960s, many of the older teachers were in mental refuge from the effects of a difficult war, and entirely unencumbered by any form of learning greater than the one book they owned – which was more than enough information to occupy 9- year-olds at thirty minutes a pop.

Anyway, Germany and back in a day! Yes, that meant: an early reveille in London at the Victory Services Club; a short yet still informative broadcast from the driver on the Evils of Multi-Culturalism during the taxi-ride to Paddington; the larceny of the Heathrow Express (the quickest way to be parted with cash per mile that I know of); the unwanted, unnecessary and certainly unrequited 'security' frisk-titivation executed by a dutiful mouth-breather in Terminal Whatever; a frenzy of bun, coffee, and easing-of-springs before the boarding fracas; the actual flight (condemned to the middle seat, sandwiched between two accomplished smoochers torn between not wanting to fill the horrid middle themselves versus tolerating fifty-five minutes without any tonsil-licking). I resolved this for them by growling like a rabid dog when any attempt to connect tongues was made across me; then a steely Hun passport check (I am officially an evil mercenary importing menace to Germany); then the game of chance to find the colleague deputed to get the hire car (as he had the 'stand aside in awe you peasants' priority card for the rental company, the wettest dream of every travelling salesperson); and finally (FINALLY) the ninety minutes dash navigating by smell on the autobahn.

The return was much the same, plus a pause for a dead horse sausage *mit pommes* in Departures, the middle seat again of course – this time with gnarly unwashed artisans for company. Finally, an hour home in a cab discussing 'Why the M25 should be shot'. So we ended up on a bit of a high, but that's a day trip to Germany. Is it just me, or was the ratio of value to activity not very positive?

The point is though, this was a *day trip* and despite the terrible battering it gives to a half decent suit and all the artery-blocking catering, we just think this is normal – except when wrestling with a pandemic. This is so different, extraordinarily different to my first encounters with Germany in the early 1980s. Then I arrived as the regiment (the truly elite 1st Regiment Royal Horse Artillery) moved lock, stock, and barrel from its bucolic burial on a former Second World War airfield in the recesses of rural Yorkshire. There we had been quartered amongst charming people for whom anyone from London was emblematic of all possible sin and uselessness. Unless a chap could prove they had very recently shot their arm up a cow's bottom for agricultural purposes (only), one was shunned as a syphilitic communist bedwetter. We, this magnificent Regiment of Royal Horse Artillery (with no horses, though the sadness lingered at their absence from modern combat) left all this behind with very heavy hearts to live a mile down the road from Belsen Concentration Camp. In fact, to live in the barracks built to house the Wehrmacht during their field training for the Last Big Tumble, in a place called Bergen-Hohne.

Saying 'Hohne' to any Cold War warrior will always elicit the response that 'Hohne was what you made of it'. This is indubitably so: as a posting it was a shithole of the first grade, and making something of it was just as our ancestors felt they must do when they found themselves in an isolated canton on a dusty plain in India. They, however, had the advantage that they could – with total impunity – shoot all the wildlife; murder, sleep with or beat local residents a choix, and drink until their livers surrendered. The rest of the day they were free to waste. We, in the British Army of the Rhine in 1982, had only the alcohol (duty-free) left from the original Garrisoning Johnny Foreigner Abroad playbook.

The Cold War has long gone and a generation has passed in significant freedom from the existential fear of war or invasion – even a proper civil war with families torn apart was totally off the cards until Brexit hove into view. As humans usually conflate what has happened in their own experience in their little adult life with the totality of history and the future of mankind, there are plenty of sensible people in top jobs around today for whom it is inconceivable that war could ever come again. Who these days worries that London, for example, could ever become a useless smoking ruin?

That sense of being 'post-conflict' is not the lived experience of 'war'n'stuff' of many millions of other adults sharing this planet today, some of whom are properly seething with rage at the West for one reason or another (lots to choose from). They don't seem to lack motive for heaping violence upon us. A handful of states and some quite bullish private organizations covet the means to commit great harm, means that are becoming more abundant as the Digital Age advances. And the opportunities for a big scrap are opening up as the twenty-first century unfolds in ways inimical to the certainties and securities of the last thirty years and more. The life we led as military folk in the Cold War seems to have a bit more resonance today with the need to manage our security and prosperity and to restore our resilience that is creeping back into fashion today. I know that this is subject still always at the bottom of the list that is headed by whatever Twitter is twittering about on any given day.

I didn't plan for lengthy stops in Germany to happen to me, in fact I had had two weeks in Hohne as a 16-year-old on a 'look at the army' as a warning. This had involved some circular hurling about at the helm of battered armoured vehicles in a dust bowl (who wouldn't sign up after that!) and a leavening of gratuitous intimidation from the resident junior officers dedicated to the ethics and customs of mid-twentieth-century all-male education. This boiled down to a rugby fetish, violent intolerance of anybody shorter than themselves and a conviction that it must be possible one day to overcome a state of perpetual virginity. On the latter point, as they lived in a closed world where lady teachers and nurses abounded, their continued failure required thoughtful introspection rather than any effort in putting the blame elsewhere. I didn't tell them this, as a guest in their mess.

Even with my nipples forcefully tweaked for wearing brown shoes after 18:00 hours, this foray convinced me that the army was still a pretty good thing, so long as it did not involve living in a shithole called Hohne with wannabe Flashmans. I think it is unlikely that any gods exist on the evidence of the last few millennia, although I concede that maybe they operate as rare visitors to Earth who drop by to check all is falling apart on schedule. But if there are any, then they have a sense of humour whatever the Archbishop of Canterbury says – and they are also a massive pain in the arse as a result. It turned out I was destined to spend some seven years of my one life in this place called Hohne, punctuating two decades.

The move across the Channel in the early 1980s was known in the vernacular as an 'Arms Plot Move', because it followed the direction of an army-wide master plan to ensure that as soon as a unit became competent in a role and comfortable in its surroundings it was uprooted and told to start again somewhere worse. Some of this rotation was to guard against the claim that joining the army in the Cold War meant emigrating to Germany. This was particularly true for those who manned tanks or other heavily-armoured equipment, for which the epicentre of the universe was the dull plain east of Hannover up to the Inner German Border (IGB) that then divided east from west. As a 22-year-old subaltern I wasn't really focused on the higher politics behind all this geography, I just knew that I was being sent to live in a foreign land and the last time I went there my nipples were sore for a week.

One of the reasons a day trip to Germany was unconscionable back then was that once 'deployed' to Germany (army-speak for being sent anywhere uncomfortable on the Queen's business) the permanently imminent arrival of the Soviet Union's Third Shock Army needed to be addressed. Another reason was that this was before budget airlines were invented. The Cold War was in many ways an enjoyable and satisfying military experience, there was just enough clear and present danger to provide purpose, resources, and excuses for some military madness, but not quite enough to put anybody off their food. This was a game played for decades, manfully out-staring the opposition just across the border, mostly accomplished by just keeping a lot of people and equipment confined to Germany at any one time. But you never knew if today might be the day.

For the first time since European empires rather waned in popularity, the British Army today is almost all housed in the UK. For today's army the idea that a hostile foreign power was poised to strike, so no one could leave the garrison to go home would be met with chortles. By 14.00 hours on a Friday, Britain's army is mostly in cars and on trains, with soldiers and NCOs heading generally north, single officers heading to Clapham with rutting on the brain, and older officers heading to the families they left in an affordable rural wilderness.

This means that if the balloon goes up, and by some incontrovertible law that has to occur on a Friday between 14:00 and 17:00 hours, the first response would come from those soldiers and officers still left in the garrison. They would be there because life had been so cruel to them that they were reduced to living full time in a MoD-leased house. They are part of an experiment to check that if a house is neglected for over forty years in every form of care save a quinquennial slathering with magnolia emulsion, it will then eventually fall down and crush their occupants. As indeed they do. The point is, those few left in quarters will be only too pleased to abandon them and dash off as the tip of the spear to certain annihilation, especially on the promise that they may find a working shower first.

The shorthand for being confined to Cold War Germany was 'ACTIVE EDGE', which summed up a massive cluster of inconveniences and obstacles to the pursuit of a balanced life. Principal amongst these was the cap of no more than 25 per cent who could be away at any one time, plus the bind of living permanently with four hours to be ready for death or glory. It doesn't sound hard, but four hours meant a two-hour travelling time limit from the epicentre of nowhere, having aimed off for the news of impending invasion to travel slowly. As this was the time well before mobile phones and personal computers, how that news would travel faster than a Russian Tank Division could trundle was always something of an unspoken crisis. We lived about two hours by Soviet tank (probably a T-72 since you ask) from the IGB, so with four hours' notice I always thought it would be really helpful if the Kremlin phoned ahead. Especially at weekends and Christmas.

'ACTIVE EDGE' was so much more than a travel ban, it captured all aspects of 'La Vie Militaire' in lovely old British Army of the Rhine (BAOR). Kit had to be kept packed at all times, and this provoked larceny on a grand scale as each of us supplemented the stuff the Queen routinely issued to us for the purposes of maintaining her realm with all the extras needed to avoid the agony of constantly ferreting about in military luggage for a day-to-day supply of fresh trousers. There is absolute joy in becoming the unrecorded owner of an illegal pair of basically rubbish army boots. And not just boots of course, we needed to be ready to fling ourselves out of the door with sufficient spare shirtage, socks, bathroom stationery, a bijou 'field' shaving kit, half a wooden spoon for all operational catering work, as well as an allotment of bullets and the odd hand grenade. A British Army officer likes to be slaughtered looking as smart as a carrot and with bowels at the top of their game.

I now know that the world is full of many lies that really do matter, but in 1982 the lie that mattered most to me was the difference between the list of kit the Queen thought I had, as listed in formal soldier-biro on my '1157' document, and the tonnes of contraband stuffed out of sight under my bed and elsewhere. All soldiers are united on the importance of having more personal kit than twenty men could wear at once. This explains to this day why when a venerable army lorry catches fire out on secret manoeuvres the list of contents to be written off as utterly vaporized would invariably require about fifteen trucks to carry if anyone paused to add it all up – which no one is ever daft enough to suggest doing.

The joy of being ever-ready to face the 'Soviet armoured frenzy coiled like a vengeful spring just a few miles away' (here I quote from memory the synthesized pre-exercise peroration of at least forty years of commanding officers) extended to more than efficient luggage drills. We had a plan, of course we did, in fact we had the magnificent, beautiful, massive artwork of the plan that left no detail untouched. It always started with the call in the middle of the night to muster men and vehicles and, if we were really going for it, to load up with all the war stock and ammunition. For an artillery regiment that is tonnes and tonnes of shells and cartridges, all of which is very expensive and so none of it could be actually unboxed. Had we ever fired it at Third

Shock Army they would have been gratified to receive high explosive more expensively packaged than a Fortnum's hamper.

Sometimes after 'the call' we just lined everything up in the dark in a long column on the barracks square, whereupon lists could be ticked. Camouflage nets would then be stolen from the neighbouring detachment, as they are a pain to put together and a bitch to store. So much better just to steal a good one painstakingly prepared by others. And, though I could never get to the bottom of it, the larceny around 'rubies' was prodigious: these are the screw-in light covers for brakes/indicators etc on veteran Land Rovers and armoured vehicles. Our fleet at the time had been issued in the 1960s (this was the kit we wished we had had for the business-end of the Second World War), it was creaking by the 1980s, much of it was still on hand well into the 1990s – and some even (and it is mad) in 2020. This is the equivalent of keeping a radiogram running for fifty years, even when Bluetooth has stolen the lead. Across half a century there might occasionally have been a shortage of rubies, though hardly an existential risk to military effectiveness, yet the enthusiasm with which Gunner Blogs would then (and now) surreptitiously unscrew any left unattended and squirrel them away was unrestrained – and completely immune to my exhortation to 'grow the fuck up'.

On a good ACTIVE EDGE, once all was assembled and accounted for and the night had given way to a grey, humourless Hohne dawn, the word would come down that we could put it all away again. Breakfast was the essential accompaniment to this news: without an immediate issue of greasy bacon and conjoined fried eggs, a mutinous spirit – a collective feeling that this was all total ass – might have briefly taken hold. But, like all hangovers and most cases of weariness, disgruntlement, and disaster, there is not much that a wedge of hot English breakfast does not overcome. However, on a less good day we were not sent off to either unpack or breakfast but to hide in a dark, wet, and muddy wood. This wood was known in military vernacular as the 'Practice Survival Area'.

It would have been poor military drills to practice surviving in the area we would actually go to if the balloon went up, even the cavalry spotted that one. The location of where we would go to be bombed to oblivion was known only to a handful of senior people in the regiment, and also anybody who could find their way into the secret room where it was all written down. The access list did not include the locally employed German cleaners, but no military clerk was going to do the vacuuming if Frau Fritz was on hand.

The surviving to be done was from the easily forecast attentions of: the massed air forces of the Soviet Union; their similarly bountiful supply of long-range rocket artillery; the precipitate arrival of hundreds of T-72 tanks and their accompanying infantry; and – hardest to spot – the Special Forces or *Spetsnaz* who would without doubt be positioned behind most trees, armed with a punishing issue of machine guns and explosives. And cheese wire. The cheese wire was not for sharing the fruity little cheddar the *Spetsnaz* had thought to pick up whilst infiltrating from the beigeness of East Germany into the luminous, consumerist West.

Compulsorily if incongruously attired as 1950s itinerant agricultural workers, the *Spetsnaz* used cheese wire was to stretch at armoured vehicle head-height across the dark tracks leading to our secret harbour. Amongst the leading dilemmas of these deployments was therefore this question: should one batten down the hatch to avoid decapitation – but in driving 'closed down' through a dark, narrow wood in pitch dark inevitably squish the soldiers sent out as guides or should one remain stoically head-out to reduce the squishing but increase the chances of a dire and very early and medal-free end to one's war?

It became fashionable for the ACTIVE EDGE experience to be embellished by doing it at the least appropriate moment. As a call-out was within the gift of every level of the chain of command that towered up from a regiment to a brigade to a division to a corps to an army to an army group to the mystery that was NATO, the scope for being novel should have been quite limited (and the number of call-outs much more strenuously rationed in my deeply-held view at the time). For some commanders, novelty was to be found in adding extra tasks to the joys of shuffling armoured traffic through a dark wood in drizzle. In the interests of economy and to avoid any drain on imagination, these extras were limited to something inordinately personal and physical. For an organization maintained to excel at armoured warfare (in which the common denominator is *driving* about the place) we did spend a great deal of time walking all night carrying full military luggage in the prescribed i.e. generally uncomfortable) manner. Brigadiers, I found – maybe because as men in their early forties they needed to get some last massive physical jerks in before their knees broke – were the worst for adding a ten-mile circular perambulation to a practice alert. We were consequently in tip-top condition for the march to the Prisoner of War cage. I doubt this was foremost in our leaders' minds, yet if they had read any twentieth-century British military history they would have seen how prudent they were.

Worse – by far – than physical embellishment was the fashion for calling 'ACTIVE EDGE' at the end of a massively successful formal evening in the officers' mess. This would not happen at a weekend, as wives would be present and no senior officer, not even the Chief of the General Staff himself, was brave enough to tell thirty comprehensively inebriated army wives at 03.00 hours on a Sunday morning that their husbands would not be taking them home after dinner for the quarterly tumble on the stairs, as mandated by the Army Manual of Dinner Night Procedure. They would now be required to totter off solo into the black on their foxy stilettos, as the regimental minibus was also now doing war. In addition, they would have sole charge of the children for every head-throbbing minute of a freezing Hohne Sunday, despite being confined largely incapacitated to a lumpy army quarter sofa and in no state for family board game hell. In sum, the chances of a Doris-wide rebellion on the spot to the certain prejudice of good order and military discipline were just too huge. No brigadier fancied being stripped from his mess dress by a baying platoon of immensely cross officers' ladies, coated with sherry trifle and deposited in a wheelie bin, naked less for a coating of alcoholic custard. So ACTIVE EDGE was a thing best avoided by senior officers if ladies were present.

Weeknights, after boys-only nights in the mess, were obviously a totally different kettle of fish. For a start, the modest inhibition against overdoing the vino that the presence of Memsahibs may sometimes confer did not apply. Very likely all present would be comprehensively shitfaced by the end of the fish course, with the compulsory beef Wellington, trifle and Stilton still to be liberally washed down. There would be a speech or two, usually sufficiently unhinged to cause real and enduring offence somewhere around the table – offence which it might take an officer twenty years of steady careerism to hit the rank to repaying on equal terms. Always, always, worth it too.

Then after dinner, it would be important to break some stuff and inflict life-changing injury through the medium of inebriated indoor sport. Mess rugby was still popular: doors smashed off their hinges, oil paintings of eighteenth century massacres either inflicted or incurred revarnished with red wine and snot, and – always – a collarbone to be broken as many stones of chunky captains landing on a thinner, sharper pile of subalterns. Elegant, bespoke, mess uniforms, designed in the 1950s to be worn in the depths of Victorian winter were first ruined by sweat and then expensively shredded in high-speed contact with economy-grade nylon carpets. At just the point when recriminations might start, the brigadier, the guest of honour for the evening, would catch the unrewarding sight of his (extended by age and weariness) undercarriage peeking through the gaping hole in what were once a fine, close-fitting pair of heavy serge trousers, and thus be inspired to say: 'Gentlemen, ACTIVE EDGE'.

This news was never greeted with total equanimity, but it was always clear that the regiment's prowess at defeating communism was about to be measured in how well it stood to arms whilst its entire complement of officers was out of their skull on Chateau Collapso. The Warrant Officers, NCOs and soldiers, at that point sound asleep in their comfy beds, were woken with the happy news of an unexpected, unwanted appointment with *Spetsnaz* in a wet, cold wood. 'Thrilled' does not capture their mood – 'Fucking Furious' was more the mark. But they also quickly realized that with all the officers completely blotto, they would have to do all the organizing, ordering, and navigating until the sun was well towards midday. And this would make everything just so much easier.

Nonetheless, when the time came to drive the regiment out of barracks and off to hide in a wood/have a painfully long walk, the officers still had to be seen to be in charge. This was the 1980s, remember, so placing a still thoroughly infused officer in command of thirty tonnes or so of armoured conveyance was absolutely fine. The drivers, able to see straight ahead but not much either side and nothing at all behind, had to work out on their own whether it was safe to proceed at each junction, etc. They made this decision safe in the knowledge that if Herr Schmidt was indeed barrelling down the road in his shiny new Mercedes and were to smack into the camouflaged flank of a British Army panzer inexplicably pulling out in front, he would most likely be pulped and thereby rendered unfit to complain. The officer rolling about blind drunk in the turret above would recall at the inquest that he was momentarily distracted by an urgent radio transmission essential to the conduct of his mission. All would be well.

In fact the only real peril would come from the Saluting Game: in lieu of being able to actually employ a sniper to shoot inattentive vehicle commanders in the head as they passed (actively keeping eyes skinned for snipers renders immunity from actually being terminated by one) the brigadier would conceal himself in bushes en route and vigorously take the name of any officer who drove past and failed to fling up his finest Guardsman-like salute. He was frequently disappointed: the incumbent vehicle commander was very likely still way too off his game to sit upright. When stopped and asked to explain, a sufficiently still alive officer could hope to explain he had briefly dropped down to consult his map away from the prying eye of Soviet satellites and was in no way bent over double in catatonic agony. In other cases, the crew wisely took the precaution of applying so much 'paint, face, camouflage, brown' to their comatose leader as to render him totally unidentifiable by his own mother. Today, apparently, this would be called out as virulent cultural appropriation, but this was war in the 1980s – and also hilarious.

I mentioned the secret room where 'The Plan' was kept for 'The Day the Soviets Come'. This was obviously more than just how to hide in a wood, hoping nobody flew over, drove through, or walked past. The Plan extended to where almost every man would be stationed in the battle for the Hannover Plain, which itself was just a 50km slice of the battle for West Germany and everything west of that at least as far as California. We were on point for the survival of the Free World.

The plan dealt with the bit of the war that started with the uninvited arrival of many sons and daughters of the Soviet Union with their tanks, artillery, and bombers crossing the IGB. It was known for sure to be coming one day, and in columns so long it would be days before everything was unfurled. It was also known it would always end with exchanges of the smaller, but no less eye-watering if present, nuclear weapons. People – like the entire population of Western Europe – could get quite touchy about this.

The plan was the beneficiary of more than thirty years of tinkering, for which new jargon had to be artlessly formulated to conceal the same tactical cobblers. Every ten years or so a new wonder weapon appeared, causing weeks of professional fretting about how 'Everything Was Now Different'. The 1980s were very excited about anti-tank missiles (so long as they got a shot from the side as the Soviet frontal armour was still really really hard), and the 1990s would have been ecstatic about the Attack Helicopter if the Cold War had not ended – though the lag in military affairs is such that a decade of theoretical ecstasy still pretty much occurred. Across military history Silver Bullets do keep turning up and for a while it is fashionable to assert this trumps everything – cannon/machinegun/aircraft/submarine/missile etc that came before), but after a while they all find their place in a rebalanced orchestra of war and everyone calms down again. Cyber war this decade's special enthusiasm, but no one got cybered to death in Aleppo.

In its bones, however, the plan was never really different no matter how many times it was re-written:

- Phase One. The Soviets get a bit arsey and things start to rumble towards the IGB. Strange stuff happens in the night in the West, there are itinerant agricultural workers lurking all over the place being militarily furtive. The decision is taken to send I British Corps to the woods. Their families are formed up in their cars and convoyed to the Channel coast, which in no way disrupts the bliss in which the local German population continue to conduct their normal lives on the Hannover Plain.
- Phase Two. More arsiness, this time with an exchange of mutual rhetorical grumpiness witlessly and transparently contrived to set the scene for a century of dispute about who was to blame for incinerating Europe. More Soviet things are rumbling towards the IGB, which will soon have to keep rolling when they reach it or an almighty traffic jam will stretch to Berlin and beyond. Which the US will have to nuke. In the Allied zone in Berlin itself, a sense of bitter hopelessness at being stationed 150 miles behind

enemy lines would be natural at this point. I British Corps is ordered from its woods to rush at 15km-in-the-hour (the whole effort confined to the speed of the slowest digger in the interests of neatness) in a vast green snail of traffic visible from space. Arrives unmolested at the newly revealed (to the British, not the Soviets) general deployment plan positions. A lot of digging happens, which is significant: digging is such hard labour it is always to be avoided unless actually in mortal danger. Mines would now be laid, great belts of anti-tank mines appearing in thirty-six hours – of course in a properly recorded way so that should the whole thing be called off someone might spend a decade digging them out again. After a hoped-for three days feverish shovelling there is almost no chocolate left across the Corps and ammunition has finally taken its place in being strapped across the bodies of a lot of now quite nervous, though still potentially heroic, British soldiers.

- Phase Three. Third Shock Army, with at least four tank divisions linking arms in the front row, issues forth across the IGB. The first shot is fired and the first cheese wire ambush occurs, a whirl of complicated messages follows to authorize new 'Rules of Engagement' that prescribe who may be shot at, by whom, and for what reason. These are received by tanks, infantry and artillery already pretty focused on being very ready to fire everything at anybody for any reason that promotes their own survival. The lights metaphorically go out over Europe once more, but actually stay on to avoid panic or getting lost – though at this point systemic panic across West Germany would not have been outrageous. The brave forward reconnaissance troops of 1st British Corps, men in tinny, tiny armoured vehicles whose regimental ancestors led charges at Waterloo and have attended every horse-based skirmish of any calibre since, are looking hard for signs of the Soviet onslaught – such as being blown to bits. They peer through binoculars and scan the flickering screens of 'man-portable radars' (man portable if you are seven foot tall and weigh 150kg), that only work in a lunar eclipse. Nothing much happens for the first five minutes, then they are swept away by a vast rolling barrage of Soviet artillery the like of which has not been seen since the battle for Stalingrad. This Phase was called something like the 'Screen Force battle', and was to inform the Corps commander, a top-notch lieutenant general, that the Soviets were on the way and where and how many had turned up so far. This picture, we always surmised, we would all to contribute to for free as we lined the bottom of our newly dug trenches with unsolicited excrement.

- Phase Four. The Screen Force was eventually vaporized (though it would necessarily turn out that to a man they then bravely exfiltrated some 100kms West to be issued with new tinny tanks and clean underwear for the Final Push) and the Covering Force Battle takes over. A brigade (5,000 blokes and quite a lot of tanks) was scattered thinly across way too much front in advance of each of the two lead British divisions. Their job was to 'buy time' for the continuing soil-based preparations going on behind. 'Trading space for time' was one of the things all officers of the BAOR were expected to be able to say with great authority, a hallmark of acquiring intimate knowledge of how I British Corps would defeat the Soviet Union by dint of only being annihilated *incrementally*.

Extraordinary derring-do was required by the Covering Force Brigade for at least the next twenty-four hours to slow the enemy advance. I particularly liked – and use in other settings to this day – the expression 'to avoid being decisively engaged'. This means doing enough to look really interested but without getting so stuck in as to be really knocked about or bothered. As a concept it works well for many reluctant school sports participants, for the habitues of Tinder, and for many politicians keen to catch the public eye but without being responsible for anything that might go badly. In the Cold War context it was never tested in anger. The military heresy of suggesting that the dictum of 'avoid being decisively engaged' simply described how too small a force should bob about for a while until inevitably pinned down and given a complete mashing can continue to lie quietly on the file.

- Phase Five Part One. Things got quite serious now. The Covering Force would be down to about 35 per cent of its tanks and half its infantry, but up a tonne of medals. It had 'bought enough time' to allow the bulk of I British Corps to have completed full battle preparations behind it, ready now to address the main Soviet thrust with stern measures. Somewhere during all this, the Territorial Army had been mobilized throughout the UK, equipped, training refreshed, and driven across France/Belgium/ The Netherlands untroubled by the attentions of the Soviet air force or premature demolition of motorway bridges with nuclear charges by preternaturally nervous European governments. They had seen the convoys of army families heading the other way, descending like biblical swarms on any *hypermarché* en route that offered wine, cheese and children's bicycles at prices unobtainable in Blighty. In that uniquely British way, there were now some trenches occupied by four privates of the Territorial Army that collectively took £1 million in salary from the City. They were ready to do their bit, a bit which could include them all being dismembered in an instant by £250 of Soviet artillery shell. Fortunately, the plan had always worked out how mobilizing and moving thousands of Reserves was fully squared with the Soviet facility for surprise and the British political reluctance to ever signal alarm and despondency by compulsorily calling out the Territorials.

Anyway, there would come a point where the Covering Force had had its chips and had to 'break clean'. In military speak this means having to stop fighting and legging it, without the enemy knowing you are doing a runner. It is performed either by sneaking off in the dark (hard to do ever since radar and thermal imaging became things) or by summoning up a massive collective blast of high explosive at the critical moment so as to stun the opposition – and then doing a runner to get well behind the division that was about to take on the squabble. The problem was always how to organize a big enough bang on a wide enough front to do this: the 'Covering Force' was more or less in bits and the folks next on to take the lead were understandably reticent about giving up their locations or expending all their stuff at this early point in their proceedings. The answer was to be found mostly in hope from the sky: this was one of those moments when the Royal Air Force might be tempted out of bed before noon. After days of deadly slogging against unreasonable odds, nothing cheers an army up more than an air force turning up in the nick of time to help the last remaining stragglers survive. In fact – and of course they are all equally wonderful blah blah – in the plan the air forces of a lot of NATO really would pitch up at this point and bomb the crap out of the front end of the Soviet push. They had the preceding days focused on the back end where the better prizes – like all the vast logistic stocks needed to get Third Shock Army to Calais – might be found.

- Phase Five Part Two. Having accomplished the 'break clean', the Covering Force Brigade hurries to the rear through the brigades bravely still occupying the Main Defensive Area to find some new woods in which to conceal and magic up new tanks and fully fit soldiers ready for the plan's finale. Meanwhile, I British Corps was ready for its Very Big Moment. Just to the East of Hannover, where life seemed to continue untrammelled by the iron and blood being noisily exchanged just outside the city limits, the heart of the British Army sat in their holes and turrets, determined (and required) to bring the Soviet advance to a conclusive standstill. This essentially meant a huge number of Soviet tanks and accompanying cast (including a ridiculous amount of artillery for such a small place) thundering into creatively located mines and big ditches between what had now become heavily defended small towns and villages, from which would now pour forth as much firepower as the British taxpayer had thought to provide. To be a player in this game it was imperative for an officer to be able to say 'enfilade fire from a defilade position' with the conviction of someone who not only really knew what it meant, but also really prayed hard that the best way of stopping a herd of tanks is to shoot at them as they pass, rather than have them roll over the top. It was also vital to be able to say, 'pin-table battle', referring to the ping-ponging of Soviet armour amongst British occupied, soon to be smoking ruin, settlements. Some grasp of what the hell an 'echelon' is was also helpful. According to the plan, the Soviets would turn up in waves, smaller ones within a day or so of each other known as Tactical Echelons and much bigger ones at some days march between them known as Operational Echelons. So, one might laugh in the face of the First Tactical Echelon, smile in the dispatch of the Second Tactical Echelon – as this completed the participation in proceedings of the First Operational Echelon – but then understandably get a bit nervy when the Second Operational Echelon hove into view and we had run out of tanks, bullets, and chocolate. But – an important but – to crumple like weeds before the First Tactical Echelon of the First Operational Echelon would mean being condemned to having one's nipples tweaked in the mess for eternity in the pantheon of military history.

- Phase Six. We never really got to Phase Six. Phase Five pretty much had to take the trick as all there would then be behind I British Corps was a lot of very vulnerable West Germany and then a motorway drive via the duty-free to Calais and Ostend. So, the plan decided we would win on the pin table and Third Shock Army would call it a day. If, obscurely, this was not how things worked out, it would mean it was time to start thinning down the nuclear stockpile. This did come in several sizes, from small enough to trouble about an English District to way big enough to consume whole cities, but the plan struggled with how this would be happening in West Germany (whose side we were on) rather than East Germany (with whom we supported reunification of more than ashes) or – a bit better – Russia.
- Phase Six (Alternative). All this being a bit sticky to resolve, the plan had an alternative ending (like any good box set this could go either way right up until the last episode is broadcast). In the preferred alternative ending it was not necessary to irradiate the land we had come to defend because (a) either the ding-dong on the pin table had successfully concluded matters or (b) a stunning counter-attack was now mounted at the critical moment to smash the Soviet advance for once and for all. The latter was much preferred. It also meant that all the troops who had suffered such a massive beating during the opening rounds and headed off into more Secret Woods to restore themselves, could now ride to secure final victory. For this they

needed a decent night's sleep, food, new clothes/weapons/bullets – and a reissue of tanks, artillery etc. It was thought impracticable with the time and technology then available to bring the dead back to life or reassemble the sorely wounded, so it was helpful that a lot more people would rock up just in the nick of time from UK. So it was, just as the battered defenders felt that their tenure of the pin table was finely in the balance (i.e. they were comprehensively done for), a swarm of fresh tanks, artillery, and – if not too cloudy or a golfing day, or at a weekend – the RAF would combine to sweep down at dawn and win the day. This version of the plan is the one that does involve final victory by dashing assault and does not involve setting nuclear winter as an objective, so we generally went with that.

It will have struck you that there was quite a lot to the plan, and so it will be no surprise that we practised it a lot. Endlessly in fact – somehow without also revealing that it was the plan. We were away from our beds for at least six months of the year doing this one way or another. Some of this practice was about the nitty-gritty of the shop floor end, mostly conducted within the confines of the pulverized woodland set aside for army training on tracks, wheels, and foot, for me days and days (and the nights in between) passed agreeably enough in rehearsing the drills involved in getting a battery of six artillery guns to the right place on the planet and sorting it out ready to fire.

When this involved live firing, in which exactly the same shell that would be used to rain objection on Third Shock Army for its unwelcome intrusion, was instead fired onto a well-defined piece of German training area the attention to detail was a bit more profound. It turned out that by 1982 the civilian population of West Germany had lost all enthusiasm for British shelling, only thirty-five years after they had apparently been only a bit keener on it than the Russian version. Objections multiplied if the shell that was meant to dig a harmless small, abrupt hole in the mud of the designated 'impact area' somehow instead took itself off to fairly adjacent German habitation. A certain amount of technology makes this harder to do these days, but in the 1980s a number misheard, a dial not fully tweaked, or a cartridge not filled with the correct amount of oomph could all lead to lengthy explanations being required in writing.

A day trip to Germany somehow feels less of a life than what once felt like a lifetime stuck in Germany. Yet nothing in this world lasts forever and who could really miss the costs and the potential for real peril that came with the Cold War? Odd too that, at the time of writing, a day trip is almost completely ruled out again by the constraints of the COVID-19 pandemic, and the papers are featuring news of Russia being disagreeable once more, and China seems to radiate some sort of clumsy menace in a world of much bigger risks. Feels like we need a plan, better than the old plan – but even that was better than no plan.

Chapter 2

Surprise

My Dear M,

Surprise comes in many forms, a standing feature of all our lives for good or ill. I am pretty convinced that it is a thing better imposed on others than on oneself, especially in a military sense – where surprise is so often the prelude to unexpected triumph or unwelcome disaster. A great deal of military doctrine over the centuries has caught the advantages of inflicting such 'total surprise' on an agile and thinking enemy that swift and complete victory is definitively wrought, followed of course by heaps of medals and parading before adoring crowds. The contrary is also well covered in the manuals: best to avoid the martial equivalent of being surprised whilst dozing contentedly under a tree by an immensely cross and hungry wild animal that nibbles enthusiastically on one's internal organs before the full gravity of the situation becomes apparent. This is a bad thing, no medals are available for being a carnivore's lunch, although a cracking defeat does still seem to make for better myths and cinema. Everyone who watches the film 'Zulu' fancies themselves as one of the VC-winning heroes left standing amidst carnage at the end, despite the statistical truth that – if actually present on the day as a British soldier, a spear in the chest was a far more likely outcome. If present as a Zulu, the limits of magic v bullet were made equally plain from early on.

Anyway, on the subject of surprise generally, I am drawn to remark to you what a defining feature it is of the human condition. No matter how clever we think we are, how much we believe we know about the world and about ourselves, the capacity always exists to be bitten on the ass by the unexpected. Sometimes this is genuinely unexpected, shit just happens, but more often it is the result of being out-foxed by complexity or a reluctance to look for or think about bad things. So often the 'unthinkable' is actually just the 'unpalatable' with a false moustache. This is true for mankind as a whole for example, some amongst us are surprised (and outraged) to find that decades of setting the gas boiler to 'inferno' so that we may walk around our quarters clad only in our pants all winter is now drowning our summer holiday prospects in the Maldives.

It is also true for states who assume their eternal comfort is not in jeopardy if they keep hold of all the water that once supported their neighbour's entire way of life. Genuine surprise (and outrage) sets in when the neighbour's army then pops over for a chat about sharing. And it's true of many people who behave as if their life and happiness is entitled to progress at unlimited cost to others. Sometimes these people are presidents of very large countries and others are just a legend in their own trousers (or occasionally both), but they express profound surprise when their self-obsessed approach to things is not unanimously welcomed, especially when this response is revealed to them by the infliction of great opprobrium and discomfort. And how we do like to share in the joy of retribution: who amongst us is not delighted to see the fraudsters who target the elderly, bullies, and fly-tippers called out, caught, and – ideally to their great surprise – hung by their nipples from a telegraph pole or whatever the appropriately safe, reasonable, and judicially-sanctioned equivalent is.

I think by now that I should be surprised by less as several decades of mooching about this planet on Her Majesty's business ought to have flushed out a few eternal truths through 'learning by bruising'. In my new incarnation as a captain of industry (Designate) – and so far it is all designate and not much captaining – there are new surprises to learn, but not that radically different.

When still in uniform (a major general in Baghdad at the time) many of my Arab interlocutors had cultivated a thoroughly charming talent for sustaining lengthy and entirely reasonable discourse in great conviviality during which they made commitments to do X or arrange Y, all communicated with a smile, a steady eye, and a lot of tea. Without intending at any point to actually do or arrange anything of the sort. This was not always because they couldn't, though it was sometimes so and this just could not be admitted, it was mostly because they didn't want to, were not allowed to, or – most often – because it would mean forfeiting an urgent engagement with viewing the back of their eyelids followed by a stroll and supper. When I charged them with this, they were genuinely surprised that I was surprised. I accept that for many of these conversations I was present in their country, like Iraq, in quite complicated and trying circumstances from the perspective of securing cooperation, without the application of more high explosive or – far more powerful – a wedge of cash from the apparently super-indulgent US taxpayer. But the fact is I was surprised, and that I could still be surprised in this way so far into my career should be disappointing.

On the other hand, in my new life, I find that the scope for being surprised in this sort of way (essentially, making a commitment without any corresponding will or ability to actually meet it) is in wider use. So many business meetings that conclude with much agreement to advance swiftly to greater things are followed, as if by law, by little actually happening. This is sometimes just a conspiracy of optimism: we are swept along on a wave of excitement and relish for What Will Be Done. We are certainly guilty of fantasizing on the spot about how much victory champagne is about to be supped from the dimples on the backs of a dozen comely maidens when the basic truth is that – whatever it is it is doomed to die as soon as we are all back in the street or clicked out of Zoom.

On other occasions I now realize that I have been manoeuvred by forces of commerce red in tooth and claw to see how much I can be scrubbed on a question of the moment, perhaps incentivized by the vaguest of promises of a tidal wave of cash and free lunches, without a single bean actually remotely in prospect of ever changing hands. This is a game best played over several rounds and the best players are the ones who inhabit the steel and glass palaces east of St Paul's and the swish offices west of Regent Street. The novelty of being surprised like this quickly wears thin, with no points for slow-learners. It's Darwin with spreadsheets. I can read a spreadsheet too now.

It made me wonder, though; when did I first really have to deal with proper, substantial, and significant surprise? The sort that makes the mouth go dry and the waterworks fizz. Probably not at all in the Cold War, as described elsewhere in these pages all the surprises during that (for me) halcyon era, as the world teetered every day on the brink of Superpower-enabled nuclear extinction, were small and predictable. The massive shock of a Soviet assault on the West really taking place never occurred of course. The final collapse of the Soviet Union 1989-90 did come as a surprise in terms of it actually happening and when, but the fact that it did happen was not a total surprise.

I remember standing in the regimental officers' mess in Bergen-Hohne at around the time the first wave of gaseous, cardboard Trabants (a form of car, but not as the West knew it) were rolling over the IGB in their thousands when the fence just fell away. Each of these vehicles potentially contained safely four and massively unsafely perhaps eight newly-liberated East Germans on their first sortie to the consumer dream of West Germany. The enthusiasm to travel was generously expedited by the West German government handing 100 Deutsche Marks to each adult as a sort of introductory offer to a new life. As quite a lot of this was handed pretty speedily to McDonalds and many other fine purveyors of fast food, history may record that the first taste of freedom was also the first step on the road to a lardy arse and furry arteries. Such are the agonies of the human condition.

There were some quite strident complaints on West German radio from the ladies who operated a very broad sweep of genitals-based professional services from a selection of fixed and mobile infrastructure across Northern Germany. Their accusation stood that all these visitors from the east had badly misplaced how pricing had been adjusted over the intervening forty years since Berlin last changed hands. There was now in way too many cases an awkward, shuffling posse of gawping window-shoppers cluttering up their enterprises. It was made plain that even all the hundred Deutsche Marks could not purchase more than the perfunctory preliminaries to sexual congress, and offering no DMs at all and pleading for a charity shag was sure to result in an interview with a baseball bat. Welcome to capitalism.

In any case, after three weeks of being visited en masse every Saturday, the local inhabitants of top tourist spots in the West, such as lovely Celle, were still thrilled at the history they were witnessing, but completely done with any Trabant owners/occupiers who did not follow the clear and comprehensive municipal parking arrangements. With great freedom came great responsibility, including parking properly, but I thought all this reckoning could wait a week or two in the circumstances – life had been hard for half a century.

The conversation in the mess was dominated by speculation over what would now happen to BAOR, it having arrived in Germany in late 1944 to, at best, a muted welcome from the inhabitants and then stayed on more or less equitable terms for the ensuing forty-five years. Even in 1944 when we were shot at with great tenacity, we were also deemed more attractive invaders than the Russians coming at such pace from the east in an attitude of really high dudgeon. The record shows that Russian conquering was abetted by a lot of rape, pillage and murder- the only point up for debate at the time was the order in which these atrocities would occur. This immense unpleasantness having been fuelled by the slaughter of millions of Russians in the opening leg of the war. (British military doctrine is mute on the batting order, but pillage-rape-murder would seem to be the orthodoxy). We forget at our peril what a bitch war always is.

1945 was a very tough year for Germany, and here we were forty-five years later with British troops still stationed in broadly the same places as their predecessors found themselves at the final whistle of the Second World War. In the case of my own regiment, this was Hamburg, and as soon as the shooting stopped the officers motored round to the poshest hotel, dug the staff out of the cellars and demanded a proper breakfast. Ironically, today the officers would need to gaffer tape all their credit cards together to pay for just one smart sausage there.

Suddenly, in 1989, the prospect of reunification was on everyone lips, with the bets on timing ranging from a year to a hundred years. So too was the question of whether I British Corps would be ordered to march east to 'secure' the rest of Germany as the Russians headed home. This was never more than fanciful: there was not much point and a whole lot of irritation would be caused. In fact, we were barred from going east in even a private capacity – so many of us immediately drove to Berlin for a look. Driving through areas on the map of East Germany that had been the home and training grounds of the 'Group of Soviet Forces Germany' against which we had plotted, planned, and trained for six groundhog months of every year for forty-five years was quite a moment. So was the revelation that there really were columns of trucks loaded and lined up to support the invasion of the West that had never come.

We had often scoffed about whether this stuff existed and hung the masterplan for victory on the thought that even if it did all exist, it would cause such an impossible traffic jam to the IGB that even the RAF would find it after a couple of tries. A cursory drive through the Russian barrack areas on the outskirts of Berlin in 1989 showed the pitiful condition of an abandoned, impoverished organization brought low by the deeper pockets of NATO. No wonder there is such a strong whiff of a score to be settled in the standing Russian lumpiness towards the West today.

This moment in world history was also a huge inflection point for the UK Armed Forces, something that is only really clear thirty years later – and still an unfolding surprise. For literally centuries, the Royal Navy and the British Army, and for literally one whole century for the Royal Air Force, there had consistently been plenty of business abroad. First in enduring, iterative wars in Europe about the ownership of land and the premier route to God, then in building and policing a global empire of surprisingly epic proportions – followed by giving it back to what has turned out to be a mixed bag of successor arrangements, and also in fending off the existential threat of subjugation and invasion from Germany for about fifty years on and off. Finally the issue of Russia as the Soviet Union occupied another forty-five years at least.

For military folk, there is nothing like a full-on existential peril to fuel all the manning, equipping, and training of satisfyingly large armies, navies, and air forces. Better still, the threat of invasion and total destruction of civilized life confers on the military man a sense of value and importance in society – 'here we are standing in the eye of the storm to protect our country, our families, our civilisation, willing – if not actually determined – to lay down our lives to save all this and more'. This narrative comes with all the trimmings of doing things like massive war games which knock any computer game out of the park for excitement at huge cost, a lot of adventurous training up mountains and along rivers, and a tonne of sporting stuff – all whilst still being paid. These really do add up to making soldiers, sailors, airmen, and marines fitter, tougher, and sharper. And it is all way, way better than knocking out another colour of flange-grubber for the international market in a factory in Reading – or conjuring up a new financial wheeze to make people borrow money they can never pay back. I miss it all every day.

So, the surprise of the fall of the Berlin Wall triggered a profound change in the military profession for the UK and many others. Gone were the pressing advantages of having a big enemy to confront at the level of real national peril every day, for years on end. As soon as this penny dropped in government and society, it was not long (about a day) before the point of having large armed forces all at a high level of readiness became debatable – and then all the talk was of what size peace dividend could be wrestled from the defence budget.

For the British Army there was the surprise double whammy of hostilities in Northern Ireland winding down in the 1990s, after a sharp start to proceedings back in 1969. This affair sometimes soaked up 50,000 soldiers, mostly infantry, in a struggle that was both extraordinarily sharp at some times and places and yet also extraordinarily bounded by a common sense of how things were to be played. Northern Ireland terrorism was certainly cunning, ruthless, and periodically devastating, but its proponents were almost always keener to get home in one piece than to die whilst engaged in a shooting or a bombing. They were also generally fussy about who they wanted to kill, which is no consolation at all to those who did die, but did mean the overall quantum of catastrophe was comparatively reduced.

Suicide bombers in places like Iraq and Afghanistan etc did not phone in warnings ahead and the terrorists there were often pretty keen on fighting for as long as they possibly could before being expedited to a massively improved theoretically-endorsed sex life at the hands of a British marksman. For the British Army I joined, however, the combination of a large, mature, and serious commitment to keeping the Soviet Union out of the West provided scale, purpose and full careers, and the commitment for thirty-seven years to The Troubles in Northern Ireland provided additional scale and a completely different, complex, and occasionally adrenalin-fuelled challenge. The whole organization, around 150,000 strong, had enough to be going on with and could hold its own as an important part of the British Establishment, pointing to several hundred years of similarly illustrious endeavour. This merited a lot of public marching about dressed for a Victorian festival with bands, usually in front of a Royal (who must find it bizarre that they have to go through all this every single time before the army offers them any lunch).

The same endurance of purpose was also true of the Royal Navy as it spent decades herding Russian submarines around the Atlantic whilst regularly pointing in a slightly needy way as far back as Nelson and Trafalgar. The Royal Air Force stood ready to keep Soviet aircraft away from UK shores and was tooled up to drop nuclear bombs over Russia, taking time and care to point over and over again back to the Battle of Britain – occasionally pausing to summon up the Dambusters for light relief.

As we now know, however, the fall of the Berlin Wall became the starting gun for a steady reduction in the size of the UK Armed Forces (the army today is well below 80,000 regulars) in the proven absence (despite attempts to find some) of peril big enough to justify keeping larger ones. This is mostly a good thing, of course it is, as it means money may be spent on more desirable things like education and health, or maybe even given back to taxpayers (though not, apparently in the UK and certainly not in 1990s Britain as public money was comprehensively splurged about until the 2008 financial crisis sharpened up Treasury pencils).

Less cash is not so obviously a good thing for professional armed forces. Less money plus more inflation means redundancies, equipment cuts, reduced training, and ever more shabby buildings. It also meant that instead of having almost all the forces ready to go almost all the time, as you do when invasion is imminent, the armed forces were switched to cyclical or 'graduated' readiness whereby parts rotated through being bursting for a fight, training to get to that state, and a period of hanging about doing PT and shitty jobs. When starting down on this road in the early 1990s there was just about enough equipment to bring the whole thing back up to readiness quite quickly, but twenty years down the road there was just not enough to go round, leaving those at the back of the queue with unlimited PowerPoint but otherwise shouting 'bang' to simulate the horror of combat at close quarters.

Set above the scrabble for size was the scrabble for purpose. If there was no big enemy to pitch against – and in the 1990s Russia and NATO were pretending hard to be mates – what should UK Armed Forces be for? This sort of debate keeps coming up in history. For example, once Napoleon was safely tucked up on St Helena there was a bit of a gap before Germany stood up to the plate as Enemy Number One. But at least back then there were still entire continents to battle over, India and Africa featuring well, and some pain to accommodate in the Americas.

In 1990s Britain the quest for Empire had certainly diluted and even the Falkland Islands were looking pretty comfy after the kicking administered to the most recent invaders in 1982. There were still a few nutters clinging to the idea that Russia was only on a pause as a source of strategic menace: how they were rubbished in the annals of learned institutions trumpeting the final, consummate arrival of post-history, post-conflict Europe. How these same nutters are being sought with pots of gold now that Russia has resumed being strategically annoying and grumpy in digital as well as Stone Age and Industrial ways.

Fortunately, certainly from the perspective of professional military people surprised to be feeling a bit spare, the end of the Cold War and some deft political handling of the consequences around the collapsing Balkans pretty quickly made sure there was some new work. This really was a surprise all round. And a bit later, in 1999 in Chicago, Mr Blair helped out a lot by talking up the 'Responsibility to Protect'; the idea that it was the right thing to do when faced with grand humanitarian catastrophe to eschew the claims of sovereign states and intervene militarily. Somehow, the end of the Cold War led to me and my fellow bearers of arms for the Queen becoming more than horrid baby-eaters, we were now a force for good. That was a cooler T-shirt for sure.

I actually didn't know how much of an angel I had become at the time, but it is good to know it now. In 1991 I attended the Army Staff College at Camberley, following in the footsteps of almost 150 years of officers marching purposefully through its portals to emerge as the Jedi knights of British military bureaucracy. Getting there involved a couple of stodgy competitive examinations and a massive amount of being clever, cute and above all Olympian-level obsequious to the senior officers who wrote the personal appraisals that simply had to contain the golden words 'must attend Staff College at the earliest opportunity'.

It's a digression, but at this time (late 1980s or so) an officer's annual 'confidential report' had a part written by an immediate superior that was shown to the subject and signed as such, and a second part written by the next up the chain of command which was kept 'blind' to the subject. In this way, an ambitious young officer could know that according to his commanding officer he was without doubt the most superb exponent of the military arts ever, the living embodiment of Hercules – and also the Spartans if the chips were really down. He was without doubt a dead cert to one day lead the combined armed forces of the entire galaxy against alien invaders and blessed with a wife who followed the flag with exquisite, fragrant, saucy charm whilst dispensing top quality Yorkshire puddings on demand (yes, this was indeed the late 1980s, things really were different). On the other hand, in the unseen second section, the same officer could not know that he was already at his ceiling, the most idle, feckless, cowardly dunderhead that ever filled army trousers, likely to bolt at the sound of a pistol being fired a mile away, loathed by his men for beating and robbing them, and married to a woman who even when sober, which was never, could be relied upon to be the social hand grenade that wrought destruction on any and every occasion. Once the idea of completely transparent reporting was introduced, a far greater proportion of dunderheads found they had careers after all, for which I remain eternally grateful.

After a year of learning by heart the stuff that was all freely available in the book we had to carry about, I emerged steeped in the ability to wave my hand over any map you might care to show me and talk about the Armoured Division's most likely 'Avenues of Approach' as it scythed through its part in the 'Corps Counter-Stroke'. I could work out how long it would take that division to pass a single point, and what that meant for clogging up the A303 in Somerset for days. Armed with this knowledge I found I was to be the 'Brigade Major', the chief of staff, of an armoured brigade in Germany – just as the Soviet jacking-in of a Third World War meant it was the wrong thing in the wrong place. Happily, back to the theme of surprise again, after only a few months the mess in the Balkans wrought some timely repurposing at the speed of bluff. War had come to Europe after all.

The thing about war is that across the whole history of mankind no one has quite fully understood it. This is partly because we know it is such a dim thing to do, yet we remain eternally fascinated by it. For the young of every generation, those who can never have felt it at first hand, it is siren-quality glamorous, a release from the bonds of daily civilized life and a thrilling test of character and skill. This is usually dressed up in fervently-trending, unhinged revolutionary or nationalist bobbins.

Militaries have always captured the market in natty clothes too. Sharp combat clothes and cool shades in battle. Generally the further a navy, army, or air force gets from actual need to fight, the bigger and more festooned the hats get, the more dangly gold accoutrements are applied, and the more medals get minted for progressively less risky activities than going head to head with an armed and professionally violent opponent. Simply getting older, still breathing, and not getting caught are amongst my favourite medals.

Over the centuries many clever people have tried to distil the essence of war into laws, like the laws of geometry or physics, or if that is too hard (and it really is) at least find some principles. Quite reasonably, these efforts have to greater or lesser degree been a prisoner of their time, but some eternal truths of wide acceptability have emerged. I cling to the Clausewitzian view (and not just because there are *always* points to be had for randomly saying 'Clausewitz' a lot at any Staff College, complemented by the 1,000-yard distressed warrior stare), that the nature of war never changes. It is always, always a brutal, feral, dangerous, unbounded, and merciless thing once unleashed, but the character of war changes all the time with technology and thinking. For example, gunpowder ended the point of castles and knights in armour, but having your head cut off at Agincourt in 1415 was just as unpleasant as it was in Syria in 2015.

Amongst the few things that are completely certain is that wars are incredibly complicated affairs once started: a blend of passions, politics, physical force, luck, and the weather that no man or organization can completely control in every way. They usually start as a result of pressure building up over time, sometimes in complex ways, and are swayed by the momentum created by people and states getting tooled up for a fight. If you give a young man a gun and some bullets he will find a way to try them out, and if trying them out brings him recognition, power, even better money and sex, it can be hard to turn the threat of war off. But no matter how complex the potential causes of war may be, they do tend to actually open proceedings for surprising reasons. Once started and the red mist descend, they become really very hard to stop until enough people have been hurt to create a majority that thinks more fighting is not going to mean better outcomes.

There is some science out there that concludes this period can be years, say twelve in the case of insurgencies and longer (maybe another five years) if they can annually regenerate by retreating to safe havens. I think I saw in the Balkans and Northern Ireland how the leaders of the fighting at the start, often in their mid-to-late-twenties, have to lose enough friends, come to fear for their own mortality and produce their own children for whom providing a future without fighting becomes important, before they trade the power and glamour of a warrior for a different and likely longer life. But by the time these men (and some women) reach this conclusion, the next generation of immortal, ambitious, and impassioned youngsters are seeing the fight as their own path to fame and fortune. Wars can be self-perpetuating if this cycle is not patiently and resolutely broken.

I am, I think, wiser about it now, but one of the failings of many people's education seems to be that they somehow become convinced that mankind has definitely evolved to the point where reasoning and intellect trump emotion, comprehensively neutering the immense gravitational pull of carnal instincts on their brain. This is despite us all knowing full well that man is still running with biologically driven emotions largely unchanged since pre-history, clinging to myths about politics and institutions with medieval origins that are as useful now as bows and arrows, and operating Digital Age technology that simultaneously massively outruns the human brain and is still basically dead thick. In many situations we know what a reasonable person should think and we know how it would be best for mankind if we behaved, yet given enough means, motive and opportunity more often than not what actually happens is propelled by forces that are the very opposite of rational.

This just can't be a shock anymore, yet every day somebody somewhere, in a position of authority – it doesn't seem to matter whether that is at the level of a family or a parish council or right up to a head of state or international organization – does something daft, by which I mean something emotionally-charged or venal that just smashes the right thing to do in the face. When this comes to light it's clear that the perpetrator really is truly sorry, and that whatever advantage or passing pleasure they had enjoyed is now not worth the trashing of their standing amongst people they know, love or are just related to. Whether or not they are truly sorry for what they did or just very sorry that they got caught can be a fine call.

I think that the expression it couldn't possibly be him/her' should be banned, in my experience nobody is immune to the potential for doing something so completely, madly at odds with the sort of conduct that fits the place in life that they are trying to occupy. It can be failing to resist dipping fingers into the till, whether an actual till or a metaphorical one of millions of pounds of other people's money. It can mean abandoning all vestiges of integrity in favouring the interests of a person, outcome, or organization in a decision propelled by lust or lucre. It can entail hurling away sensible mores about how people should relate to each other – and this generally involves applying a hand to another's nether regions uninvited, satisfying the criteria for being 24-carat pervy or much worse.

I imagine you are now asking me what does this have to do with surprise or the business of surprise and war? Well, my first point is that war may bring out the best in some people in a way that Hollywood is delighted to milk, and this is a good thing as most wars are a bit better for an element of heroism and stiff integrity. But for every genuine hero amongst the sea of chaos and tears at the heart of fighting on any scale there are many more people who behave like utter shitbags. This is not because they think it's necessary or unavoidable in the circumstances to be shitbags. It's because when war releases the brakes on normal civilized ways of living, the temptation to exploit what feels like glorious, liberation from being ordinarily normal becomes irresistible – especially if the chances of being found out are small and the chances of being judicially spanked even less.

War has unquestionably demonstrated that it can bring out the very worst in people, the same people who would behave just like anybody else in a stable, secure normal environment. It can be explained by fear or outrage in some settings, it can be mitigated by the real threat felt from others claiming to be on the same side, it might just be a massive dose of red mist descending in the heat of clearly difficult and trying times, but the result is that apparently normal, thoughtful people who claim to be decent and respectable are burning their neighbour's house down whilst shooting and raping the occupants. This comes as a surprise at the time, every time, and it will happen next time.

The surprising capacity to do this is always amplified when one party starts to see another as 'the others', somehow different or lesser and threatening to 'us'. This is clearly easier when people look different, hold to different flavours of God, or exhibit any visible characteristic that sets them apart. These differences, which we tell ourselves are irrelevant and wrong and lead to discrimination or harm as we try to build complex, multicultural twenty-first century life, quickly rocket to the surface as soon as shots are fired. Despite several thousand years of evolution, the battle to contain mankind's innate predisposition to discriminate on a physical or psychological basis is really only rarely and barely kept under a veneer of civilisation. The rapidity with which states shafted their neighbours in the scrabble for facemasks and hand sanitizer when COVID-19 besieged the world in 2020 shows how little it takes to dump the talk of fraternity in favour of – as the Scottish like to say – 'taking a shite in next door's kettle'.

If making war against 'the other' is easier when they are something different or lesser, the temptation to wrap this up with hardcore demonization is hard to resist. Much easier to shoot the 'handmaidens of the devil' in the face than the 'other' people you see around town being ordinary albeit in a different type of hat. The capacity to demonize makes it easier to do much worse things, and normal people are certainly capable of this even though they know that it's not just wrong, it's massive gold-plated wrong. Of course, demonizing 'the other' also increases the chances of reciprocation in kind, and certainly makes the challenge of finding an end to fighting without slaughter or capitulation much harder. When tired of shooting the devil's emissaries, how do you then convert them back to the status of normal citizens and neighbours with whom it will be possible to chat about peaceful coexistence?

This dichotomy, the struggle to balance the human capacity for considered reason against the grip of reflexive emotion, partly explains why wars often start for pretty shoddy reasons that then cause the whole head of steam to bust out of its container. I can't see too much difference between a seven-year-old boy who loses his temper at one slight too many and hurls stones at his assailants across the playground, despite the walloping that will follow, and quite a lot of history. It also partly explains why once wars have got going, they are so hard to stop. Sometimes they are just not going to be stoppable until enough steam has vented, even if this venting shapes the future as far forward as one can see in comprehensively unsatisfactory ways from any reasoned perspective. It is perfectly possible, I have found, to look a protagonist squarely in the eye and explain why more fighting is just not in their or anybody else's interest, with which they agree for a moment – before again submitting to the urge to smash in some more skulls.

Some wars do finish in an emphatic outcome, which usually means the losing side has been comprehensively defeated, destroyed, slaughtered, or fled. None of the wars of my personal acquaintance have ended in this way. Even if there has been some sort of clear outcome at the level of military fighting, the questions that remain about power, politics, justice, reconstruction etc are far from resolved. In almost every case when the actual fighting is brought to an end, the protagonists are just as enthusiastic as ever to secure and advance their interests by any and all other means. Only now, of course, they bear all the scars of the fighting, which will of course inhibit their ability to be rational about their future. Sometimes the only way to peace is for the generation that fought to grow old and die whilst their children are encouraged to focus on building a boring normal life where the prospect of a owning a newish BMW supplants the enthusiasm for shooting.

We shouldn't really be surprised that the leaders of the fighting are not ideally placed to be the leaders in settlement and peace. Applying the general precept that turkeys don't vote for Christmas, where the leaders of the fighting have become accustomed to power, money and impunity, their heart is just not in giving it all up to be normal and poor, and especially not if it might mean going to jail. Where they can convert themselves from warlord to politician, they are likely to feel better about it – politics is a career one can pursue until quite old and doddery, being a street fighter tops out where kneeling to shoot requires a twenty-minute yoga warm-up.

Becoming a politician also usually means that there are the resources of a state to plunder, with the delicious prospect of these coffers being regularly refilled with international money for post-war stability and reconstruction. Profit for very little effort or risk is a big driver for peace. If the newly minted warlord-cum-politician can delay or avoid entirely the need to submit themselves to any sort of decent or fair election that threatens to pass judgement on their past and current life so much the better. What then follows is that they surprise even themselves, as well as many of their followers at home and their supporters in the international community, at just how *rubbish* they are at running countries. Quite a lot of African, Balkan, and Latin American history illustrates the point. Given that they have had neither training nor experience in their entire adult life in much more than fighting, I don't think the surprise at how poor they are at organization and administration ought to be quite so widespread.

I think there is a particular problem here in the way that western militaries deal with the administrations of countries either still at war or just emerging from one. For a start, one of the first things that generally happens when war breaks out is that many talented people who can leave do so as rapidly as possible. This is of course particularly true for the middle and professional classes, those who have the will and the money to get out and build a new life elsewhere exit quickly, either as commercial migrants or refugees from genuine persecution. In some cases, parents stay but they dispatch their children abroad – who then build different lives that rapidly deplete the prospects of them ever returning. Amongst those who remain there will be a few very dedicated, brave, and capable people, but also some fanatics who may be gifted but are essentially deeply unhelpful to the cause of trying to restore stability, and an awful lot of people who couldn't leave but now find themselves in roles that would not previously have been within their compass. As I saw in the ruins of Bosnia, taxi drivers appear as Chiefs of Police because they are a local enforcer, clerks are suddenly running the town council. In some cases, full marks for effort even if the results are poor; in other cases no marks at all.

To the newly arrived British, French, German, Italian, US officer etc, usually sent to impose or maintain a fragile peace, the person sat behind the desk marked 'Minister' wearing a suit looks just like a minister at home in a peaceful and mature liberal democracy. But what is under the suit may have nothing more than ambition, an education from watching *West Wing* on Netflix, and possibly a sense of duty to offer. They have authority, but in terms of vision, education, and training there is very little to work with. Worse, in some countries this minister is operating on entirely different assumptions: he or she understands that this job has been bought or awarded on the traditional and still prevailing basis that it is mostly a platform for personal plunder and abuse. That is after all the way it has been in these parts for as long as anyone can remember. Western diplomats, officials and military officers who either don't know or choose to ignore this are very likely to find themselves comprehensively done over and swiftly robbed of any money that they may have to bring to help the work of the ministry.

The expectation in stabilizing war-torn places is that things will improve as time passes if effort is applied, but unless a very long time indeed is allowed my experience has been that things can get quite a lot worse for quite a long time. At the outset, say when fighting has just subsided enough to begin to establish the renewal of civil administration, the newly employed ministers and their teams are weaker and more malleable. As they grow in confidence in their own abilities to see off the attentions and criticism of their international minders, whilst still maintaining the flow of foreign cash, the pace and scale of plunder and malfeasance tends to rise. Even if the international community sees this, and it generally doesn't very clearly, it is torn between withdrawing support and money, thereby causing political and social progress to stall, and other less principled sources of revenue to fill the gap, and keeping the money and advice coming in the hope that things will change over time. This is hope priced in millions of dollars.

We also know that one of the reasons that these new administrations prove so hard to steer onto a more honest and righteous path is not just the difficulty of knowing what is going on and applying a degree of necessary conditionality, it's also because the behaviour of the national and international representatives working alongside them can set less than a gleaming example. One of the cardinal principles for nations who agree to deploy their forces to places like Bosnia, Iraq, and Afghanistan is that these troops will not be subject to arrest or detention by the host nation. There are pretty good reasons for this, high amongst them the horrifically broken nature of the judicial and penal system, but where it confers a sense of immunity and impunity that is gratuitously exploited then the incentive for the locals to change their behaviour is diminished. This can be in small things, such as the way international forces barge through local traffic, or in big things such as how very large sums of money are spent and accounted for. Contracting practices that involve handling large bags of cash without the ability or even the requirement to produce either proof of outcome or auditable accounts have made some international organization staff in loosely regulated environments such as Afghanistan personally very much more prosperous, as well as their local counterparts. Should this be a surprise after so long?

Looking back at the preceding few pages I may seem a bit sour? If so, I apologize as the experience over thirty years or so was always exhilarating, sometimes a joy, and occasionally successful. Almost nothing I learned at Staff College got under the skin of what being in and around a war really meant, though it certainly helped me to turn up properly dressed, with some methods to apply and enough sharp pencils. So much of my contribution was about trying to make headway amongst all the surprises and the bruises. As it was not possible to know then what I think I know now – and as every campaign has unique characteristics – perhaps the surprise is that so much of the business of war will always just be a come-as you-are party.

Chapter 3

Bosnia 1992

My Dear M,

I would be lying if I said that I had ever given Yugoslavia much thought before I found myself heading there as it comprehensively fell apart thirty years ago. It was another of those salutary lessons in life, military and personal, that the things you most expect to happen and prepare for don't materialize and what actually happens just smacks you between the eyes with neither warning nor mercy. There are big exceptions to this rule, mainly applying to the things that you know are very likely to happen but which are way too unpleasant to contemplate and expensive to prepare for. These are parked in everybody's 'too difficult' tray and given a stiff ignoring, buttressed by hope and prayer. This pretty much ensures that they do materialize and do become more than a bit tearful and costly, like a global virus pandemic.

Anyway, my own part in the dismemberment of Tito's Yugoslavia was really a confluence of accidents. I was an energetic chief of staff of an armoured brigade (normally around 5,000 people) garrisoned in a charming part of Germany called Minden. The brigade was heading towards being closed down following the Soviet Union's unhelpful (to me) decision to cease cooperating in an infinite Cold War with the West on the grounds of being broke (and communism being found to be a nutjob). Quite a lot of the brigade had very sensibly already found better employment than maintaining vintage armoured vehicles in barracks for a war that had been called off, by being dispatched (yet again) to bring harmony to the streets and fields of Northern Ireland.

Some of the rest of the brigade was busy working out how to take all the stuff accumulated in houses, offices, stores, and vehicle parks over decades and get shot of it. There was way too much to fly-tip. A few opportunists would find a way of adding a bung to their pension in how a thousand 'chest of drawers, upright, three drawer, soldier' left the taxpayer's books by magic. Army furniture is sourced specifically to be as devoid of style and homeliness as possible, clinging to the worst of 1950s enthusiasm for all things brown and box-square well into the 1990s, so its brightest post-Cold War future was probably as firewood. However, there was the odd piece of genuinely nice stuff which had usually been informally liberated from the Third Reich and then employed to adorn the houses of the more senior officers for half a century. We can be pretty sure none of this ended on a bonfire, judging by the rash of brand new cars that seemed to appear amongst some sections of the 'Accommodation Services' staff and their German counterparts – one shining example of effective Anglo-German cooperation in the latter twentieth century.

With only some formulaic trundles of the remainder of the brigade around the usual dusty hell-hole of Lüneberg Heath training areas to look forward to, I thought that the violent thrashings of the unhappy constituents of the former Yugoslavia became much more interesting. When it looked like some sort of half-baked UN deployment was being conjured up, I took the unusual step of dispatching an advertisement for the services of a top-grade brigade HQ around the palaces of the mighty in army command circles. Warlike business is not normally transacted like in a bazaar and it was no more than a certain bored wistfulness. I thought no more about it. Which of course meant that a short while later the phone rang and within about a week we were climbing aboard a plane to Croatia/Bosnia (at the time the distinction was a bit lost on me).

That week in Autumn 1992 was my first live encounter with the truths of most 'unplanned' military deployments. It was only loosely orchestrated chaos, starting with two quite important questions: where was this place and what were we supposed to do there? The first, this was pre-Google, meant getting some maps sent to us. All wars need to allow time for a lot of maps to be sticky-taped together or pretty much nothing can be got going. So we knew after a day or so that we were going to the right of Italy, a bit above Greece, and well below Austria. We knew a lot of Germans liked to take their summer holidays in parts of it, because we found a guidebook in a local shop. We pretended to understand the wisdom it conveyed through our extensive beer, sausage, and sex-focused military grasp of the word-elongating, verb concealing mystery that is the German language. As long as we wanted to know the best places for a dawn raid to deploy towels or get our Mercedes fixed, we were now off to a flying start.

Eternal Truth One about professional military forces and the prospect of deploying on an operation, especially a new one, is that no matter how ill-informed the preparations or bizarre the mission, no matter how big a gap there is between aims, methods, and resources, no matter how tiny the chances of success, once given a sniff there is no way we are not going. It's what we do. I am, therefore, much struck by the agonies my new commercial colleagues submit to when making decisions about whether to invest in a new project or a new market, or buy a company. They seem really bothered about whether it will succeed, or make a profit, or add value to what they already do. They often decide not to do these things. You just can't do that in the military line of work, especially for top-notch opportunities like invading somewhere, or you would never do anything.

Eternal Truth Two is that when all wars start, there must be an obviously short, certain step to decisive victory and home by Christmas. If we acknowledged that getting anything done would take a minimum of ten years, cost billions, and involve a fair bit of death and injury, what government would put that in the papers as it sent us off?

So, of course, the week before we flew was just this blur of well-intentioned activity. There were some quite important things to try and get straight, like what was the problem we were trying to solve and what was the plan? The first needs to be reasonably clear or dumb things generally ensue, and it was immediately clear that what we were being asked to do sounded simple enough but was actually papering over a lot of strategic fannying about.

Our mission, which we were going to accept whatever its merits on the basis of Eternal Truth One, was to 'support the delivery of humanitarian aid' to the benighted victims of the war, still very vigorously underway in Bosnia. This was a bit novel: generally speaking, one might wait for a war to finish up enough before committing to get food and blankets to the disadvantaged (of which there would be many). An alternative is to make the war stop by turning up mob-handed and forcing hostilities to conclude at the point of our more, bigger guns. But deploying military forces to alleviate just the symptoms whilst the causes of those symptoms were still very much alive and well was bound to have some challenges, mostly because – whatever we did – we would change the situation on the ground and that would never please everybody. It's hard to be everyone's friend and no one's enemy once the throat-ripping has started.

This middle course was the result of the government of the day in the UK and others elsewhere being stuck with popular revulsion at what was being portrayed on telly in living rooms across their countries every night. Bosnia is, after all, part of Europe – in fact it was a part of Europe that many people were used to taking their holidays in. Stoked by centuries of troubled history, the violence was as brutal and feral as had been seen so close at hand in Europe since the Second World War. In particular, the eruption again of 'ethnic cleansing' – the wholesale displacement of entire communities on the basis of their ethnicity in order to establish control over exclusive mono-ethnic areas – was particularly shocking. The sight of thousands of women and children being forcibly removed at short notice from their homes and basically chucked over the nearest front line to join their ethnic kin was inevitably going to spark a powerful 'something must be done' lobby. The fact that their menfolk had been carted off to certain unpleasantness, even massacre, was even more outrageous. Hard to argue with that.

On the other hand, if in doing this 'something' the UK and others were drawn into a messy, expensive and bloody conflict of no material use to national interests the nobility of the original purpose would quickly become lost in the lack of progress, casualties, and no clear sight of an achievable end. As is traditional when problems like this appear, it was not long before some observers were talking up the prospect of Bosnia becoming 'Europe's Vietnam'. And it would be Europe's Vietnam because the United States was making it pretty clear that they had enough on, this was happening in Europe's backyard, as problems go it had only modest proportions, and so Europe should please kindly just get on with sorting it. The US approach partly reflected that it was the German recognition of the existence of separate states called Bosnia-Herzegovina that had caused the neighbours on either side, (Bosnia, Croatia and Slovenia) all of whom had long cast covetous eyes over this region, to assert their interests as forcibly as they considered necessary. In fact, there were still deep scars from the ravages of the Second World War amongst all parties and no love would be lost in having another go at each other.

If something had to be done, and that something was certainly not going to include taking part in the war, then would doing some muscular humanitarian support do the trick? Specifically, if the United Nations High Commissioner for Refugees (UNHCR) was struggling to keep people from starving and freezing as the war rattled around them, perhaps European (and Canadian) military could help them get the stuff through? The counter-arguments to this included the point that all we could be doing would be keeping people fatter and warmer for longer before they were shot or shelled anyway.

Sitting in a quiet market town in Germany with about a week's notice of heading down to Bosnia, it would be fair to say that this was the most flat-footed of flat-footed starts to an UK military intervention for some time, certainly since the Falkland Islands briefly changed hands in 1982. Despite the excellently taped up paper maps, it pretty quickly turned out that we didn't know where we were going. Where we first decided we wanted to go (Tuzla) was flatly rejected by the Bosnian Serb side, the first sign for us that working for the UN and claiming neutrality was not a total Gold Card. It was also the first indication that we were not anywhere near clear about who was who in this bitter conflict, which is never the brightest start to a military intervention.

We could see that there were three principal protagonists: the Bosnian Serbs who had by now left the capital Sarajevo and adjourned to the surrounding mountains from which they engaged in prolific sniping and shelling of their former neighbours. There was now quite a large Bosnian Serb enclave across

Bosnia and Herzegovina from which large numbers of 'others' were being forcibly ejected. The 'others' in this case where the Bosnian Croats, clearly well-connected and supported by Croatia, and the Bosnian Muslim – or Bosniacs – who had no contiguous neighbour to call on for support but plenty of help from elsewhere in the Muslim world. Any war with godfathers like these is bound to thrive.

The politics sounded quite complicated even before we got to grips with the problems of terrain, climate, and infrastructure – and how we would forge effective relationships with the UNHCR and the rest of the 'UN family'. This family would include a large clutch of 'Non-Government Organizations' taking on part of the aid delivery workload, ranging from large professional groups to two blokes with a school atlas and a shabby (stolen) van. The one thought that united most of the 'aid' fraternity was that 'All Soldiers Are Thick Bastards'. Sometimes this was genuinely believed because the only military they had ever encountered had indeed been slow on the uptake and often hugely obstructive. For others, the hippy grief-junky tossers as we came to know them, it was just cool to be army-allergic. That didn't extend to objecting to us rescuing their crappy vans from snow drifts or feeding them en route when they had run out of their survival cheesy Wotsits, I recall.

Our initial view was that the problem of getting aid to the victims of war meant forging a path through the testy Bosnian Serb areas, to locate the needy amongst the more friendly and disadvantaged from the other two factions. This predisposition about who was more friendly was reinforced by an earlier recce being modestly strafed by a Serb aircraft ('modestly' in this case means there were no casualties, but those present could still be forgiven a laundry crisis). In fact, over the ensuing first few days of examining the problem it became increasingly clear that the Serbs were much less of a problem as they simply were not going to allow the passage of any the convoys we were meant to secure. No meant no. On the other hand, the Bosnian Croats and the Bosnian Muslims were also now apparently fully committed to tearing at each other's intestines with spoons across the areas they had shared for decades, so our passage to any intended beneficiaries of all this food and blankets was never going to be straightforward.

The original master plan that had the British deployment entering Bosnia from the north, or indeed by any route up there that worked, in order to establish a presence around this place called Tuzla, was thus swiftly binned in favour of approaching Bosnia from an entry made in Croatia, through the lovely coastal city of Split. This would limit the challenge of getting into central Bosnia to securing a way through the squabbling Bosnian Croats and Bosnian Muslims, generally maintaining a healthy distance from the nearest

Bosnian Serb tank or artillery piece. And starting one's war from one of the loveliest recreational coast lines in Europe got my vote anyway.

My grasp of the speed and uncertainty surrounding organizing ourselves before we had to get on a plane (to wherever we were going) was a tad unhinged by the army's insistence that we were immediately inoculated against every possible disease or lurgy known to science that might conceivably pop up. Given the premium on time it was not possible to allow lengthy clinical intervals between the constituent parts of what became a massive cocktail of drugs, so we basically lined up and had the lot in one go. The medics mixed it up a bit by jabbing in as many different parts of the body as possible. I have never been tempted to try any form of recreational chemistry, but if the effect is anything like half a dozen army vaccinations competing for attention, I can see why some succumb. It is entirely possible that the first instructions I wrote or briefings I gave were more than a little tinted by being off my head on army-provided chemicals.

To make things just a bit more interesting it was decided that now was the right time to rotate the brigadier who would be my boss and who would lead the adventure. Doing this a week before departure meant uprooting staff from a very able commander whom we knew well in order to attach them to another equally able man whom we knew not at all. Military staffs are like Labradors: they are programmed to deliver unquestioning adoration of their master and invariably reflect their moods and idiosyncrasies. So we dutifully went through some of the pain of a rescue dog adapting to a new master on the very eve of the biggest dog show of our lives. This was not an impossible ask, but it was still one I resolved to try not to repeat.

Common to all outcomes was the immense personal predicament of what to pack for the war. There were some basics of course: a huge sleeping bag, a helmet, and a pistol with enough ammunition for a small siege were all high on my list. Ordinarily, the army (any army except the US) is very reluctant to give its people all the stuff that they would like for a war, in order to keep the burden on the public purse manageable. But when the balloon goes up a magic door opens somewhere in middle England and unleashes a tsunami of kit for every occasion. We knew from the guidebook that it could get quite chilly in the middle of Bosnia in winter, so we were awarded the right to draw all the equipment one might need for Christmas at the North Pole. The right did not quite extend to all the stuff actually being available, though we appreciated the thought, so things like insulated boots were not immediately to hand – to my great personal regret later on and ever since. Bosnia in winter did bad things for my feet that have never gone away.

The packing conundrum is that there is only so much space in the military baggage one is able to take, which is essentially as much as a very big and very fit man can stagger with for about 10 yards before collapsing in a sticky heap. This is quite a lot by holiday standards, but this holiday was going to be at least six months, very likely going to involve a fair bit of camping and bound to span from the depths of winter to the height of a Mediterranean summer. Worse, there was a huge question mark over the availability of a laundry and every likelihood of there being no chemist at which to replenish the supplies that keep a man looking sharp and not rotting at the edges. Small mercies like an emergency Mars Bar or ten must also find their place.

In a very human way, there comes a point in the preparation for battle at which every soldier just needs a few hours at home to pack his kit and prepare to exit the bosom of his family, for what will certainly be a protracted absence and may possibly include some lumpy consequences. The lumpy consequences for me included leaving a reasonably stoic wife with one toddler on the ground and another in gestation in a German town, a long day's drive and a ferry from any family. At only about a week's notice there is not much that can be done to alleviate this scale of administrative vortex, but fortunately a small rear party remained in the garrison to take the flak. As this was all before email was much of a thing or mobile phones were really common, we who deployed could take comfort from the fact that once safely in Bosnia we would be shielded from the worst of the drama and misery that would burst around our households. It could catch up with us later, much, much later.

So, the day came on 15 October 1992 when I and my fellow warriors of what was once headquarters 11 Armoured Brigade mounted the steps of a C-130 aircraft and instantly became Headquarters British Forces Bosnia on OPERATION GRAPPLE. That sounded great, though we were surprised the aircraft was from the American air force – quite why I don't recall, but maybe our own air force had better things to do. Might have been a golf day.

Literally as we mounted the steps, I was handed a large brown envelope which contained the first written instructions for the deployment we had received. Fortunately, these affirmed that our destination was still Bosnia, or rather Bosnia via a firm base which we were to establish on the Dalmatian Coast in Croatia. These instructions had a lot of standing military blurb about all the magnificent things we were to accomplish and all the terrible things we were to avoid, and amongst all this was the key fact that we had about three weeks before the first ship would arrive in Split carrying the heavy equipment. By then we need to have worked out where to send it, how to get it there and what it would do. There would be no end of help coming from the whole of the military architecture in the UK, some of which we would probably welcome. All I had to connect to it was a phone number in my notebook that would perhaps connect to a Royal Marine bloke I knew from Staff College in an operations room in Wilton near Salisbury. This is how history is made – for good or ill.

After four hours of flying sideways on the haemorrhoid-inducing plastic fabric seats of the C-130, we touched down at Split airport. In normal times this airport handled waves of largely German sunseekers easing off to parade their loveliness on the beaches along the coast. We were travelling out of season, but the only waves currently being handled were more C-130s flying humanitarian aid into Sarajevo. I was expecting to be met by a small British Army Advance Party, hoping very much that they had resolved where we were going to set up shop at least to start with. More than that was an open question, so as the aircraft unloaded we really didn't know whether to expect a marching band and an adoring crowd of relieved Croatians, or to have to skirmish our way into the terminal in the face of a hostile, armed reception. I hoped not to have to skirmish as all the Arctic kit I had to wear because it wouldn't fit in a bag was already causing some crevices to crust.

One of the major advantages that a C-130 has over anything British Airways usually employs is that as well as seating some fifty people in great discomfort it can carry their wheeled transport. As it would be incredibly painful and slow to get things organized if we had only our feet and perhaps some bicycles, turning up with some Land Rovers (stuffed to the roof) was impressively useful. Actually, we didn't have far to go as the best available accommodation to get started in turned out to be a collection of beach villas not far up the coast from the airport. If this sounds a bit bizarre to you, and I agree that it might, the fact that other villas were still occupied by people catching the last rays of summer alongside some unhappy-looking genuine refugees added an extra layer of weird. It was also very quickly apparent that unless we quickly discarded all the Arctic clothing we had been so thrilled to receive, the first casualties of the deployment would be the entire brigade staff collapsing from heat exhaustion.

The occupation of a set of beachfront villas possibly indicated that the risks which we faced in that area were more social than martial. But it also revealed the next Eternal Truth of military deployments, that prosecuting war depends quite a lot on the availability of water and shithouses. There is, for example, not much to be gained from deploying 100 brave warriors into the thick of the fight if they dehydrate after twenty-four hours and subsequently collapse with dysentery as a result of poor plumbing arrangements. The villas solved this problem, at some modest cost to the British taxpayer, until we were ready to occupy a suitably ramshackle but basically functional, more overtly military solution and adopt the full combat camping regime. No rush, I thought.

By nightfall on the first day we had established Headquarters British forces. One villa now served as the hub of intelligence, planning, and operations. This was my domain and relatively straightforward: when you know hardly anything it is quite hard to plan, and as the force was still in bed in England and Germany, our operations were understandably a bit thin. Next door, however, my counterpart Jim – the deputy chief of staff responsible for things like logistics, infrastructure, and medical support was beginning to address a hat-full of really substantial questions – with the three-week deadline of a massive ship full of armoured vehicles arriving uppermost in his mind. Neither for the first nor the last time in my career, I was content with the thought that all this 'log shite' was best left to others.

We could now at least ask our superior headquarters in the UK for help, because our Royal Signallers had established full satellite communications. 'Full' at this point in proceedings meant that a commercial satellite dish was balanced on a windowsill in order to get a shot up to space, connected to a telephone held in panting anticipation of receiving orders to dial by a bright member of the Royal Signals stationed in the villa's kitchen. It was also possible to connect the world's most irritating and slow laptop computer to the satellite. This became my primary source of gloom and frustration as soon as it started to deliver a ceaseless demand for information and updates to feed ministers, officials, and senior officers scattered across the entire firmament of the UK Armed Forces and NATO. My ability to type being as limited then as now to my two fairly unenthusiastic index fingers, many, many hours, long into the night, were to be spent reporting that not much had happened so far, but we were really busy planning to do something.

The next Eternal Truth of military operations that we encountered is that when something gets going, especially if it is new and exciting, everybody at every point in the entire 'chain of command', which extends from a corporal managing a checkpoint on a road in the middle of nowhere to the most senior four-star general in his swanky office in London, is certain that only they are truly in charge. This sentiment proceeds in inverse proportion to the scale of the operation: the smaller it is and the less that is going on elsewhere the more desperate the quest to take charge at all points on the 'chain of command' of whatever is actually happening.

The military have spent centuries conjuring up structural ways to divvy up the work, generally settling on the notion that there is a strategic level (what goes on in capital cities and at the top of alliances), an operational level (what goes on at the level of the particular theatre or country of operations), and the tactical level (which is everything to do with the fight itself). The lines between these strata are easily blurred, so the opportunity to stray with great abandon is easy to create and irresistible to ignore in practice. There is a drill that everybody is schooled in, that is actually worth sticking to. But Corporal Wheel Nut thinks the Chief of the Defence Staff doesn't know his ass from his elbow in matters of military strategy, and General Throat-Tangler thinks Corporal Wheel Nut should stand a bit to the left and carry an extra bandage.

So, of course, from the very first minute of a British military boot touching Balkan soil, the flow of help began. What was in reality just about 100 quite confused people sniffing the air and wondering how to make progress, was immediately augmented by several thousand supportive minds elsewhere. Because military organizations theoretically work as culturally disciplined hierarchies, the prevailing view along the length of this chain was that whatever they were offering was clearly not only the best thing to do but also non-discretionary.

As the chief of staff, a major, my incapacity to tell the tower of talent above me to please just fuck off was limited, so I needed more subtle ways of keeping so much help at bay. My greatest ally in this was just how pants our communications back to the UK were at this time. The single satellite channel I had access to had the dual advantage of being hugely expensive per minute and extremely fragile. Whenever I used it I was meant to feel as if the Chancellor of the Exchequer himself was sat on my shoulders beating me in the face with a calculator. The number of beatings was reduced by the number of occasions on which the thing was dead anyway. My relish at this state of affairs was undone in a matter of weeks by the Royal Signals turning up with a simply giant satellite dish, boxes of telephones, and miles of cable. Happily, even this was not immune to a timely tug on the right junction box.

Meanwhile back in the UK, as we got going the queue to shovel help across the single space-based thread must have been huge. There was probably some arrangement whereby a really Big Cheese in the Ministry of Defence could pick up his or her office telephone and demand that some magic was done to get HQ BRITFOR on the other end of it. The magic needed was for some clever youngster in an exchange to gaffer tape bits of wire together and pray, thereby generally establishing pretty quickly the limits of the power of prayer when it comes to wrestling with duff technology. This suited me well, and if there was a real crisis I could always call from a phone box down the road.

The other vital weapon in containing the support and enthusiasm of the entire British military establishment was that we controlled the flow of information about what was happening. As the only source of reference at that time actually on the ground we could recommend what we really needed and what needed to be done. The medium for transmission of all this gold-dust was a daily Situation Report. Forming this into the right package of truths, half-truths, and wild-assed speculation was generally the thing that kept me out of my bed most nights. My beauty sleep was certainly not helped by the initial requirement to inject the wisdom into the dimmest laptop in NATO, print it out at the speed of a striking slug on a tiny thermal printer, and then *fax* the damn thing back to Wilton. Once received in all its smudgy glory at the other end, it was the work of moments for a squadron of clerks to get it photocopied and distributed at the speed of light to everybody who thought they needed to know what we were up to (which was everybody except some parts of the Army Cadet Force, who were just not trying hard enough).

A corollary of everybody feeling that they needed to be in charge was that everybody felt compelled to join us on the ground. The roll of unsolicited volunteers was unceasing. There was no part of the UK military firmament that did not think they needed to be amongst the first to deploy, in fact the more obscure their function the more vibrant and urgent was their plea. Sometimes we were the beneficiaries of very senior (= immune to my 'please just fucking fuck off' stratagem) officers urging people on us, always with the best of intentions and always accompanied by the sense that they would take rejection badly. In other cases, people tried to infiltrate themselves onto the mercifully few seats available on what was becoming a regular flow of C-130s. It was definitely not on the syllabus at Staff College, but one of my key duties was to survey the manifest listing the next arrivals and to delete the names of anybody who was a surprise. Those who did slip the net were awarded the shortest operational tour of their lives, ideally no more than the time it took for the aircraft to turn around and take them back to Blighty. I still get hate mail for this alone.

It wasn't that we didn't appreciate all this largesse, nor that we didn't need to expand our resident capabilities. It was just that unless this torrent of expertise was prepared to sleep standing up outside and live off the sandwiches they brought with them, there was nowhere for them to go or to work. I quickly discerned the pattern whereby officer A would somehow succeed in getting the authority to join us, promising to be no bother at all and provide us with a truly vital edge. As soon as their luggage was located and sleeping bag unfurled they would be upon me, more in sorrow than anger, to point out that they needed 'resourcing'.

'Resourcing', it turned out, involved: a bed in a bigger space not shared with others; a desk centrally located in the operations room so they could play their instrumental part in the campaign; a laptop we didn't have, connected to a network that didn't exist; exclusive priority and urgent access to the satellite whenever they thought essential; obviously their own dedicated Land Rover and driver – with no question at all of them having to share – let alone (Heaven forfend) that they may have to sit in the back; first dibs on the rest and recreation flights when we got those organized; a tour of duty that must be shorter than the allotted six months given the catastrophe that would unfold back in the UK without their personal attention (or cause them to miss the two weeks in a caravan in Dorset they booked just before they left); a comfy chair (for which they had a chit from the doctor); and obviously a very high chance of securing their long-overdue OBE.

As noted above, I had always considered myself more of a Jedi warrior than the sort of soldier who gets himself steeped in stuff like logistics, it was something of a disappointment to come to terms with seeing that almost the very last people we needed in the first few weeks was anybody whose core skills were at the front end of offering military violence.

This was not so much because we couldn't see who we were going to shoot at, indeed the list of candidates for that seemed to grow exponentially as we felt our way into Bosnia, but because without laying the basic foundation for bringing the force in, the entire enterprise would simply get stuck in Split docks and shortly thereafter expire from a mixture of disease and constipation. Nobody 'up country' was going to get their flour or blankets that way.

We arrived on 15 October and we knew the first ship would arrive on 27 October, carrying a starter pack of light vehicles and stores. We also knew that 200 containers would arrive on another ship on 7 November and two days after that would be the big moment when the fighting vehicles of 1st Battalion the Cheshire Regiment finally rolled into action off their vessel. Only there wasn't going to be any rolling anywhere unless we had built enough of a ramp for them to drive off the ship onto dry land and then park somewhere without bogging-in.

Once we had done that, the wheeze was to get this 'battle group' about 125 miles, as the crow flies to a place called Vitez in central Bosnia. Today that should take about three and a half hours in a decent car, but in 1992 it meant easing a lot of armour over some mountains on a forest track that needed significantly improving in what were becoming very damp and chilly conditions. At the other end of this journey this brave little band needed somewhere to park, sleep, eat, repair, and organize that was big enough and secure enough. It would also prefer to have electricity, water, and bathroom plumbing – because without these things a long winter in Bosnia would struggle to produce more than a hard-lying camping expedition. We had come to help the seriously vulnerable and disadvantaged, not become them.

So despite the great enthusiasm from Whitehall and all points in between to see fighting men thundering into Bosnia and bringing succour to a benighted population, ideally soldiers with a blanket in one hand, a bowl of soup in the other and a bayonet between their teeth – the reality was that to start with we really needed much more prosaic skills. Top of the list were a couple of civilian contract experts from the MoD, because unlike soldiers they were encouraged to dispense bags of cash in a decently formal way. Not far behind them were the specialists in converting broken, filthy buildings into something basically habitable, and their associates who are good at providing power, water, and sewage. I am sorry to keep coming back to plumbing, but if you feed a few hundred soldiers at one end with the finest combat curry a military chef can conjure up from packets, then some hours later most of it has to go somewhere sensible. Without these arrangements, basic as they may be, things will fall apart pretty quickly.

It was apparent as soon as we arrived that the vast majority of the population of the former Yugoslavia had been unacceptably idle in grasping even the rudiments of the English language. Those that did were almost all quickly marked down as spies, thieves, or charlatans. In order to converse satisfactorily with the people who really mattered we needed interpreters we could trust. Some of course could be hired locally, with the caveat that in many cases they would be reporting to more than one master. The other caveat is that if a hot-blooded male British Army captain is paired with an adult female interpreter not old enough to be their grandmother, they do seem to feel compelled to sleep with them and then to try and sneak them back to the UK. The hot sex approach to asylum never really won the Home Office over. But to find interpreters who could be trusted with the most privileged information also meant looking back to the UK for native speakers, or trying to grow some ourselves.

The field of native speakers in uniform was very small, exactly three, and they were swiftly pressed into service. Two, both officers, went on to make major personal contributions to the British engagement in Bosnia and were lucky to escape without being completely worn out. The third lasted for only a short period before he was outed as having Serb family connections, which – it was made pretty clear by a messenger – placed his mortal longevity in great risk. So it became inevitable that we would have to teach military people to speak at least some colloquial Serbo-Croat.

There were a couple of problems with this, first they were initially taught the Serb dialect which immediately made them suspicious and even dangerous in the eyes of the other two flavours. Second, Serbo-Croat is a very challenging language to learn and achieving anything like a useful degree of proficiency was beyond most of the students unless they really kept at it once deployed. In many cases, the colloquial speakers were good enough to say a few words of hello, none of which rendered anything meaningful to the intended recipients. Their interpretation of what local people then said to them probably had as much to do with their vivid imagination as anything that might actually have been spoken. The moral here is that campaigning in somebody else's country without speaking the language is fraught with peril, so roll on the universality of 'Google translate' embedded in a chip in the skull.

Amusing though villa life was, we would have to find a more martial home for the force than a beachfront, and to do this we would need the help of the local authorities. Fortuitously the recce party, that small gang that met us on arrival, had already been ambushed by a couple of geezers claiming to be our liaison to the full panoply of the Croatian state. To facilitate their work, they had sensibly taken up station in some rooms in the very comfortable and beachside Hotel Split. This had the principal advantage of being an easy place from which to affect their business of relieving the British taxpayer of as much cash for as little help as possible. I should point out this is common ground in any warlike deployment.

On arrival at the war, men like them appear in suits a little too tight and shiny who claim to be Your Guy. Their principal attribute for this role is that they speak a version of English (we, of course, know nothing of their language, but we are confident in speaking our mother tongue slowly, loudly, and with pauses). The Guy will be responsible for three things: he will be able to mire the simplest request – for convoy movement for example – in astonishing bureaucracy; he will be able to secure any resource or service on payment at well over market prices to people he is personally related to by blood or alcohol; and he will try to steal any information that might please the men in shinier suits who are convinced we are a conspiracy against the state.

The other reason for being in Hotel Split was that it also accommodated the staff of the legion of international and other aid-related agencies. There is some good sense in this as hotels provide sound accommodation and catering, parking for the vast fleets of gleaming, rarely used four-by-four vehicles that are the sine qua non of any self-respecting emergency relief effort, meeting rooms, and decent telephone lines. They also provide the opportunity to create a lively community of aid-deliverers, some of whom have a depth of experience and expertise that moments in history like this really need. Others only bring a prodigious capacity for the consumption of cappuccino on a warm terrace whilst talking ignorant bollocks about the situation and what must be done. This group is often supplemented by the summer vacation intern grief-junkie tidal wave, all on a break from their degree course in something ethereal or cuddly. There is great value in how the combo of the permanently useless and the temporarily useless energize the after-hours social programme of the entire aid effort, mostly by sacrificing their livers and enthusiastically sharing their genitals in support of the morale and welfare of the expert community.

There were to be no such temptations for us, although I did notice that many on the staff found a deal of essential business to conduct in the Hotel Split. But we needed billets for at least 650 people, plus parking, stores, catering, ablutions, and lots of office space to match. We also needed a home for 845 Naval Air Squadron and their fleet of Sea King helicopters. In 1992 the Sea King was technologically the flying equivalent of a 1960s washing machine, but they turned out to be brilliant workhorses – so long as one ignored the oil and other fluids dripping from various working parts. But we couldn't shoehorn all this into any hotel.

The answer to our accommodation dilemma turned out to be right opposite the airport that we had arrived at, in a barracks (Divulje Barracks) then occupied by assorted Croatian troops but previously the home of the Serb-oriented Yugoslav Army. On vacating the premises in something of a rush the previous owners had still taken the trouble to carry off anything they could, smash up the rest, and evacuate their bowels in as many conspicuous places as possible. The current owners were better, I sincerely hoped, at the business of fighting their neighbours than their form to date at DIY – for there was no sign of even a broom being used in earnest so far. The place was absolutely minging and would need considerable effort to make it habitable to even basic military camping standards. When I considered whether we should speedily depart from our beachfront villas in exchange for sleeping on the concrete of a rat infested, poo-decorated shell of a barrack block with no windows, doors, running water, or electricity, I was pretty much of a mind to drag out the moment of moving for is long as possible.

In the interests of dreary expense, I didn't get my way for long, and we were soon all finding floorspace in a barrack room that had at least been mopped out, enjoying the closest proximity of around thirty other officers and their various domestic peccadilloes. I fancied that as chief of staff, regularly knocking out 20-hour days at this point, there should be a law against me trying to sleep against the backdrop of a clutch of wheezy officers well into grunting middle age and all snoring in disharmony like a rhinoceros with flu.

Even when more cleaned-out space became available and we could start to spread out to sleep, we were still hostage to wobbly infrastructure for some time. The water supply worked on an algorithm (before algorithms were invented) to ensure there wasn't any when the need for a cold shower was at its most desperate. The power supplies' greatest sin was to cut out just as a lengthy document was about to be completed for urgent transmission, at least until early one morning when a young Royal Engineer given the task of getting the generators going twiddled some knobs so inexpertly and inquisitively that about 1 million volts shot through the entire system. Anything that was plugged in, including those things that made the odd quiet moment more relaxing – like the novelty of a very cute mini-CD player I treasured – was instantly and irrevocably destroyed. The military lesson to be drawn from this is to hang on to the beachfront villas for as much of the campaign as possible and invite the bean counters who want you to move to a shithole to occupy said shithole first.

Whilst the race to be ready to receive a force that would quickly nudge north of 2,000 was on, the important struggle in parallel was to work out what would be done with it and with whom. Two days after we first arrived the brigade commander (Andrew Cummings) headed into Bosnia with the commanding officers of the infantry, engineer, and logistic units that made up our contribution to the war effort. The man on point was the Cheshire's commanding officer, Lieutenant Colonel Bob Stewart (who subsequently exchanged his uniform for an especially noisy seat in Parliament).

As they travelled on the routes that kept mostly well away from the line held by the Bosnian Serb forces, they expected to have to focus mainly on just getting through some difficult country and finding potential operating bases. In fact, they were quite forcefully struck by just how much effort the Bosnian Croats and the Bosnian Muslims were putting into fighting each other, as well as keeping their common enemy, the Serb, at bay. We found that wherever these two groups shared a village, which they had shared in many cases for many years without really being too conscious of their particular ethnic predisposition, now was the moment when they had decided to fight for exclusivity. How neighbour set on neighbour was a remarkable feature of this conflict, even allowing for the pressure brought to bear on them to behave like utter shits by outsiders. It was one of the first occasions where I saw people doing terrible things that were positively not in their own best interest and certainly not in their children's interest, where they knew this very well and just did it anyway.

The next military Eternal Truth to acknowledge is that whenever a war turns up the imperative to get as much military kit there as possible quickly takes hold. If there is new kit, the urge to try it out will be irresistible (partly from natural curiosity, but also very definitely driven by the need to show that spending all that money was worth it). In addition, as soon as the war starts, every bit of an army (and navy and air force) feels a dose of existential peril if they can't find their part in it – even if the war on offer is, as was the case in Bosnia, really somebody else's war, and what we were doing was by design small and niche. We were not planning to need tanks, for example, though as things turned sour we did get some artillery. Can't have too much of that in my view.

Even allowing for the novel role we were given, plus the joy for the armed forces of some work turning up now that the Cold War had resolved itself, it is still hard to explain why quite so much military hardware ended up focused on this small quarter of Europe. The imposition of a no-fly zone over Bosnia (a good idea) led to aircraft carriers squeezing themselves into the Adriatic as well as fighter jets filling several airfields in Italy. The Serb air force probably didn't merit quite so much discouragement.

A war also gives free rein to people who must try out their latest gizmo, always well-intentioned and always touted as 'battle-winning'. Quite apart from the bits of communications wizardry we received (though a telly with Sky News on was the most helpful to me), my personal favourite gizmo was the arrival of eight brand spanking-new, specially-equipped, one-tonne trucks for our United Kingdom Liaison Officers. These were the wheels for pairs of a young officer and a sensible soldier who would sally forth to remote parts and report what they saw.

To help them report they were equipped with the very cutting edge of information technology in 1992, consisting of some sort of fiendishly inoperable laptop and a telephone all wired into a satellite dish. This satellite dish took up the whole of the back of the vehicle, where it was mounted on something so magical that it would allow the dish to whirl about whilst in transit, tracking the right part of space to maintain constant communication. This required some massively complicated gimbal arrangement. It might just have worked when travelling on a perfectly smooth road at 5mph with no wind and no sudden movements. But on a Bosnian track, the equipment's useful life expectancy was proven to be about three seconds. After that the satellite dish was generally found some distance back down the road in a twisted heap of 'gimbalgeddon'. It wasn't all for nothing however, the 'United Kingdom Liaison Officers' (UKLOs – an officer for glamour and a senior soldier for making stuff work) did a great job by relying on the miracle of High Frequency radio, the occasional landline telephone, and a biro. They might also have squeezed some basic computer game out of the laptop for recreational purposes. Most significantly, once the extensive load space was liberated from a useless satellite dish it made excellent sleeping quarters and a dry place to hang their washing.

The British Army's newest excitement at the time was the Warrior Armoured Infantry Fighting Vehicle, about twenty-six tonnes of quite well fortified tracked vehicle with a decent 30mm gun in a turret on top. It had just about made it into service in time to see the end of the Cold War and make it to Gulf War One in 1991. There was a view that taking a tank-like thing to a place like Bosnia to accompany food and blankets was a bit over the top, especially as we were not to be drawn into somebody else's fighting. On the other hand, as it would be a big and powerful thing it would insure against a very bad day and we could be confident that the battle group could extricate itself from most drama without too much fuss. This would certainly be true if caught up between the Bosnian Croats and Bosnian Muslims who generally fought with small arms, some mines, and light artillery rather than tanks. Absolutely *not* true if we ended up mixing it with the Bosnian Serb elements who really did have tanks. For that moment, we really would need the Royal Air Force in a screaming hurry, weekend or not.

The much more immediate problem, however, was that these warrior vehicles would start their Bosnian Odyssey in Split docks and their intended place of work was the other side of some large and snowy mountains. For all their impressive capabilities, these vehicles were never intended to make good toboggans and the 'road' they would have to travel included several opportunities for a short skid to a long drop, with only poor outcomes for the crew. When the day came for the convoy to drop off its transporters at the foot of the mountains and began the slow climb towards Vitez, an awful lot relied on the skill of some young soldiers having their first experience of armoured tobogganing. The draft note I had written explaining why the first deployment had started so tragically even without the intervention of one or more potential enemies ended up in the bin, thankfully.

In parallel with resolving our strategic plumbing crisis, we needed to find who we were going to work with and how. Humanitarian aid delivery was the responsibility of the UNHCR, who ran their own convoys and loosely coordinated the efforts of many other providers big and small. Some of these were really professional, well used to working in tricky environments and competent at it. Others were borderline lunacy, invariably fuelled by an intense desire to do good things but so woefully incompetent and ill equipped that sooner or later they would crash and burn (metaphorically at least, and frequently literally). It was in any case, to say the very least, disconcerting to hear from the UNHCR people who actually ran convoys daily into Sarajevo and elsewhere in central Bosnia that the very last thing they wanted was to have a military vehicle, even a splendid British military vehicle, travelling with them. They didn't want any more bullet magnets.

They had some pretty practical reasons for this. First their trucks ran on wheels at speeds no warrior was going to match, so even if they were minded to be escorted one immediate result would be a dramatic drop in the efficiency of their delivery. Second, they were already being shelled a bit and held up at various checkpoints where the trump card was their unarmed neutrality: they were just helping people and not taking any part in the war raging around them. Asserting neutrality, they argued, was a tad harder if you turned up with soldiers insisting on freedom of passage with some implication that the issue would be forced. As soon as the issue was forced, the notion of neutrality would be lost for the duration. If the threat of force really was hollow, what was the point of all that hardware anyway?

Some of the edge was taken off this argument by the effort we had put into painting our vehicles UN white and adorned them with as much UN insignia as possible. We had also exchanged our usual random selection of British Army headgear for UN blue helmets and berets, but this didn't appear to be convincing anybody. So the idea for which we had been dug out from Germany and UK, that we would be in Bosnia to escort humanitarian aid, was being complicated by the realization that the aid didn't want to be escorted.

After all this effort, we were definitely not minded to just report failure and go home. Happily, in the best Staff College fashion, there was a way forward with a little bit of imagination, some crafty words, and a bit of conceptual fluff. Instead of escorting humanitarian aid, that is driving around with it, we would 'create a climate of security' through which the convoys could more safely run. However, as we were strictly forbidden from any sort of peacekeeping or peace support mission (there being no peace to keep and no enthusiasm in London for the risks and costs of either making or keeping one) how would we create this climate without getting entangled in somebody else's fighting? The answer was to walk a very fine line in the way the various local factions were *persuaded* to shoot less, talk more and embrace the advantages of their own people neither freezing nor starving in front of their eyes. This was a relatively easy proposition to run in a part of central Bosnia, less so where all three parties converged in considerable bad humour around Sarajevo and some of the Muslim enclaves surrounded by Serbs in eastern Bosnia.

This adroit redefinition of how we needed to work highlighted the challenges of explaining the rules of the game, known as the Rules of Engagement (ROE), to our soldiers – especially the infantry and reconnaissance elements who would be daily tested by the circumstances they found. The profound wish of Her Majesty's Government that in achieving the desired level of 'something being done' we would not stroll into anything that look liked taking sides, was pretty stridently and regularly emphasized. The ROE allowed us the inalienable right of self-defence and pretty much nothing else.

This meant that if any of the parties to the conflict should fire at us, we could respond appropriately in kind. Hard to argue otherwise. On the other hand, if we saw party A firing at party B as they went about their business of destroying their own communities, then we had no authority to intervene. On the occasions where party A and party B were both at least pseudo-military and had freely entered into fighting each other this didn't seem too problematic for us. But, and it was a huge but, what if we saw party A, a clearly military organization, mowing down the women and children fleeing in front of them that constituted party B? Getting in the way of that would be the right thing to do and as it meant clearly taking sides it would have all the consequences that came with it. Neutrality is like virginity, it is very difficult to have it in half measures and once lost there is really no restoring it.

The truth, of course, was that we were – none of us – going to be witnesses to a massacre of women and children whilst we stood by with far more firepower and armour than anybody else present at the time. Squaring the circle was partly resolved by the protagonists recognizing that massacring their opposition in front of us would have much wider consequences for their general position at all levels. As we were not able to be everywhere all the time and escorting humanitarian aid didn't really justify much activity at night, it was pretty easy for them to postpone the most appalling acts until they could be carried out unobserved.

Nonetheless, it didn't take long for soldiers to work out that when faced with a situation where they simply could not stand by, for their own sense of themselves as much as anything, the answer was to manoeuvre quickly to a point where party A could only fire at its intended victims in party B by also firing at us. At which point the rules for self-defence became operable and would result in as much British ammunition as could be decently expended in the circumstances heading as quickly and accurately as possible for party A until they desisted.

The last great hurdle to overcome before we actually started doing anything useful in Bosnia was to come to terms with the fact that this was a UN operation, not a British one. The authority and the direction of military activity was going to sit with UN headquarters, nothing nicely national. This was a matter of law, and almost entirely lost on most of the British public, press, and government. In the early days it didn't matter at all as the UN headquarters that was going to take charge of the British contribution didn't even exist. Our sense of independence was reinforced by the mercenary fact that everything we did was being paid for by the British taxpayer and by every single thing we did being subject to the obsessive interest in London and across the entire British Armed Forces. I lost count of how many times I was encouraged to recall who paid my salary, wrote my personal appraisals, and would find my pension.

The UN authorities were fairly quick to point out that as we were operating under their flag, wearing their badges, and using their name a lot, following directions that emanated from New York rather than London was going to be non-discretionary. Within a few weeks, UN HQ Bosnia and Herzegovina Command began to take shape and to take charge of the British battle group's operations, arrangements that were aided more than a little by the fact that there were now British officers in HQ BHC too. They saw that they were now lawfully in charge on behalf of the UN, 'not all the bastards trying to do their job for them in London'. Good luck with that one, I thought.

The reality of our mission, to do something but not to get involved in the war, was brought home to me when I stood on the famous (and subsequently destroyed) ancient bridge in a heavily contested town called Mostar, wearing my blue beret and surveying the scene at a time when there was no fighting there. A young woman stopped by me and in perfect English asked me what I was doing. I trotted out the carefully crafted lines about supporting the delivery of humanitarian aid blah blah, anticipating this may enable better understanding – maybe even gratitude? In this I was sorely disappointed. The young lady calmy explained that as we had turned up with so much more military power than any of the protagonists, including the Serbs if we put our mind to it, what did we think we were achieving by watching people like her die in front of us? We were either guilty of an act of *omission*, i.e. we were meant to do something and could do something and we just chose not to, or we were guilty of an act of *commission* where we were effectively cooperating with those who committed slaughter. To this day I have never found a satisfactory response to this, but for the ensuing twenty-five plus years in uniform I was never going to let it happen again.

Chapter 4

Travel

My Dear M,

Every life has to contain some disappointment, no matter how hard we strive to shovel it all into the path of others. I am terribly struck this dank London morning by the one I have inflicted on myself. For ignoble and inescapably mercenary reasons I am subject to the full horror of being on a commuter train in rush hour. It was never meant to be like this, I successfully prevented it from being like this for well over half a century, but it is now unquestionably the case. Forty years of wearing the Queen's boots in contented, sometimes even satisfactorily violent duty as an officer of the British Army kept me safe from the depredations of modern civilian life. This insurance has now expired.

This explains why I am writing to you from a train stuffed with humanity, wandering in its own sweet way towards a randomly selected arrival time at Waterloo. Some bits of Britain's railway system have elected to cooperate this morning, just enough rails and signals resisting the greater attraction of lying uselessly inert and indolent whilst the remainder heap gratuitous unhappiness on the travelling public. My co-travellers and I are locked in silent communion longing for journey's end, most – thank God – maintaining the expected British icy refusal to acknowledge the existence of their fellow sufferers, despite being rammed close enough to exchange a full range of whiffs and fluids. Imagine what this would be like in the grip of some terrible global pandemic?

It's not the first time I have travelled without the trappings of gilded celebrity, in fact I have only the briefest acquaintance of, say, barrelling along in a private jet in the company of the Beautiful People plumping myself up with bits of posh dead fish and lashings of Bolly. I have, I will always be proud to say, sat on occasion where HM The Queen sat on the RAF's Royal Flight jets when they are pressed into service on military foreign adventures. A frisson of nobility should course through anybody's veins when that happens. For me though, this was sometimes dented by focusing on the fervent hope in dodgy foreign parts that the thing would either get up off the ground or back down on it in one wholly intact piece.

Take, for example, Banja Luka airstrip in Bosnia one very cold, snowy day, where the vital objective was to get going fast enough down the runway through snow – possibly (definitely!) more snow than the RAF Big Book of Rules permitted the pilot having read this out to us. I forget what the precise difference was in inches or centimetres, but a Hawker Siddeley 125 was not built for wading through drifts of more than a dusting. This day was several dustings to the good, but none of us – especially not the aircrew who didn't really do 'outdoors' much – fancied a few more days of hanging out in the Metal Box Factory which served as British HQ waiting for spring to arrive. Yes, there would be passable beds and respectable doses of food, but – a big but – owing to the Balkan freeze using the plumbing required a will of steel. We are back again to the first principle of war: get the shithouses sorted out. The choice between a) more encounters with the consolidated efflux from many, many army suppers and b) a sudden, unprogrammed, and no doubt fiery runway death, felt like a fifty-fifty call we were more than willing to take at the time. In the event, we found that by holding our breath, reducing our assholes to 100 per cent watertight, and gripping the hell out of the Queen's chair we provided enough additional lift to help the aircraft make it enough inches off the ground before the end of the runway became decisively difficult.

That same aircraft type in August in Basra, southern Iraq, in 2003, was having a similarly tense battle with the physics of heat and humidity challenging the limits of British engineering designed for a different clime (defined as 'summer in Swindon'). As explained to me by the pilot, in part to justify why I was the one and only passenger he was going to take, the first challenge was this: would we get off the ground by the end of the really very long runway? Yes, we would: although it was well over 100 degrees Fahrenheit and the humidity was 100 per cent, Mr Rolls Royce had aimed off for that – provided we held our breath, screwed-up sphincters, gripped hard etc. The real problem however was this: if one of the two engines Mr Rolls Royce had carefully provided chose to cease working in the middle of all the effort what would occur? What needed to not occur was an immediate reduction in altitude and certain death in collision with a camel. What did need to happen is that the one remaining good engine dragged us up to 500 feet sufficiently quickly, so that we might pop back to Basra intact for a word with the engineers. If both engines gave up, we all agreed, the gliding talents of a HS-125 at 10 feet meant definite instant blazing death – no hope at all of making lunch in Baghdad.

The thing was that in these steamy conditions just one working engine meant reaching 500 feet would occur by about Iran in one direction and Syria in another. This calculation was before any consideration of the predisposition of some of the population of southern Iraq to want very much to shoot down any coalition aircraft that offered itself up, and a HS-125 travelling quite slowly just above roof top height for miles was fair game. Being shot down was usually avoided, on cooler days and with two good engines, by shooting off the end of the runway at hardly any feet at all, turning violently to a flank, then pursuing several miles of hugging the ground at top speed (passengers exhibiting all the sangfroid they could reasonably muster as there was a war on) before rocketing up as steeply as possible to get beyond machine gun/small missile range. Only then would RAF tepid orange juice and pre-curled cheese sandwiches be allowed. Anyway, on this day both engines clung on and we made it to Baghdad in time to be heavily patronized by the usual combo of political, diplomatic, and military genius lodged there, so all was well.

On the subject of getting down I am always inclined to support the view that this must be harder than the getting up. For a start, there is no doubt where the aircraft has to go: it must the very start of the runway without equivocation – and it has to get there at the right speed and rate of descent to fit between 'smashing into the tarmac' and 'continuing to fly until the runway is to the rear'. In many settings there is always, the additional challenge of local unhappiness taking the rude form of people anxious to bring down any plane in order to curry favour with their God or their peers.

In the early 1990s, flying was the only way to get into Sarajevo without a long drive over the mountains that involved several interviews with armed representatives of the Bosnian Serb following. These ladies and gentlemen made high theatre out of the absurdly quaint notion that you might (as a UN representative, with papers and an official light blue hat) be allowed to pass. These interlocutors were the masters of all the tools of passive aggression available to minor officialdom when stuck operating a freezing mountain checkpoint, genetically filled with huge dollops of irrational yet no less visceral loathing for all non-Serb mankind. Of course, the magic of the US Dollar in note form or the handing over for safe-keeping of a liver-destroying quantity of any alcoholic beverage with a proof rating above anti-freeze would expedite passage, but the precedent would be unsustainable for those that followed. So, it was a whole lot better to fly.

Flying meant boarding a Lockheed Hercules C-130 transport aircraft in Zagreb, filtering through a bureaucratic web so dense that only the UN could possibly construct it. It drew on the rigorous help of every state on the planet to add at least one unnecessary detail or barking-mad procedure. This is not luxury travel either: luggage strapped under a net on a pallet at the back and passengers on seating like camping chairs (camping furniture in long folding-down rows of small seats with metal frames specifically designed to stem the flow of blood to legs, the designer made no concessions to any human passengers who might insist on bringing their feet with them). The couple of hours of flying down to Sarajevo could pass easily enough (i.e. asleep, after four hours of form-filling, luggage searching, frisking and hanging about), but always at the back of one's mind was the thought of Mount Igman.

Mount Igman (4,954 feet) does provide the burghers of Sarajevo, when not focused on genocide, with something splendid to look at, ski down, and take water from. For a C-130 on a dark night it also provided the opportunity to make 120 people an indistinguishable part of the Dinaric Alps. It wasn't that anyone was trying to shoot the plane down, that would be really hard and bound to have difficult repercussions for the general situation, it was just that dodging the mountain and finding the runway in cloud and in the dark really was quite hard. Not hard for the passengers, we were only there to supply additional fear and incontinence, but certainly for the pilots. The standard of night vision technology at this time was pretty basic (one amorphous vast green blur in a massive headset looks much like another at 250 knots when peering through intermittent cloud). The quality of instrument landing system may have been a bit better globally, but the one fitted to Sarajevo in 1991 was by all accounts what Bill Gates would define as 'technically shite'.

As explained to me, there were a couple of needles on a dial that needed to point to the same place. When they did, all was well and a runway threshold would duly appear. If they just looked at each other blankly, the system was not helping avoid ground-induced sudden death at all. If midway through the descent the hitherto cooperative needles pinged apart without warning or explanation, all was most definitely not going well – and Mount Igman was not about to pick itself up and move out of the way. When this happened, and it seemed to happen a lot, the news was conveyed to the passengers by the aircraft exchanging a gentle downward sensation for a violently upward surge at max chat from four very excited turbo-prop engines. Not as excited as the pilots though, who were already exchanging notes on how much of a laundry moment each had just incurred.

Sarajevo had its moments, but for the combination of the snow, cloud, and ice of hard winter weather, plus big mountains, an airfield on the very edge of a crowded city, and very great local enthusiasm for shooting aircraft down, travelling to Kabul has few peers. This time the aircraft of choice would be a Boeing C-17, much bigger than a C-130 and therefore a little fussier about how much runway is a good thing. As described elsewhere in our correspondence, when we first started out in Afghanistan in late 2001 someone thought it was a cool idea to precision-bomb holes in the runway at intervals – although at the time neither the Taliban nor Al Qaeda were making much use of air travel. The resulting gap was enough for a C-130 to land but not enough for a C-17, which was not funny as we shivered and ate lukewarm food from foil bags for weeks until the holes were mended and more stuff could get in on more and bigger planes.

Anyway, arriving at Kabul when times were hard meant only landing in the dark, so on an overnight flight usually from somewhere outside Asia. My particular favourite was departing from Cyprus or Oman in winter as it meant sweating in Mediterranean-style heat in Arctic kit for a few crevice-disturbing hours whilst waiting for the plane, then about five sleepless hours squished on a C-17, before an arrival early enough to have a camping-style wash and shave before cracking into a long day of whatever needed doing. (Helping make Afghanistan 'better' has been a vexatious undertaking since pre-history, so it is usually sensible to be a bit vague about one's 'value proposition' here).

The final act of flying to Kabul in a C-17 involved sitting in complete darkness, in fact sitting in complete darkness in body armour and helmet. The point of the darkness was to make the job of the Afghan warrior stationed on a mountainside in the pitch black with missile or rifle a tad harder. As he (invariably he, as no female Afghan warrior would be daft enough to commit to this literal shot in the dark) would have clambered up in the expectation of hearing a jet coming his way in pitch dark at 350 knots, with enough aural precision to point his weapon of choice, and launch a projectile in time before the moment passed. If lucky enough to be the bearer of a heat-seeking missile, the type that latches on to the engine exhaust, some of this would obviously be easier – but a RAF C-17 has a 'defensive aids suite' that whacks out reliably distracting flares if an approaching missile is detected. Or whacks them out anyway if there is the chance of freaking the passengers out. And in any case, the point of the passengers sitting in total darkness remained moot. Some did suggest that the obvious thing to do was to sit on one's body armour as any bullet was more likely to arrive from the ground than the stars. This must be so, but the obvious unstated advantage of putting the human cargo into Kevlar wraps was that should things not go well, by which I mean should the aircraft decelerate from 350 knots to zero in 2 feet of rock, then identifying our bits became less time-consuming.

There is something disturbing about the military mind when dropping down blind through an occasionally turbulent Afghan night. It's not just that in the absence of all visual clues nobody has any idea where the ground is or when contact, for good or ill, arise. It is perfectly possible to sit in the blackness and convince oneself that the trajectory is somehow upwards, right up to the point when a smack in the pants announces the runway. No, the disturbing factor is how total darkness is unanimously taken as a signal for the collective unleashing of unbridled flatulence. Like knowing which stall to take up in a half-occupied gentleman's lavatory, nobody ever teaches you the rules, but everyone knows them. Lights off in a C-17 about five hours out of Cyprus, when more than one RAF packed meal will have been consumed by each protagonist (a critically dangerous tonnage of hard-boiled egg, comprehensively processed cheese, and the sort of fizzy pop favoured by the destitute), and suddenly it is OK to let fly enough gas to keep a Zeppelin aloft for days. Maybe this is why landing seemed to be such a wobble, so much gas probably threw all the pilot's dials off. Anyway, unlike landing at say Dubai in a 747, when as soon as the doors open a mandatory waft of expensive eau de something shoots in, when a C-17 lands at Kabul in the dark, a massive waft of strangled lower intestine shoots out.

At least when flying on a C-17 with all the exigencies of military service, accompanied by a lot of biggish blokes all wearing body armour, the squeeze is explicable. But why, I now wonder silently and back in the present, is this train equipped with seats that speak of managing five sets of cheeks across, when it is obvious that the asses here present will bulk out at just four Standard British Pairs? Somebody did this on purpose, which surely raises the question of who and why? Was it designed by a team of Munchkins? It does not work for ten British adults, none remotely acquainted, travelling to London whilst overlapping prodigiously at the ass. There are giant sheep transports plying the oceans from Australasia to bring us our lunch and new cardies that allow their cargo more elbow room.

I also observe that there are different rules amongst my new civilian peers on this train about what constitutes 'being ready and on parade on time'. The military are accused of overdoing things on this front: there is an immense collective enthusiasm for always appearing at the time stated, washed and (if applicable) shaven, in the uniform of the day – a uniform that has met very recently with soap and an iron. Hair will be properly sorted out, which spans having it shaved to the skull – especially in the infantry – floppy within tolerable limits for the cavalry or a Guards officer, or for those military ladies operating long tresses hair is wrestled into a steely bun (aka a 'Falls Road facelift' for our Northern Ireland veterans).

Shoes or boots will be as prescribed by thoughtful Dress Regulations and very familiar indeed with the attentions of polish and a brush. In many cases, and I recognize the pleasure that this imbues, shoes will be burnished to a mirror-like finish – using the high craft that only water and wax can achieve. Resorting to chemical polish solutions that the darkest corners of the internet try to sell is the mark of a complete cad, not just the RAF Regiment. (It is easy to tell the True Believer in a well bulled-up shoe as the index finger of the dominant hand will be permanently stained 'cheap duster yellow'. Do not be fobbed off by feeble suggestions that this condition is somehow linked to tobacco abuse – it is Military Footwear OCD.)

There is common belief in getting up and out in the right order for the day across the armed forces and in all conditions. I have seen soldiers rise from a listless night in the steamy jungles of Belize, in the mosquito-infested hell of a summer dawn on the Canadian Prairie, on an icy, dark Bosnian January morning, on a stinky Kabul daybreak, and on many other uncomfortable starts around the globe. In all cases steps were immediately taken to restore order and look the part. 'Shaving is worth two hours sleep' is the mantra – obviously also a lie – but there is no professional doubt that a wash, a shave for those who subscribe, and clean footwear unless actually stood in a bog are an important part of how a soldier prepares to go out and expedite helping the enemies of the Queen meet their maker.

Anyway, my point to you this morning is this virtue does not appear to apply to a voting majority of the 800 or so of my co-travellers on this slow, overheated, and crammed commuter train. Some, I observe, have minimized to just seconds the interval between being horizontal in bed (whether their own or the one they tumbled into in vigorous conjugation with a partner of fleeting choice, it matters not at this juncture). This is the only possible explanation for their being here in attire that discriminates in no way between work, study, sport, leisure, or sleep. They have stumbled out in universal kit, an order of dress therefore equally wrong for all seasons and purposes, probably highly inflammable, and certainly conspicuous in its lack of acquaintance with a washing or a pressing. But it is clearly not prohibited here.

As I am new to this, I could be missing the point that this casually attired group are all total geniuses, so preoccupied with the deepest and most pure thoughts that distraction by worldly obligations like 'washing' and 'dressing' would be a gross disservice to mankind? Are these the ace creative types one glimpses in the pages of *Wired* magazine, living in converted factories where the echoey, dank, freezing white wasteland in which they have parked their futon and wok is – as Gunner Smith would say – the 'dog's bollocks' of modern domesticity? If I think I am sharing this space with people who appear to be slipping down the evolutionary ladder, it could well be my co-travellers are concealing (comprehensively) the talent that will reverse climate change and induce global harmony? Or, may I legitimately think to myself that they are just grotty little bastards, unaware of how looking less tattered and grimy would help us all rub along in this sweaty carriage?

I see there are some around me who (good) have made considerable effort to spruce themselves up from what was prima facie a modest state of repair before leaving hearth and home. However (a pity) some have still not completed the job and consider (no!) that it is perfectly in order to renovate and embellish when closeted with the travelling public (me, but not just me). When did this become a thing? My daughters, with whom I have argued the point intensively see no ill at all in sticking their face on whilst travelling with others, so I know I am the social outlier here.

I have seen no sailor, soldier, airman, or marine – of any sex – arrive on parade (that is, at work in a condition to actually work) incomplete. Yes of course things may sometimes be forgotten in the haste of responding to the pressing claims of a hostile force. When being shot at, no British military person hesitates to suspend their ablutions to join the fray. In the wildest parts of Helmand on the hottest days of fighting the Taliban in the latest Afghan campaign, there were certainly times when soldiers fought bare chested wearing budgie smugglers and flip-flops. This is the price of being summoned at a clip from dozing in their scratchers or struggling under a solar shower. Such are the exigencies of operational life, things happen, people get hurt, bathing is not inviolate. Nor will a submarine captain pause in his cabin to put his trousers on when informed the boat is thirty seconds from ramming Africa (though if in another's cabin without his trousers he really should snatch the time required to reassume them). But, here's the rub, neither that paratrooper nor the submariner would ever consider grooming themselves on a commuter train to be an acceptable course of premeditated action. The appropriate alternative course of action is to heave themselves out of bed just a few minutes earlier.

Not so for the young lady opposite, whether or not sleep was genuinely in short supply the number of minutes from bed to platform was insufficient for a complete rendering of the public face. Instead, the job is being brought to a snatched conclusion as we trundle along. I wonder if it is just me that finds this a difficult concept to grasp – though based on the nonchalance of my neighbours it really is just me – is there not something a tad reprehensible about inflicting aspects of getting ready for the world on the travelling public that one happens to be involuntarily squeezed amongst on a rush hour train?

Just past Woking, we also confront the question of food in transit. Like most of my comrades on this train, I eschewed breakfast on the promise of being able to celebrate making Waterloo alive with a cup of expensive froth covering just enough life-enhancing caffeine and artery-blocking patisserie. The only available alternative is a pre-departure bowl of wheaty-bangs taken at speed in the comfort of one's own kitchen. There is, I thought, no middle way – no opportunity to dine en route now that these commuter trains have long since dropped the dining car in order to create more space for ten cheeks of seat into eight cheeks of width.

It seems there is a middle way. The gentleman opposite wears a suit that indicates deep misery in employment as a counter of beans or stacker of dockets at a major London enterprise, complemented by his choice of 'I am a serial killer' shoes. He is deliberately making his life more unsatisfactory by breakfasting on board from his own plastic box. Whatever it is, moderately viscous and predominantly beige, it certainly has not benefited from the journey – and my journey is not enhanced by having to absorb the sights and sounds of this stuff being spooned into his face.

I am not arguing here that it is not sometimes essential to eat on the go. Enough nights in the turret or hold of an armoured vehicle crawling through the blackness of a German, Polish, Bosnian, Kosovan, Iraqi or Afghan night (they do share many characteristics, mostly just being dark and long) has long settled that. My gratitude for mobile catering in those circumstances will never recede. A hot beverage of highly questionable brown provenance washing down a clever facsimile of a sandwich, signed off by the provider's oily fingermarks, was always a little dose of joy.

The steel and character needed by the appointed 'chef' to operate deep in the bowels of a packed vehicle to get all this together is medal-earning stuff. Catering in the constant pitching and tossing, encumbered by helmet and body armour and equipped with only a bent plastic tea-spoon and a biro is cooking on the edge. I would like to see any celebrity chef knock up a half decent egg sandwich in these conditions. But the point here is still one of *necessity*: in that panzer we needed to fuel up and we were running all night, the commuter train to Waterloo lasts about an hour and there is food at either end, so would it not be possible to hold out in between?

It never occurred to me that this commuting thing would ever be part of my life until very recently, in fact just the hint of this prospect sealed the case for continuing to follow the flag for as long as possible (that, and the prospect of lawfully eviscerating more of the Queen's enemies). Getting to work in the 1980s, for example, involved a lot of living in a British military garrison in Cold War West Germany, and the distance between bed and duty was easily within the compass of a bicycle. It required a little innovation: I misemployed a bracket designed to hold a tennis racket to carry my sub-machine gun, which I thought was highly practical but some of my peers thought a bit louche.

Loucheness may account for why my bike regularly moved itself to hang 15 feet in the air in the workshop, to the surprisingly deep amusement of my soldiers. In fact, the novelty of this just refused to diminish, no matter how stridently I informed them it was both juvenile and tiresome. This short bike commute also led to my first brush with the Royal Military Police, as pride in my performance at cycling from office to officers' mess (set off, turn left, straight for a bit, turn right, stop) without touching the handlebars was not shared by the senior warrant officer of that corps who stopped me en route to lunch and offered his views on road safety. I assumed he was taking the piss, until it became substantially clear he was being lawfully earnest in the way that only police officers can be. Thereafter, I maintained my trick-cyclist proficiency more carefully when passing any red-caps, if you live by the sword these things have to be accommodated. But the point stands: commuting by bike under the shadow of a menacing Soviet Union was a doddle compared to my new struggle to Waterloo.

Fast forward a few years (about twenty) and 'commuting' meant hurtling down Route Irish in Baghdad – the road that connects Baghdad airport to the 'Green Zone', with home in the enormous US Camp Victory off to one side. For some time, it was thought too dangerous to drive at all and the trip meant about four minutes thirty seconds flying in a Blackhawk helicopter at rooftop height. I took the view that as my Close Protection Team dropped me off at the flight and then had to make the road trip to pick me up anyway, I could balance the risk of either hitting an Iraqi rooftop at 100 knots or being shot out of the sky by Al Qaeda against being impact-welded at 60mph into a roadblock, or shot from the flank, or smashed by a bomb placed in the road, on a passing truck, or in a hedge. Anyway, driving was actually less faff and quicker – and avoided the 100 degree hairdryer treatment of flying with the doors open on a summer's day in Baghdad (or in spring, autumn, or most of the winter for that matter).

This time the Royal Military Police were entirely on my side, in the six men and women of my Close Protection Team. They fully shared my lack of enthusiasm for being shot or blown up and were steeped in the art and science of avoiding it. Two armoured Toyota Land Cruisers, a bit of electronic inhibition (sorry again to all those citizens we passed who had their mobile phone calls so rudely cut off), and a lot of military dressing up all helped. Wearing full combat dress, a helmet, full body armour, gloves, ballistic glasses, and hearing protection inside a heavily-armoured car sounds like overdoing it, but any first-hand acquaintance with explosive gases at supersonic speed and pressure enough to crush concrete and induce a horrid combo of splintered vehicle and people is compelling education. Some experts advise keeping your mouth open to reduce the effects of the pressure on being blown up, and I agree that the unpleasant surprise alone warrants such an expression, but the very few milliseconds in which to elect to drop the jaw make it unlikely. Driving about with everyone permanently open-mouthed is not a cool look.

Besides all the protective clobber, the close protection team would bring along as much weaponry as there was space to carry it. Long-barrelled automatic weapons for a proper firefight, all manner of grenades, a smallish sub-machine gun for a spirited, shorter-range encounter, at least one pistol for an entanglement at about ten paces, a decent fighting knife for a proper rumble, and a Swiss-army penknife – in case my lunch came entombed in clingfilm. I was allowed one pistol and enough ammunition to die fighting with dignity without endangering the rest of the team as they sensibly abandoned me. As a travelling ensemble we were pretty well sorted, but none of this stuff was any use against our principal enemy – the roasting, boiling, endless heat of Iraq. Mr Toyota made some effort equipping its vehicles with decent enough air conditioning, but this was no match for a vehicle already cooking its occupants with armour plating, occupants also done up in enough kit to hit 'boil in the bag' status after just a few minutes outdoors. And on the days when the aircon gave up, the twenty-minute dash down Route Irish was exactly nineteen minutes way, way too long. Amazing how much fluid one body can emit in that time.

I doubted at the time that I would miss commuting in Iraq or the rough side of travelling by air on military business, and I guess I really don't. But UK rush hour commuting is no less taxing in many ways: squeezed, hot, malodorous, uncertain. I still don't plan to make a habit of it.

Chapter 5

Afghanistan 2002

My Dear M,

Sitting in a hotel room somewhere close to Bergen-Hohne, near the lovely town of Celle in Germany on a chilly Tuesday evening in early December 2001, I think I might have been forgiven a small glow of satisfaction. This was my last night as commanding officer of 3 Regiment Royal Horse Artillery after a bit more than two years in command, including six months away saving the Balkans from themselves and quite a lot of mud-infused, cold, and extraordinarily dark tramping about in woods in Poland, rehearsing the art and science of field artillery with as much discomfort as possible.

It is surprising how small things stay with you, but 'Polish wood dark' really is definitively dark: it is literally not possible to see your hand in front of your nose. Given that using torches is military poor form as grisly sniper-death tends to ensue, without a carefully laid trail of army string between workplace and bed it was common to spend most of the night hopelessly entangled in pine trees mere inches from one's intended destination (importantly, this was usually my bed in my case). But on this particular December night all that now stood between me and a return to my own house in England, a family skiing holiday, four months on the Higher Command and Staff Course (my route to Jedi status) and a warm, stimulating, well-illuminated winter mostly indoors was a farewell dinner, a tearful (me) parade to mark my departure, and the ferry-flog back to Harwich.

The phone rang just as I was slipping like a gilded fox into my dinner jacket. On the other end, to my surprise but not immediate alarm, was one Major General John McColl, the commander of 3(UK) Division based in the very military town of Bulford on Salisbury Plain. We had spoken a couple of weeks before about the dimly emerging prospect of British forces being dispatched to Afghanistan to establish, from nothing, an international force in Kabul. This would prop up the security of a new Afghan government that was being created in the aftermath of the Taliban being chucked out.

It would be one significant step on the journey that began on 9/11 and had already featured a lively US-led campaign to support the Afghan Northern Alliance advance south to eject the Taliban government – not only because most people found them weird and disagreeable but mostly for harbouring Osama bin Laden and his crew. I knew that the chances of this deployment happening were disappearingly slim, usually ideas like this die quickly as nobody wants to take part or pay the bill. The US was there already, but apparently keener on just rooting out Al Qaeda and Talibs than 'doing security' for the proto-government they had just installed under the (still pretty surprised) President-Designate Karzai.

I was due to take up the post of chief of staff of HQ 3 Division once I had qualified as a Jedi, but this would not be until Easter. John McColl had told me some weeks before that in the very, vanishingly remote possibility of a deployment being required, I would be on the first plane out as his chief of staff because the incumbent needed some medical attention. He assured me, not quite on the blood of his children, that this was so far-fetched a prospect that I should forget all about it and enjoy the next few months. So that is exactly what I did, but now, according to this phone call, the plane was leaving for Kabul on Friday with me on it. I was to carry enough socks and sandwiches for several months of Afghan winter excursion.

There are shades of administrative nightmare that range from mild inconveniences to massive trauma, but I am claiming the next few days as a Code Red Cluster. The dinner in Bergen-Hohne was lovely, although being transported there in a dinner jacket on the back of a thumping great motorbike on a freezing December evening did terrible things to my bladder. Icing it down to thimble size is no help to lengthy formal dining. I know I made a speech, which I hope was as moving and amusing as the diligent author (me) intended, and I know there was an exchange of military gifts. The aim of these exchanges is to deliver a large lump of martial ugliness, deeply significant to the recipient and wholly appalling to the spouse who must graciously assent to giving it house space in perpetuity. I still have and treasure a very large bronze model of a thumping great AS90 155mm armoured self-propelled howitzer. Table decorations don't come cooler than that.

There was a short night in the hotel, a final parade during which I had the great pleasure of promoting my driver to Lance Bombardier as my final act in command, and then an overnight journey via Bremerhaven to Harwich. I was not really following these events closely, my head was a tad preoccupied with how to reacquire the kit which was already on a removal truck somewhere towards England, whilst concurrently finding out enough about HQ 3(UK) Division and whatever this mission to Asia was about in order to make that plane without feeling completely at sea. This included urgently finding a map that showed where Afghanistan is on the globe and getting a clue about the weather. The latter may sound incidental, but it's really not if you can only pack what you can carry. Nobody likes to dress for the wrong season – especially if it means freezing your tits off for weeks.

On arrival in England there was a detour, wife going one way to collect children from school and me another to acquire keys to our house. In the absence of any household goods and chattels that first night in England was passed in another functional motel. The army was paying and so 'warm and dry with working locks' is the benchmark. The moment came to convey the happy news that not only was Christmas cancelled and so too was skiing to my two instantly and understandably quite put-out daughters (9 and 7). I was also more than concerned that all this ill-timed moving activity was burning time that I didn't have to get myself adequately sorted out.

The next day involved abandoning wife and children to receive the removal truck in any way they wished (which they didn't much), the crew was instructed to unload everything as quickly as possible as my military luggage was located somewhere in there at random. This they did with commendable speed and alacrity, mostly by dumping any box anywhere floorspace could be found, ensuring that everything that should have gone upstairs was downstairs and vice versa. I think it was at least a year before that was undone, if ever.

Meanwhile, I had located HQ 3 Division in Bulford and introduced myself as their new chief of staff. The staff and I were joined immediately in silent communion that my untimely appearance was potentially complete arse, but in the circumstances they would have to give it a shot. Some novel aspects were immediately apparent, for example secure communications then relied on a system called Brent, designed by experts to induce fury in the user without fail. Due to some sort of shortage of electric string, at this moment the fury could only be accessed by lying on the floor of the grubby conference room that had been pressed into service as 'HQ'. There was a map, Afghanistan at a scale that covered an entire wall, but as is usual at this point in any new military excitement there was near total uncertainty about everything else.

The points I recall being impressed on me forcefully and regularly as I got started were that Her Majesty's Government's preference was for this to not happen at all, for it to be short if it did happen, that it was not to cost any money, that it would be best by far if no ammunition was expended, and there should certainly be no casualties. For sure, make no mistake, this would also not last for more than ninety days as Turkey was guaranteed to come and take our place.

The clock just ticked around to Friday and an early start for RAF Brize Norton. One of the few constants in deploying somewhere in the world at rocket speed with the British Armed Forces is that catching a flight from RAF Brize Norton will require at least four hours in the departure lounge, six is often better. Nobody really knows why this is, particularly when so many people are pretty used to the challenges of making it through a security inspection, walking some yards to an aeroplane, climbing the steps, and sitting down, without a great deal of drama. And whilst this is happening somebody else loads most of the suitcases into the hold, exercising some discretion on what items to choose to send (perhaps to the Falklands, wherever was intended).

Even taking account of the need to travel with a lot of firepower, there is additional magic that only the RAF can bring to the flying process, beyond the ability of anyone not admitted to that circle of trust to know. It includes the mandatory opportunity for a young man or woman in the first blush of their RAF career to patronize in gritty detail a packed room of already tired travellers (who have just left their families for probably six months or more) about the immensity of making it from a sticky plastic seat in the terminal to an uncomfortable fabric bench on a C-17 aircraft, without committing any sort of war crime (such as wearing a soft hat or soiling the tarmac with a loose paper hanky).

One of the best things about a C-17 is that it is so noisy in the back that conversation is impossible once the first engine has roared into life, following the minimum thirty minutes of exploratory knob-twiddling by the drivers, so once in flight there was plenty of time to speculate in great ignorance about the task ahead. Speculation was richly enabled by a generous flow of RAF pre-curled sandwiches and fruit-coloured, fruit-exempt drinks constructed specifically to clog -perhaps fatally -the human waterworks. In fact, this diet was just as well as where we were going had no functioning plumbing. We were about to be reminded that the first principle of war is always to establish the shithouses or everything else will turn to tears – doubly so in winter. Remarkably, both Napoleon and Hitler had made this schoolboy error when invading Russia in their turn.

Normally a C-17 is such a magnificent thing that it can land on a sixpence. Unfortunately, a number of Allied forces, principally those of the United States, had bombed all the sixpences on Kabul airport. This was done with the best of intentions of preventing the Taliban, perhaps not famous for their air power, of taking advantage of the miracle of flight to fuck off to Pakistan. It meant that our arrival would have to be at Bagram, some 30 miles to the North of Kabul. In any case, we staged through Oman and swapped to a RAF Hercules C-130 for the leg to Afghanistan, as this would be slower and more uncomfortable – though maybe less prone to being blasted from the sky.

Not for the first time, this transfer involved being in a very hot country for slightly too long whilst dressed for the Arctic, and it certainly meant flying without much sleep in the small hours of the morning in order to arrive at

Bagram in the dark. As recorded elsewhere in our correspondence, the RAF sensibly reduces the chances of a plane moving at several hundred miles an hour being shot down by a sniper standing on a mountainside in pitch black just in case, by turning off all the lights inside the cabin.

So it was that about five days after I was sitting in Germany as the commanding officer of the finest artillery regiment in the world, I found myself on the tarmac in Afghanistan as the chief of staff of whatever this international force would be named. At this stage we didn't know what it would be called, and there is so much that hangs off a name. Our mission was going to be something to do with establishing 'a climate of security', which is one of those expressions that could mean something different to every single person who employs it. So far as we could tell, the job was to help the newly installed interim national government get going (i.e. not get too shot/blown up) and start to deliver a sense of a better future ahead. This was for a country that had been tearing itself apart for at least the past twenty-two years, either fighting with the Soviet Union or amongst itself, and sometimes (quite often) both at once.

Establishing this 'climate' was not going to involve mounting major offensive military action, partly because it would be self-defeating and mostly because the international military presence on the ground would be massively outnumbered by the various flavours of Afghan forces in and around Kabul. The Afghans would not have the very beneficial advantage of having the US air force close at hand, but they would have a big handful of tanks and artillery. So we would be establishing a 'climate' by consent more than force of arms, though we would have the muscle to deal with small and localized squabbles. In short, the trick was to help the locals have the confidence to stop shooting at each other (and/or us) and invest their energies in constructing from scratch a more peaceful way of living. In ninety days. Then go home as someone else (Turkey was still the bookies' favourite) would pick up the gig.

It was always going to be the case that upon this tiny bandwagon that we were going to create would be heaped a mountain of differing expectations and aspirations. Afghanistan is one of the most impoverished and underdeveloped countries on Earth and mostly a committed subscriber to the most conservative forms of Islam, particularly beyond the cities. A traditional way of life exists in how communities and families function largely untouched by change for many generations. There is a collective and rather vague Afghan sense of a golden era in the 1960s when there was much less death and much more by way of economic progress. The myth is more powerful than the reality merited, but the myth is enough to be important.

It was also the time that some of the senior members of the world's governments, civil services, and other institutions were remembering that they had travelled to Kabul as young adults in order to consume as much of the locally produced opium crop as their then skinny and bronzed frames could manage. The reality of these fond memories had long since been trampled on by a full generation of the equivalent of a vicious standing national knife fight in a phone box. We were not now going to be buying kaftans on Chicken Street after dining on goat and hashish pudding. Nonetheless, there was still a firm impression in the presumably chemically quite damaged mines of some world leaders that Afghanistan could quickly resume a life that was all peace, love, weed, and pomegranates. And flared denim trousers.

We found that in the intervening years Kabul had been comprehensively smashed by its own leaders deploying special savagery against people and habitat. The fissures between the largely Pashtun south and the rich mix of northern ethnicities had become immense. On top of this the Pashtuns had become split between the Taliban and the non-Taliban, fuelling a degree of bitterness that only proper family feuds can rise to. And everybody hated the Hazarah, who not only made the genetic mistake of looking a bit different but also earned remarkable opprobrium for following a different shade of Islam.

Kabul, long established as the national capital, seemed to be the thing to fight over as it came with the traditional authority to at least claim to act as the national government – even if the authority of the national government most dribbled away at the outskirts of the city. None of the opium that fuelled much of the rural economy and financed endemic corruption was actually grown in Kabul, but the money and the power that flowed from the narcotics trade infused almost every corner of national political life. Kabul was the key to riches, power, and flights to Dubai to launder cash somewhere nice.

We absolutely didn't understand it well at the time we arrived, indeed we didn't understand it properly when we left, but the problem we were taking on was certainly complicated. It was about helping the interim Afghan government that the international community had created out of thin air as the Taliban reluctantly retired from office to get started and to do something useful, without it being ambushed either metaphorically or physically by its many detractors. We had to do this in a way that was mostly about encouragement rather than force and this relied on our 'Afghan partners' sharing not only the objective but also a keen sense of what 'getting there' looked like. We were, obviously, culturally from the equivalent of another planet and not a single one of us spoke Dari or Pashto, so arriving at a consensus about what to do and how to do it would be a novel ride.

In these early stages, we quickly found, that what our partners in the government mostly wanted was for us to ensure that the Taliban didn't come back to Kabul. We should otherwise keep out of the way as they restored traditional governance across the country which, as it turned out, would still mostly involve a lot of them robbing and beating the people we thought we were there to help. Having to work with partners infused with venality, some acutely dysfunctional cultural boundaries, and masters at systemic incompetence had not featured much in the Staff College literature. As usual, the fact that we could only communicate through the handful of local people who spoke some English meant that we would come to understand all this only slowly through a very narrow straw.

The first night in Afghanistan, kept very short by having to arrive aircraft sniper free in the middle of the night, was spent on the floor of a freezing hanger at Bagram airfield. This was home to a significant US and UK Special Forces contingent and had the memorable downside of being one of the coldest places on Earth I had known in which to briefly inhabit an army sleeping bag. After a brief opportunity for ablutions and access to some shape of military sausage-oriented breakfast, we were on the road to Kabul in a small road party to work out against the clock what sort of plan was needed and what sort of force was required to execute it.

It would be lovely to think that we had a free hand in designing all of this in the way that any decent military manual will prescribe. We certainly would have a view that people would listen to, but so also had many European capitals looking to contribute to the force. Each one was busy managing its own particular degree of ignorance about Afghanistan, distilling competing domestic political circumstances and a fuzzy bundle of thinking around what the mission should do. We knew we would be in for some heavy-duty bargaining.

There is quite a lot you can get away with in these circumstances by being the only voice in the room that has actually stood on the ground and spoken to local actors, especially in terms of influencing military detail. This advantage never entirely outweighs the potential for someone senior in a big government to assert their opinion, (unfettered by any significant contact with reality) to shape our lawfully binding instructions. Mostly, over the course of my career, this second-guessing has been performed by a clever-clever policy wonk, wrapped in high-street polyester and tugging at the elbow of a minister who is also having a big moment in the sun. For both, nothing in their ascent to date up their respective ladders of power had necessarily equipped them to add much value, but then we were winging it quite a lot too.

Every nation that chose to contribute to the force would officially submit to the clear leadership of the appointed multinational commander, in this case John McColl, whilst also being perfectly confident that each national contingent commander knew full well who paid their salaries, managed their illustrious careers, and owned their pension rights. We knew we would repent this dichotomy at our leisure, but coalition operations are always a bit of a knitting circle, less so perhaps when the US is in charge and doing all the heavy lifting. The US can pretty much just chin-off anybody who isn't playing the same game. We were so small we really needed the help.

What followed is now just a blur of meetings in my mind, including the opening audience with the brand spanking-new President-Designate Karzai. There was head-scrubbing deep into the night to try to distil a complicated moving picture into a manageable plan. Our home for a couple of nights was the British Embassy in Kabul, which had only very recently reopened for business having been firmly closed during the tenure of the Taliban government. One faithful local staff member had secured the premises throughout, keeping things ticking over for five years or so. When the day came that one of the more adventurous types of UK diplomat appeared at the heavily shuttered gate, it wasn't long before the white-jacketed stewards were eagerly back in action sticking their thumbs in the gravy. British embassies have a long-established way of operating, which includes taking a certain pride in being able to offer residents the comfort of a modestly but efficiently run small hotel. A very great deal relies on the dedicated support of local staff, especially those who toil in the kitchens. At this time in Kabul the Embassy was attracting a steadily expanding crew of people from various bits of Her Majesty's Government, all of whom needed to be on the spot to make history, some actually for good reasons (i.e. for more than curiosity or their enthusiasm for paramilitary tourism).

In December 2001, the ability of the staff to manage their clientele with decorum and largesse was inhibited by the mismatch between the number of beds and the number of people seeking one. In the circumstances the bedding supply was doomed to lapse into medieval standards of cleanliness. Bathrooms there certainly and wonderfully were, but just not much water to operate the equipment. Even when there was, it was so absolutely freezing outside that any form of effluent was very reluctant to move on without stiff encouragement. So the basic grandeur of the building, itself only the former staff accommodation and stables of a once much grander establishment now occupied by Pakistan, was a tad diminished by too many residents contributing to too much stink.

Nonetheless, gloriously, there was hot food served by the men in white jackets who knew well from which direction the food was to be served and from whence a dirty plate was removed. A table was made to cope with the expanding numbers and orders taken, despite everything. Whatever happened on the other side of the kitchen door, stuff appeared that looked like decent rations, gratefully received by all. The supply of electricity held up pretty well and one way or another heat was generated in some places. But not, as it happens, in the stable to which I was allocated at some point with my sleeping bag, where the floor had everything in common with its cousin, the hangar floor at Bagram.

At this stage of proceedings there were two big trades been constructed before much soldiering would get done. The first of these involved establishing the terms and conditions by which a bunch of international troops could operate in someone else's country, even if that someone else was extremely new to the running of anything. The resulting 'Status of Forces Agreement' (SOFA) was a really important thing to get right as it set the broad parameters for whatever was actually going to be done.

It needed to cover things like what happens if a soldier from country A commits something that looks like a crime: does he/she get investigated, tried and jailed by the Afghan authorities or is this reserved to his/her home state? Anybody who has seen the inside of an Afghan court or jail knows the answer to that question, nobody from Europe and North America would deploy their forces if they did not have immunity from Afghan jurisdiction.

Just as significant, and a very difficult sticking point, was to agree and establish the roles of the international military presence and fix the limits on the use of force to which it would adhere. Self-defence in any circumstances was inalienable, but permissions beyond that needed careful negotiation – we were neither invaders nor occupiers (in our eyes anyway). The SOFA also determined the rules for Afghan forces in and around Kabul, and here we very nearly came unstuck. Our view was that the best thing Afghan forces could do, bearing in mind that these were still the forces of the Northern Alliance which the US-led effort had facilitated in kicking the Taliban out, was to leave the city completely to the local police and us. Leaving the Northern Alliance in total charge was unlikely to be an exercise in magnanimity or charm. As far as the Afghan leaders were concerned the best thing their troops could do as the victors was to stick around in town as much as possible, really making the most of having seized the capital after years of wilderness living and a lot of death. Their view was also that the best thing for the foreigners to do would be to adjourn themselves to just outside the city limits and they would call us if they had a problem. And they were never going to have a problem.

For pretty good reasons, not many nations were going to make contributions to a force until they knew what these terms were. In some cases these terms would need to be approved by national parliaments, if and when they could get round to it and actually agree. In the UK system, troops can be pushed out the door on a phone call from the PM, in some European countries everybody down to the last barista in the Parliament's cafeteria has to concur. The rush, the urgent imperative that we saw to seize the moment, deploy and get going quickly enough to be present for the formal installation of the new government in early January, was thus at odds with legal wrangles around Europe. There was also the small logistic challenge of deploying troops from Europe to Afghanistan in the middle of winter without a properly functioning airfield.

Fortunately, the man charged with sorting the SOFA out was the then Brigadier Peter Wall, commander of 16 Air Assault Brigade (and who later became Chief of the General Staff in the UK) for it was he who was doomed to Christmas in Kabul whilst all this was thrashed out. The thrashing-out actually took well into January, and in the event – as we know now but did not then – was resolved partly through a translation error. The English version of the SOFA says there will be no Afghan forces in Kabul, thereby satisfying our wish to have them outside the city. The Dari version says there will be no Afghan forces *on the streets of* Kabul, thereby ensuring that there would be plenty of Afghan troops in the city in various barracks, just not very much seen on the streets. As fundamental arrangements go this was clearly bollocks, but as we were never going to be able to eject the Afghan forces by force, nor going to deploy to do anything until a good enough SOFA was resolved, it was handy enough.

To my entirely unconcealed joy, the possibility of staying in Afghanistan without pause for at least six months was leavened by the clear (I thought) imperative to head back to London after only a few days in order to present our findings and an outline plan to all the nations that were considering making a contribution. The passage back to Blighty included one of the longest nights I can recall, as after another thunderous four hours on a C-130 to Seeb in Oman, we flew on one of the RAF's tiny HS-125 to get back to Northolt. This involved stopping en route for petrol, a leg-stretch, and to ease-springs at Cyprus and Bari.

I cared little about the return itinerary as I was charged with writing our report overnight on a clunky army laptop perched on my knees, accompanied by some PowerPoint wizardry prior to making landfall in the UK. The many people who have subsequently come to my rescue in the construction of elementary PowerPoint expositions will know just what torture this was for me. In any case, given the lifespan of the battery in a clunky army laptop is about forty minutes on a hot day, none of this was going to happen unless we resolved the challenge of how to acquire electricity at 25,000 feet. Crucially, the RAF base commander in Oman, Wing Commander Simon Bryant, succeeded in acquiring a shaver socket adapter from somewhere. It was only this masterstroke that meant the presentation the following day was not an entirely oral adventure given from memory. Simon Bryant subsequently became an Air Chief Marshal, obviously for more than just digging me out of a hole in December 2001 – but in my view this was plenty enough.

We ended up at RAF Northolt around dawn a few days before Christmas, with just enough time for mobbing a hot shower and welcoming some clean clothes motored up from Bulford. As we drove the short distance to the Permanent Joint HQ at Northwood, I was of course conscious that what we were about to say would shape the course of history in Afghanistan, but mostly I just wanted a cappuccino, a comfy poo, and a snooze. We played out as much as we knew to a large audience of representatives from many nations, many of whom had looked at an atlas and read *Time* magazine and so knew far more than we. I wish I could recall anything that was put across at this seminal event, but by then whatever the strategic and high military issues surrounding the proposed deployment were, they seemed much less interesting than seeing my bed for a good long kip. And anyway, once we were back in Kabul we would have it our way more or less.

The big play to be made now was in the horse trading between the various states thinking of offering troops to the enterprise. The enterprise was becoming known, after a great deal of trial and error, as the 'International Security Assistance Force' (ISAF). This captured the desired sense of only being there to help rather than take charge. It's a name that stuck to the end day even through the toughest years 2006-2014 when the force became much bigger, covering almost all of Afghanistan one way or another with a massive American lead. When we ventured out in 2002 there was no American contribution as their military effort was very firmly still focused elsewhere in Afghanistan on assisting the remnants of Al Qaeda and Taliban out of their mortal existence. But back with ISAF in Kabul in January 2002, the serious business of who would do what, where, and when was underway.

This trading is an aspect of military alliances that invariably arises at the outset of any excitement and then plagues the enterprise in one way or another for its entire existence. The Second World War was no different. One might have thought that everybody would sign up to the same game and the same rules, but in fact most participants come along with their own versions of the game that they would like to pop under a common banner. In Kabul in 2002 the UK was the 'framework nation', providing the commander and the principal headquarters (and me), a big lump of the troops on the ground and quite a lot of the logistics and other supporting effort. This meant we acted as the clearing-house for what others would do, or more likely not do. This we did by military speed dating in a small tent on the site of what would become the first ISAF HQ.

The first battle is over turf as nations decide which part of the available landscape they would like to call home and to catapult to success. Like anywhere, there are nice places where everyone would prefer to be and there are dire places where no one hopes to go. Experience shows that the UK takes so long to decide what it will ask for that it then finds that all there is left is the most miserable festering shithole. Other nations, I think the most admirable are France, Germany, Canada, and Australia, seem to get their towels on the beach before the bidding is even open.

Military forces and all their clobber take up quite a bit of space, so there is a preference for empty warehouses or former schools. Occupying the latter is generally at odds with the task of trying to restore some sort of normality, not many 'normal' countries have foreign troops sleeping in all their best classrooms. There is always a massive fight over who gets to live on the nearest airfield, as this offers slightly greater reassurance of being able to leave if things go pear-shaped. Once the squabble over who gets where is resolved, and sometimes that involves head of state-level intervention, the next question is what has to be in place on the ground before the soldiers can come and start work.

This is always an interesting dilemma. In Kabul the Brits – who are basically happy to kip on a gungy floor if there is interesting work to be done and a medal at the end of it – thought there was no other option but to arrive with what one could carry whilst better facilities were gradually built up around them. In this case it was a slightly bold assertion given that it was absolutely freezing at night and there was almost nothing locally to procure that would speed up getting better organized. But Paratroopers being Paratroopers were never going to sit idly on their Thomas the Tank Engine duvets in Colchester if there was a brand new war to get stuck into somewhere in the world.

Such commendable enthusiasm had to be moderated by the hard logistic fact that every drop of water or fuel and every ration and bullet had to come in by air at night, and the capacity for this was limited by the holes still very inconveniently dotting the runway. The holes excluded the bigger, heavier planes anyway, but as we were well into the Christmas holiday period, it also seemed that every plane/crew in NATO had something better to do. It wasn't true, some planes really do break down en route over the Caribbean – stranding their crews there for Christmas however reluctantly they want to be at home in Slough. But it just felt like we could whimper in an unheated hanger whilst anybody in NATO who could fly something useful over to us finished their leave in the Alps or the Bahamas.

Just as I had done in Bosnia eight years previously, I found myself as the chief of staff having to take charge of the manifest of every single inbound flight for the first period. Once again this involved me moderating with extreme prejudice the enthusiasm of many officers to insist that there was not the slimmest prospect of this operation succeeding without their immediate and prominent personal participation. Once again, this included the promise that they would be entirely self-supporting, if necessary just sitting quietly in a corner of the headquarters we didn't actually have until their enormous wisdom and energy were required. Once again, this promise would prove to be a sham as anybody who succeeded in breaking through my cordon would immediately demand an office, a toasty bed, a dedicated Land Rover, and the best soldier to drive it. Happily, for me anyway, I had the benefit of both prior experience of this phenomenon and also now being a lofty colonel, so the task of deflecting so many offers of help became a favourite part of my day. We didn't quite reach the point where the Archbishop of Canterbury and the surviving Beatles were ringing up to press the case of particularly worthy candidates, but we had pretty much everybody else try.

Anyway, back to dividing up the turf: everybody rolled out their preferences. For France this meant that they were having the airport, or at least the bit of it that didn't involve running the airhead (a military term for 'just like an airport') itself as the Brits were going to do that, and anyway they were not working Sundays. This turned out to be a good thing, lunch at the French contingent on Sunday was epic, always accompanied by a fresh delivery of decent champagne. The Germans, who were going to take on a bigger role as time passed, decided they were going to have a massive warehouse as their home and fortify it against a nuclear attack. They were happy enough to get out and about, just not on their feet as they would only drive, and they were definitely not up for going out after dark. The headquarters I was responsible for would be protected by a mix of Italian Special Forces and Carabinieri, truly excellent people if a bit obsessive about their immaculate uniforms – complete down to nonchalantly and identically slung sunglasses in all weathers. There were many smaller offers, I think the smallest was just one bloke from New Zealand. (New Zealand later won my special visitors prize for having a contingent of visitors that was larger than their contingent on the ground.)

Each contingent reserved the right to deploy its own 'national support element' (NSE), not a bad thing as every country had to sort out its own spares, hats, and diet. The NSEs were responsible for providing the 'real life support' (i.e. food, shithouses, medical evacuation) to their contingents and this is where the battle over time and timing of arrival was fought. At the opposite end to the British enthusiasm for being cold and grubby was the German way of having almost everything immaculately prepared before the first infantry soldier stepped off a plane. Medical provision, which in Germany's case was outstanding, made sense – but as we watched the *Schützenfest* (German festival involving much beer and sausage) benches come off a precious aircraft before anything too martial had turned up, some concerns about relative priorities arose.

It quickly became clear that some participants kept really valuable capabilities in their NSE because they then did not have to share it with the wider force, or because there was some national activity that they wanted to pursue under the cloak of ISAF. This too always happens and is sometimes innocuous enough. What was not on was one particular contributor deploying small intelligence detachments around Kabul to talk to key figures acting as if they were us, when they were operating on entirely closed national business to which we were not privy, i.e. doing their own thing with our badge. Everybody tries this a bit and only one European nation I know of can be totally depended upon to completely tear the arse out of it. Once detected, it is fairly easily shut down by the promise of massive public embarrassment, but annoying nonetheless.

Each contingent's NSE enthusiastically made sure that some core national preferences were sustained even in the most stringent conditions. There would be proper beer for the Germans (behind closed doors of course), a variety of cold wet and dead fish for the Nordics, obviously a sauna for the excellent Finnish Civil-Military Integration Team, and for the Italians – of course and thank the Lord – a proper coffee machine. This was a wonder of chrome and steam: in the middle of a prolonged winter camping exercise with very modest facilities a large tent appeared in which was installed a proper, functioning commercial grade coffee machine operated by a bearded expert. The machine provided essential cultural support to the Italian contingent, who were kind and neighbourly enough to share it with the Brits otherwise blessed to receive an occasional battered can of fizzy pop and a squished Mars Bar. On the other hand, it also established a deep cultural schism when, to the utter horror of the Italians, the Brits insisted on asking for cappuccino not just after 11.00 hours in the morning but well into the evening. This division, serious as it was, was quickly papered over by shared grief when the machine spontaneously ceased work for want of a part needed from somewhere in Italy. I need hardly record that practically everything else that might have found a place on a crowded aircraft to Afghanistan was much less important than that missing spare part.

Which brings me to the realities of camping in the depths of winter in Kabul. Part of getting organized was to find a spot to build HQ ISAF, with the facilities to keep around 350 people secure, fed, and usefully employed. It would have been lovely if there was a building ready to move into, ideally one with its own power station, water treatment plant, a heated indoor swimming pool and a nightclub. We didn't find any of that, most places were badly smashed about shells. Those that had survived the fighting were usually needed to establish the new government operation anyway.

It was bad enough that we were depleting the stock of capable officials by hiring interpreters (i.e. any Afghan who spoke reasonable English even if they were very senior professionals in their own discipline) at rates that massively exceeded the pay (though not the pay-offs furnished by the opium trade) of even a very senior official. We couldn't really compound this by demanding they evacuate one of the few functioning buildings in Kabul too. We are also very mindful of the benefits of not being blown from our beds, which meant having enough of our own space and the ability to assure – with terrific prejudice if necessary – that only the right people got in. Not the car bombs or other versions of suicide bomber that would seek us out for sure.

The solution quickly came in the form of what was known as the 'Military Sports Club', a building with land in central Kabul which had actually served as such for the Afghan army at some point. There was what was once a fairly splendid building, though now much dilapidated and full of a combination of refugees, shit, and explosives. It was built sometime around the 1930s as a wedding venue for Afghan aristocracy so there were some sizeable rooms that could be converted into open-plan operations rooms and separate office space. It was going to take some weeks to do the renovations and in the interim we were stuck with military tentage and everything that came with it – or rather didn't.

At this point the most important thing in my life was a certain hole in the runway at Kabul airport. Filling this in stood between me and all the stuff that would be needed to build an elegant, tented headquarters, fit it out with communications and computers that could occasionally connect us to the rest of the world (or at least the UK headquarters at Northwood that would connect us to the rest of the world), some traditional camping furniture, and the wherewithal to enable around 350 people to eat, wash, and sleep. Somewhere in amongst this would have to be the means of generating some warm air to combat what was clearly going to be a pretty frigid Afghan winter. Massing all the staff's capacity for capacious oral opinion would not be quite enough to heat a big tent.

Filling in the hole was not just a question of hoofing in enough earth and stones, the requirement was to restore it to the billiard ball smoothness demanded by the Royal Air Force so that a thumping great transport aircraft wouldn't get upset by a weenie lump or bump. This meant calling in some specialist Royal Engineers, expert in top-class runway hole-filling. Whilst they got their magic spades out, the force we could deploy remained balanced by the capacity of the flow of available C-130s to bring in pretty much everything.

There was also, fortunately, a UK military logistics expert on hand trained in the art and science of shopping. He or she was empowered by the Minister of Defence to sally forth into Kabul armed only with an interpreter, a gun, and a bag of cash to see what the local merchants could rip us off for. It turned out there was no shortage at all of local merchants steeped in the skills of ridiculous prices, but quite a big shortfall in anything we might want to buy. In any case, mindful of the shocking effect the arrival of an international force in the immediate aftermath of decades of fighting will have on local prices, we needed to be cautious about who we let rip us off. Nonetheless, if there is an entrepreneurial opportunity to be seized, an Afghan businessman will always find a way and messages were already flying around Asia and into the Middle East about establishing the best mechanisms for relieving ISAF of as much hard currency as possible. Their helpful list started with nuts and bolts and extended all the way to selling us unwanted relatives if we needed domestic help or maybe a brothel, etc.

By around the middle of January the runway was all tickety-boo, so the bitch-slapping could really start over the allocation to nations of the available landing slots. Although Kabul airport was no longer runway deficient, nor short of mountains in its immediate environs to fly into, it was definitely short of parking space for transport aircraft. There could be no hanging about for leisurely unloading, but that would mean a proper scrap over who was allowed to land their stuff and when.

Pretty soon RAF C-17s were beginning to fly in our vehicles, each one loaded to within an inch of its mechanical life with precious kit. I have a photograph of me walking from the gate at the Military Sports Club as the very first Royal Signals truck drives in. The look on my face reflects my thought at the time that it would no longer be necessary to doss on the floor of the stables at the British Embassy, because on that truck were the means to get our winter camping expedition properly sorted out.

Our runway joy was significantly enhanced by the discovery that there still existed in the world a fleet of truly massive Antonov 124 cargo aircraft. These seem to spend their lives circling the globe carrying an immense amount of stuff (150,000kg) in one lift at prices even Ryanair on Christmas Eve would be embarrassed about. Acquiring the services of even one of them meant we got a lot more beans and kerosene faster, but no more people. Although these camels of the sky could carry maybe 400 souls at once, it was likely to be with such a thin guarantee of actually making it in one piece that Her Majesty's Government couldn't swing with it. This obviously didn't bother the Ukrainian crew, who essentially lived on the aircraft whilst on duty and treated it as their home, office, laundrette, salon, café, and pub.

With enough stuff piling up on the ground the Royal Signals could now have their big moment and construct us a big enough, working tented military headquarters. This may sound to you as simple as: sticking up some quite good and insulated tents in the chosen pattern; filling them with wooden tables and canvas chairs broadly unchanged in design since the Second World War; placing on these tables rugged laptops and telephones to match the number of staff; and connecting all this up with some light, electricity, and heat generated out of large inflatable plastic sausages. It actually is that simple, but after generations of practice the Royal Signals know perfectly well how to make it sound hugely complicated and to take an age. It was not as if anybody thought being in tents in January was a great idea, but until the adjacent buildings could be made safe, bastardized with enough plywood and the cheapest possible plumbing by rogue Afghan contractors, and filled with knock-off office furniture sourced from somewhere dodgy in Asia, there really wasn't an alternative.

We also needed somewhere to sleep, eat, and wash. The first of these was satisfied in my case by taking the shell of a room in what had once been a concrete hostel of some sort in the Military Sports Club. By 'shell' I mean concrete space without windows, doors, lights, or indeed anything other than an unlimited supply of stinky Kabul air. But it was enough space to stick up a camp bed, upon which a thoughtful Signaller pretty quickly placed an Afghan horse-hair (probably) mattress liberated by our military shopper. Some clever and attentive work with polythene at the hands of another Royal Engineer sorted windows out until spring and a bit of basically lethal wizardry with electric cable and exploding lightbulbs finished the look and feel.

As anyone who has camped for more than a few days will know, and we were looking at an indeterminate number of months, whether one is freezing cold or boiling hot it is imperative to accept that one's ablutions will take longer. They need to be conducted as a drill. Failure to attend to operationally imperative levels of crevice management very quickly result in disturbing manifestations wherever the sun rarely shines. In the absence of plumbing, this means coming to terms with bodily maintenance courtesy of a single bowl of (ideally) warm water most days. Making the water warm was the task of a Puffing Billy device thought to be unchanged in design since the Crimean War. It works on the basis of dropping a very small amount of petrol onto a naked flame loosely connected to a metal bin full of water. It has to do this dripping at a rhythm that is sufficient to generate heat without explosion. Needless to say, the ratio of successfully generated heat to potentially catastrophic explosion was never that good and the consequences of the latter plastered anyone assembled nearby with a deleterious amount of unwanted soot – if they were not actually mown down by shrapnel from an explosively-terminated galvanized dustbin. For these reasons, I have never seen the attractions of camping holidays.

It is important to record here that the reason we were going to such lengths to live on basic scales was far more than about the limitations of the air-bridge. London had agreed that we, HQ 3 (UK) Division, would rush out and set up ISAF in Kabul as a going concern and that *after strictly no more than ninety days* we would hand over to another nation to lead. That nation, apparently as a matter of cast-iron consent, was widely thought to be Turkey. But Turkey was in no rush to pitch up until it was absolutely certain it was not taking on a complete crock of shit. Turkey wanted evidence that success on this relatively simple if novel mission was assured, and that it was sufficiently well equipped and recompensed by others to bear such heavy responsibility. 'Others' in this case was clearly intended to be the US taxpayer.

Consequently, the ninety-day mantra meant that nothing was going to happen which might indicate in any way that we might be ready or willing to stay for a minute longer than our ninety. The provision of plumbing and comfy beds definitely fell under this prescription. Needless to say, in the end we went home bang on day 186 and at no point in this six-month adventure did we manage to wrest a working tap, shower, or water closet from the UK MoD – munificent though they were in other areas. The UK MoD did particularly excel at sending us an endless stream of visitors keen to scrutinize our work at first hand and to buy a heavily discounted authentic Afghan carpet before the flight out.

Our combat plumbing dilemma was shared by the rest of the city, a city by now teeming with the flow of returning citizens and refugees encouraged by the sense of security our arrival had somehow already conferred. Basically, Kabul manages without the sewers and waterworks common in most other metropolis, meeting the obvious waste disposal challenge this poses by everybody setting fire to as much shite as possible after dark. There is, after all, not much to do after the sun goes down when there is no power and a curfew is strictly enforced, although the huge squadrons of children on the streets indicated that people did still have some time on their hands once all their poo had been incinerated.

The sewerage (lack of) situation gave us two substantial challenges. (I'm sorry to keep going on about this, but in my view it is impossible to exhaust the subject of the first principle of war – get the shithouses in early.) First, all this nocturnal burning has to go somewhere and as Kabul sits at 3,000 feet in a bowl formed by mountains the basic answer is that the atmosphere, especially in cold weather, clung onto whatever nature of smoke was sent to join it. We essentially recycled Kabul's sewerage through our lungs, leading to an early and earnest medical recommendation that we should cease our obsessive jogging in circles around the perimeter (a feature of any military deployment) as it only served to expedite the quantity of deep lurgi each of us was processing anyway.

The second concern is that an inevitable consequence of life in a city like this, at a time like this, is that no matter how conscientiously one tried to avoid a poisoning, one way or another it was inevitable that we would all suffer catastrophic arse-strike. This is not a once-in-a-lifetime event either, fervently though we wished it to be so. We were doomed to iterative rounds of internal explosion, the like of which had rarely been seen in England since the Dark Ages.

There were clues we learned to look for when one of our number became close to an involuntary trouser detonation. First, a glassy thousand-yard stare conveyed both the imperative to adjourn far faster than only 'immediately' to an appropriate facility, with huge harm befalling anyone obstructing this manoeuvre. No room for any error of drill here. Second, it became necessary to master moving faster than Usain Bolt whilst keeping both legs clamped firmly together from the ankles upwards. This is not effective over great distances, but I have seen as much as 100 yards traversed in this format at just short of the speed of sound.

Given that we had been granted no porcelain of any description, the destination in these dire circumstances was an artfully constructed wooden cubicle placed over quite a deep hole in the Afghan terra firma. There is nothing a Royal Engineer cannot do with 4" x 2" timber and a box of nails. These cubicles were built as terraced rather than detached dwellings, so the opportunity to suffer alone was rare. Whether it was the tear-inducing effects of army sponge pudding gumming things up that drove the sounds of a man pushing a grand piano across a ploughed field, or whether it was the heartfelt 'Yelp of Jesus' (Jeeeesuuus) on making it to the instant of detonation without a laundry catastrophe, this was rarely a quiet or happy place. Whatever the occasion, the first imperative was always to identify a spot that was not occupied by another comrade. Thereby arose one of the first international incidents amongst the ISAF brotherhood.

It transpired that our Italian security force, truly expert military professionals, were not thrilled by the British ninety-day embargo on anything that looked like permanent plumbing. In particular, the necessity to rely on the fine wooden thunder boxes that centuries of accomplishment in the Royal Engineers had created did not play well – a little surprising perhaps to anyone who has toured southern Italy. On one chilly day, a very large US liaison officer, well above 6 feet and very much broadened by serious work with weights and hamburgers, was observed moving with that look and the tethered legs towards the facilities. The Royal Engineers had thoughtfully cut off the bottom half of every dwelling's door to reveal whether anyone was resident – the sight of a pair of shabby combat boots with crusty army trousers rolled on top being enough of a clue to try elsewhere.

On this occasion, a quick scan revealed a vacancy and without breaking momentum a very large US paw seized the door in a state of highly urgent concern. Exactly as he did so, a pair of small pale hands appeared from inside, making the unforced strategic error of grasping the top of the door. It was now clear – but way, way too late – that there was an occupant, albeit one on the small side, who had avoided the trauma of placing lower cheek on well-trafficked plywood by perching on top of the facility. In taking a grip on the door he was thus perfectly positioned to be ejected horizontally at great speed – his trousers arriving last – falling perfectly horizontal some distance into the open. Man really can fly when powered by such a vigorous American intervention. I can only say that witnessing moments such as this in the depths of a Kabul winter provoked a joy amongst us that very little else in life can surpass.

Amongst all this domesticity there was actually some work going on, let's not lose sight of that. Troops duly deployed from several nations and set about helping their designated patch feel less at risk of imminent and grisly death and destruction. A sense started to take hold that it would be possible for the interim administration under President-Designate Karzai to survive, get organized, start to deliver services to a benighted people and convene a *Loya Jirga* to talk about a new constitution. (A *Loya Jirga* is a giant meeting of Afghans from all over the country, mostly self-selected by virtue of being in the 'Elder' bracket.) As is often the case in situations like this, the presence of an international military force soon led to expectations that far more than security would be provided.

A capability/authority gap then appears. The military can see what needs to be done to provide for the basic needs of the people they are now living amongst. Once the need to focus on quite so much shooting diminishes, the troops do begin to have some capability to help with other stuff. On the other hand, this help is bound to be limited and bound to be a bit amateurish – and it certainly does not come with authority from either the new but still feeble government nor the many international and national development aid organizations who normally do this other stuff.

A row then ensues in which the military argue pretty unsuccessfully for more money to spend on making local life better as part of building a climate of security (with the exception of the US military, who really get this). The aid and development experts say that 'doing more' is unhelpful because it might skew development or create an unsustainable dependency. The military then say ... so will you please now pull your finger out and come and do something? The aid and development experts assert that it may be secure enough for soldiers (with guns, who are paid to be shot at) but it's not safe enough for people armed only with designer jeans and expensive sunglasses to dispense the hope'n'woke. (On the latter, there are many genuinely appalling things out there to address, sexual slavery for a start, but given the choice most people who are starving and freezing prefer to see a sandwich and a blanket before a video about health and safety in the workplace.)

Nothing much then happens for about a year, during which the military generally find one of their more redundant or hopeless officers and tell them to fix up a school. They do this with genuine enthusiasm, but also without establishing where the teacher and the books will come from to fill what will have become a magnificently whitewashed shed with some new chairs. Whilst all this is going on, the local population's expectations begin to exceed reality, and slowly loses faith in the early promise of the intervention. Some of the space left vacant by ineffective government is filled by very effective criminality, and the international community will then try reforming the police force, a force which really does see its traditional primary purpose as robbing and annoying the citizens in their area.

Working through this knotty mix drives an endless stream of high-level visitors to 'Theatre' (as in 'the operational theatre of war', not a cabaret outing). As we were in tents and it was freezing, I had hoped that this would deter all but the most fanatical, amplified by the necessity to fly the four hours from Oman in the small hours of the morning in a C-130 ideally filled with highly toxic chemicals.

The only other visitor deterrents I could come up with were to place the visitors' tent between the generators and the shithouses and to make sure this tent was leaky, free of all forms of heating and furnished with campbeds whose long service to military medicine bore all the hallmarks of their previous residents having comprehensively and frequently expelled all of their bodily fluids. None of this seemed to work, as every week brought another tidal wave of senior people looking to be informed, to be helpful, and to buy a dodgy carpet on Chicken Street. Chicken Street, Kabul's equivalent of Oxford Street, didn't last that long as an amenity for us as it became clear that our regular custom was acting as a magnet for those who wished to discourage us, ideally (in their view) through the medium of decapitation. Our departure from retail tourism was much regretted by the many Afghans who were making a tidy living producing the stream of genuine antique musketry and other equipment in the vast numbers that had somehow been salvaged intact from various nineteenth-century British excursions in the country.

We really did start to make progress with improving security in Kabul by forging decent partnerships with the various flavours of Afghan police and military. It quickly and predictably became clear that if we ever wanted to leave (and we were still being told ninety days was our max), then a great deal needed to be done to improve the capacity and capability of our hosts. If this wasn't done, we could be absolutely confident that the day we left was the day the status quo ante was resumed to the general misery of everybody except the newly reinstated warlords. There were, as ever, many aspects of the 'security sector' to reform, including the army and police of course, but also the ministries that sat over them.

The habit with a big task like this is to start at the shopfloor and then embark on a voyage of discovery up the chain, as it quickly becomes evident at every turn that a more systemic fix is required. This habit is generally accompanied by senior political exhortation to accomplish wholesale and enduring institutional reform in about a year without anybody (except the US taxpayer again) having to fork out very much cash. In Afghanistan, let the record state, the US, German and even British taxpayer (and others) did an amazingly generous job and continued to do so even when it became clear that a great deal of the robbery and other larceny that was feeding off all this bounty was being executed by our partners as much as opponents.

Fixing the military is the easier debate to settle between allies as it is clearly going to fall to the international military to lead. At this very early stage in what became a twenty-year effort, the only candidate to do anything was us, and as we were such a small force we could only contemplate making a small start somewhere useful. The harder debate is always about who leads police reform.

What the Afghans had was police in the traditional Afghan way, mostly formed around leaders buying their position at any level from whoever could claim the authority to grant it, supported by foot soldiers recruited because they had a complete set of limbs, and their own firearm and some bullets, generally an AK-47. If they had a Rocket Propelled Grenade (RPG) launcher, in case any citizen went shop-lifting in a tank, so much the better. Policing to Afghans meant guarding things (the things that mattered to them) and fleecing the local population at checkpoints as some sort of quid pro quo for maintaining a very individually defined sense of law and order. This is not, by the way, to say that they were not some very committed and altruistic police genuinely committed to serving rather than robbing their community, indeed there were – just not that many.

So although the Kabul police at this time were really much more of a paramilitary security force than a constabulary, the international community desired that Afghanistan had a police force which could succeed in Berkshire or any leafy, peaceful, law-abiding, and prosperous part of Europe. This indicated, correctly, that it should not be ISAF who led the reform, although it was still only the international military who were actually present on the ground at this time or for the foreseeable future.

In most countries, the police are accountable to the Interior Ministry, as is the case even in Afghanistan. But Afghanistan, being abroad, was also generally regarded as a basket-case to be fixed by the foreign rather than home ministries of supportive nations. Most foreign ministries do retain some small capacity for policing matters, because if they didn't how would they be able to lock themselves into a furious squabble with their sibling home and defence ministries about who does what?

We found after only a few weeks that the stage was set for years of trying to entice proper police officers from places like Berkshire to go to Kabul to transform a *force* equipped with not much more than a few of their own teeth, sandals, and rifles into a police *service*. The number of civilian police officers who want to leave their homes, families, and careers to spend a year away watching their back on the streets of a lively town like Kabul is quite small and the cost of inducing them to do so is considerable. Quite a lot of this work ended up back in the military lap anyway, where the Royal Military Police took this new hobby in their stride.

Fortunately, and very generously, Germany soon elected to take the lead on rebuilding the police in Kabul quite early in our stay. Still, the conceptual and capability gap between a German police officer, arriving with perhaps twenty years of education and access to the full panoply of the policeman's inventory, and his Afghan counterpart was considerable. So obviously amongst the very first things to do was to send us a fleet of top of the range Volkswagen police minibuses. These created a shiny, colourful opportunity to establish some sort of mobile, reactive police presence. The prospects for this actually happening diminished every time one was commandeered by the local police boss at his personal heated/airconditioned bedroom with kitchen en suite. And anyway, as no one in Kabul has a driving licence though everybody somehow knows how to drive, the life expectancy of a pristine police bus is to be counted in hours.

Back in the military lane, Major General McColl spotted that we needed to do something useful and quick. The thing we could actually do was create from scratch the first unit of what should become a spanking-new Afghan army, representing the embryonic new nation rather than slaved to a particular warlord. Looking to create a small force for the new president of around 650 men, we may fairly be accused of underestimating quite what 'from scratch' really entailed. Finding volunteers would not be hard, but finding volunteers who were: sufficiently ethnically diverse; had four working limbs; capable of absorbing elementary military training; neither too traumatized nor basically as mad as batshit; and (vital) sufficiently well-disposed to the presence of ISAF not to shoot us in the back on the range was much harder.

Money or gifts in kind had to be sourced from all over the place to provide uniforms (thank you, Turkey), quality weapons, buildings fit for habitation, Afghan-style kitchens (which send a British environmental health inspector into a complete tizzy), rations, bedding, and medical supplies. And of course, pay, which in a country with a devastated economy and very weak immediate prospects was the primary reason for the queue of thousands who wanted to join. A small team of British instructors was found from within the UK contingent, none of whom had any formal clue in how to go about creating and training this unit, but they knew a good soldier when they saw one. Happily, they quickly identified that some of the Afghan officers appointed to this task really did know their stuff and had a wealth of relevant and recent tough combat experience, Afghan style (which is Olympic standard brutal). There were inevitably some recruits who were complete oxygen bandits and a danger to themselves and everybody within 1,000 yards, but the imperative of maintaining consent through ethnic balance could not be easily diluted and so some of these members had to be found safe things to do that didn't involve ammunition.

I was happy to be awarded the task of maintaining some broad supervision of this project, which if nothing else provided me with a credible reason for getting out of the headquarters to visit training and other events. My first contribution, however, was to come up with a name for the thing. I settled on 'First Battalion Afghan National Guard', partly because it conveyed a meritorious image and mostly because it abbreviated to: 1 BANG. I found this just as hilarious then as I do now.

As things turned out, every day brought something new. There was general progress in keeping things calm and secure in the city, even when this produced a vast number of refugees and internally displaced Afghans flocking to Kabul as it gathered a rumour of security and safety. This was despite there being almost no intact buildings in much of the city to occupy, the result of being shelled by Afghans not Russians, and of course no jobs existed other than those people could create with great ingenuity on the spot. Amongst all the real human drama playing out, the Afghan national cricket side found a day to absolutely trounce an ISAF XI – with kit provided by the MCC.

We also measured progress by the rapid increase in traffic and the pollution from thousands of catastrophically out of tune ancient engines grinding in convoy along broken roads. I discovered that in former times, black vehicles were strictly reserved to senior officials and the population at large was still conditioned to get out of their way. The black Land Rover Discovery that Her Majesty's Government lent me was afforded the same privilege, at least for a while. My ability to cut through traffic like butter was significantly enhanced by a blonde female driver of the Royal Signals: in a country where females didn't drive, were fully covered up outdoors and definitely not ever blonde this was a magic solution. It was all a far cry from the situation twenty years later, before the 2021 ignominious exit, when international staff would be flown by helicopter around central Kabul even if the distance could be measured in only hundreds of yards, to reduce the opportunities for being blown to smithereens.

Departure in 2002 only came once we had satisfactorily seen through the holding of the first *Loya Jirga*, a new constitution. We also had to complete the handover of the leadership of ISAF to our Turkish successors. Just to illustrate the diversity that exists even with NATO, we turned up in Kabul with some ragged equipment, no plumbing, and fully resolved to work ourselves to the point of collapse. Our successors appeared with the most impressive array of brand new stuff, built Afghan bricks-and-mortar accommodation with actual running hot water for their officers before there was any question of turning up (this block then fell down quite quickly), and as soon as we had completed the handover they took the rest of the day off to rest up. In any case, I was in a truck heading for the airport about a minute after the change of command was sealed.

The excitement didn't end even when in the departure shack at the airport, packed and ready to fly home. The unstoppable flow of genuinely grateful Afghans who dropped by to say farewell to General McColl included presenting him with a working revolver and a supply of ammunition as a personal gift. This was not the easiest thing to explain to an RAF policeman manning pre-flight security, but then most things really are different in Afghanistan.

Chapter 6

Work

My Dear M,

Wednesday, and a full day in World HQ. World HQ is the weeny glass bubble in the City of London from which Universal Defence and Security Solutions Ltd is sallying forth, our mission to bring truth and light to the planet (though only in defence and security matters, usually a little light on joy I admit). Forging a path through the Afterlife is well underway. Progress is moderated a bit by doing it with no money and all the vicissitudes of a learning-by-doing-by-accident approach to grubby commerce. There is no doubt it ticks in a different way to the business of soldiering – killing in the workplace, for example, is really frowned upon – and the flip from life at the top of the military to starting afresh in the primordial ooze of Planet Start-Up brings many surprises, usually bitch-faced ones. But a stand has to be made, which is why World HQ is established, in a tiny glass bubble capable of exhibiting never more than four distinguished gentlemen at once. We are immense military provenance marooned amongst a throbbing hive of incurious youth. I guess the neighbours do look at us and wonder if we are on a daytrip from the home to stare at the living, chucked into some weird business-centric extension of God's waiting room until Nurse picks us up again.

There are some other grey-beards on the floor, usually the proprietors of small enterprises staying afloat by relying on the willingness of twenty-somethings to thrash themselves into permanent psychosis in return for a free MacBook, somewhere dry to go during the day, and monthly survival cash. We, on the other hand, rely on second-career mature ex-military and Civil Service types, so we are already each a bag of career-induced trauma and pleased to thrash ourselves for the whimsical promise of immense riches before we die. That means we need to rush.

Perhaps these other mature business owners hereabouts would be our kindred spirits, so should we ambush them in the kitchen? But I notice that these others keep their eyes firmly on their personalized hilarious mugs as we pass. Is this because they too are wrestling with their own grand personal crisis: are these people also conditioned over decades to know that work means a suit and an office with a door, who are like us now self-seducing down a slippery slope from 'open plan' to the humiliation of hot-desking?

Sartorial degradation has most definitely got a grip of them already. It must be that 'they' (co-residents over 40 years old and clearly losing the battle against the ravages of early middle age) believe that adopting the fashions and accoutrements of the post-millennial will make them richer, thinner, and live longer. The financial and clinical evidence for this actually on display here is thin. Yet still they take up arms against the conceit that the more seasoned male body is not easily rendered fashionably contemporary. This contest is unnecessary bollocks. We all know the natural law that a good suit never goes out of fashion, even on the last limo ride to the crematorium. And do wear a tie: nobody wants to see a wispy chest monster spiralling up a wrinkly neck to throttle its host through an unbuttoned collar in the workplace; this is the City of London not a Greek nightclub.

I know too that US males must wear jeans until death liberates them from constant and severe undercarriage compression, but UK males who have gone sensible chinos-only from age fifty to fifty-five are in great, avoidable peril if they think they can carry off a return to the devil's cloth just as significant bits of limb start to wither and wobble. They may well have seen George Clooney tart about Las Vegas robbing casinos, but he has a trailer full of make-up artistes, Botox on his cornflakes if he wants it, and always a defibrillator close at hand. The UK male's beer-pies-and-crisps-based diet is indeed a heritage glory, but the legacy is a frame demanding a great deal of elasticity in the trouser department after the age of twenty-five, plus a belt prepared to live for eternity in the clammy darkness of a massive fleshy overhang. So, even though they may get the denim up, over, and into place, the chunky dumpling on stilts look is not for everyone. Or anyone.

This idea that work and leisure do not now require different orders of dress must have taken root whilst I was away in foreign parts smiting the forces of darkness for Her Majesty. Such dissolution is certainly deeply entrenched on Planet Start-Up, even allowing for the number that are so fresh from the egg that surely their mothers still collect them at the end of the day and they should be expected to possess only short trousers? No such excuse for fully adult males, sensible blokes advancing smoothly into their second half-century, easing about this place content that they look cool and hard at work in weekend trousers and holiday shirts.

Some of this elite also think they can carry off commuting in sparkly bicycling Lycra with the same aplomb. They convey only a 'badly packed luminous sausage close to rupture' meme, but the recreational dressing phenomenon clearly extends beyond the office walls. Perhaps offenders with children older than eleven (the point at which a parent transitions from unconditionally adored superhero to spectacularly obstructive curmudgeonly asshole) should be required by law to bring an offspring to work on the first Monday of each month, to point at their parent and loudly demand that they get a grip of themselves and go home to change into a suit of material that does not conduct electricity?

We do go out from our glass bubble occasionally, this is essential in a fledgling organization where a compressed prostate is pretty much mandatory, but otherwise we only see what we can see peering out from World HQ. I have found that there is no parallel provision in civvy street for lining the workforce up and inspecting their working parts for malfeasance, such as wholly overdoing the tattoos and the piercings – usually after overdoing the falling-over water on a night out. This is a pity, the line-them-up approach was hugely useful in the military of the past for combating the prevalence of a spectrum of militarily-inefficient and socially inconsiderate sexually transmitted diseases.

A junior army doctor would take himself down a line of 100 naked men employing only a single MoD pencil as an aid in effecting a proper rummage. There were 416,891 hospital admissions for VD in the First World War, so quite a lot of pencils saw quite a lot of gungy genitalia back then. My colleagues do wonder what manner of fevered crevices are passing by World HQ minute by minute, but to be honest they all look so healthy these days perhaps medical science has found the way to keep it all tickety-boo all the time. That could have ended the First World War a year early.

Beards are now big too I see, in fact growing a virgin beard and heading to Amsterdam for a massive ceremonial bong and an encounter with 6 feet of obliging Amazonian lovely are on the preliminary bucket list for many officers leaving the armed forces after their thirty to forty years of gruelling conformity. This is a healthy thing, unless subsequent employment ambitions hinge on beatification. Beards are anyway now allowed in uniform, apparently because there were no good reasons not to allow them, which is no way for a military hierarchy to think at all. I would have thought that hysteria brought on by uncontrollable itching whilst wearing a rubber gas mask would have counted, apparently not.

My firm view remains that not having a good reason is no bar at all to banning all sorts of unpleasantness. One is left to marvel at how some of the gentlemen here on Planet Start-Up have unleashed their full castaway look without let or restraint. They now view the passage of their lives through a veil of latte-infused stinky whisker. For a few, not even rigorous investment in the power of prayer combined with liberal applications of the sort of unction advertised exclusively in the naked boob-based media can get their chins even up to wispy puberty. A miserable scrawl of a thing hangs like a dead plant on random bits of their face. In some of the more disciplined parts of the world these would be forcibly removed by the police with a Stanley knife as a public nuisance. What other follicle catastrophe exists elsewhere on those same bodies, because the visible indicators are certainly not encouraging?

Whatever degree of recession the beard habit is imposing on the barber trade, other artistes are making a killing in tattoos and piercings. These bodily accoutrements were once the preserve of Enid Blyton's pirates and gypsy fortune tellers, certainly forbidden to the soldier (who often 'forgot' this whilst out socializing). Judging by what parades past World HQ, there is now a consensus abroad that this artwork is indeed most fetching in the eye of both the owner and the owner's preferred circle of admirers. 'Preferred circle of admirers' these days is as cheerfully wide as the oceans are deep.

A casual survey (we are not actually using clipboards here) of the legs and arms passing World HQ in the ceaseless convoy of youth that ebbs and flows between desk, loo, beverages, and lounging about locations affirms that there is a lot of mutual tat/hole-based admiration around. Some work is neither bounded by spelling commended by the *Oxford English Dictionary* nor showing much evidence of any great skill at drawing, but no doubt all have special meaning for the wearer.

I do hope this meaning is greater than 'don't engage your arm with a tattoo needle at 03:00 hours when completely off your trolley on recreational chemistry'. As seen from our bubble, the bits and pieces from which rings dangle and to which studs are stuck are surprisingly varied. Ears are well in the lead as the orthodox and common starting point (for all sexes) and noses next in line. A small metal stud inserted in homage to a seventeenth-century beauty spot maybe, a large metal hoop conveying a more bovine motif. We have heard, but have no evidence to offer, that nipples are also firm favourites for accessorization. Is this just good drills, allowing the bearer to clip keys and a small torch to their chest when out and about after dark, especially when accompanied by brain cell-extinguishing liquids?

Anyway, on the subject of work, our business in World HQ is about making the world a safer, calmer, and more balanced place. Both objectives rely on transferring cash from rich nations and big industry to our empty pockets in exchange for our wisdom, which ranges from expertise in the laying waste of entire nations to bijou bumpings-off, and all the supporting cast stuff that goes into the global industry of defence and security. We obviously don't do the slaughtering thing now, though we would still be brilliant at yelling encouragement from the touchline at any clash of arms, like those uninhibited Dads at school sports urging their offspring onward to a stress fracture. Mostly we are really good at helping others avoid too much unpleasantness or fisticuffs by being better informed, prepared, equipped, and realistic. We are pretty sure that our comrades on Planet Start-Up don't do this sort of work, and so we pass as many contented hours wondering what the hell are they all doing as they may spend on us.

As I look out at our co-workers there are two principal schools: those who stare silently at computer screens and those who shout into telephones. There are some, not many, who have mastered staring at a screen whilst simultaneously bellowing into a phone, and most of these have enabled themselves to bellow better with a headset. As the isolation a headset confers entails losing all sense of personal volume control, I think we hate these multi-tasking bellowers most of all. None of us within the 25m collateral damage zone of the serial bellow-merchant are interested in purchasing elements of an exciting new range of Digital Age plumbing supplies. So being offered the opportunity, unbidden and relentlessly, to acquire the magic of automated flushing is tiresome. Just occasionally one of us will snap and exit World HQ to walk slowly past the offender administering a stare capable of chilling molten lava, not concealing especially well the longing to follow this up with 9mm of bullet travelling at 1,500 feet a second through the offender's cranium. The occasional, feeble and totally ignored pleas from the Administrators of Planet Start-Up for less bellowing and more consideration of fellow strugglers are a very much less effective alternative. The 2020/21 pandemic lockdown that emptied Planet Start-Up has saved many lives, including those of at least three headset bellowers – whether or not they got the lurgi. We all have our breaking-point.

And this brings us back to the subject of plumbing, one of the recurring themes of our correspondence. Locations like Planet Start-Up do offer sanitation facilities for the inhabitants, but – I sense – this is intended more as a token supplement to daily ablutions than a dedicated commitment to provide total real life support. This infers that everybody plans to arrive at the office having spruced up and moved bowels before departing their dwelling-place. On this basis the ratio of facilities to users would be reasonable. Not so, however, if many many people assault the 'light-touch' provision at the work place with their own personal daily Armageddon. The plumbing on Planet Start-Up is a horror-show by 10:00 hours. Not because the gently needy have popped in for a little light easing of tension, but because a band of dedicated and expert enthusiasts have committed to a daily fly-tipping from their entire intestine in one tumultuous blast. They are evidently so proud of their achievement that they insist on leaving the record prominently available for independent verification. We are totally prepared to take their prowess on the basis of trust – a tweet if they must.

This cannot be just a casual thing, so much work goes into the results it has to reflect a steely commitment (admirable in almost all other settings) to saving up for the really big event – quite possibly for a week. We might be more sympathetic if their procedure was supported by the sounds of a man in genuine distress. We would all bow our heads in silent empathetic communion on hearing through the door all the anguish and frustration of a man pushing a grand piano across a ploughed field in a storm in a snorkel and flippers. That is pain we all relate to: who amongst us has not wrestled with the consequences of dining on a tonne of beef curry and chips followed by a wedge of plum duff? We know this sort of fine dining is always followed by a lesson in the difference between precision-attack and carpet bombing. But this is different, in the tiny and insalubrious conveniences of Planet Start-Up we hear not the sound of a brother human in distress, we hear the sounds only of immense triumph.

Perhaps we should be more sympathetic, because many hours are lost to the ancient dispute between senior military men over whether service in a jet fighter, a tank, or a frigate incurs the biggest haemorrhoidal penalty. I cannot prove it, but I have long suspected that war crimes have been occasioned by the need to get done, get home, and take the pressure off – and I very much doubt whether any Court Martial would refuse such a reasonable explanation for hitting the 'fire' button in conditions of immense arse-based duress.

Setting aside plumbing matters albeit likely only briefly, the art of meetings in this commercial life seems quite different to the military experience. Not in every respect of course: meetings in military life are convened just as thoughtlessly, frequently, and pointlessly as in the very best commercial environments. Sometimes meetings about military matters are so comprehensive and so lengthy that they totally remove the time or energy to act on any of the learned deliberations, ensuring the longevity of masterly inactivity no matter how dire the circumstances.

In a really big headquarters, the more senior leadership can sustain a punishing regime of coordination between themselves without end, jabbering away safe in the knowledge that this is the top-cover that leaves their supporting cast at full liberty to really get on with the important stuff, free from adult direction or interference. Whole countries have been successfully invaded on this basis. As artificial intelligence removes most of the supporting cast, the machines will just crack on even faster and better as the remaining humans 'do meetings'. Whole continents will fall.

When the victims for military meetings form up, the military people are brain-washed in basic training to be there five minutes before the stated start time (whether physically present or virtually assembled), MoD civil servants are compelled to rise from their desks at the appointed start time and process in serenity in the direction of the meeting, heading for a ten-minute late kick-off in accordance with the Civil Service Code. The chair of whichever tribe will adopt the Arab formula of arriving last and as late as seniority and importance demands. This is between twenty minutes and six months.

The truly magnificent, a Big Cheese usually defined by ministerial rank, will adopt the principle that it is enough that they appear a minimum of ten minutes late in order to emphasize their greater proximity to the Divine. Their role is to: set out as many bland and misleading tenets of whatever is needed to establish a truly inept framework for the work ahead; provide a moment or two for some gratifying public simpering from the more insecure attendees; and then get out before a clever box of shite in the cheap seats can ask a pointed question. It is then quite in order to come back for a few minutes at the end of proceedings to hear how their magisterial opening has been totally ignored in the interests of progress and justice. This will be artfully concealed in a superb bundling of vapid rhetorical tosh and buzzword crapola such that the Big Cheese cannot possibly spot their systemic irrelevance to proceedings, even if they were listening. Which they are not: it is enough that the room is able to bask in the radiance of a super being moving amongst them, consenting to share the same air.

Purely military (i.e. no civil servants or any other civilian lifeform present) meetings will follow their own protocol. First, the senior officer present is in charge – of the agenda, the discussion, and the conclusions. This is an immensely satisfactory way of working if you ask me (as a four-star general): it very quickly cuts to a solution by ensuring anything hard or involving unpleasantness like money is left hung up outside with the hats and coats. There is just an audience of disciples to enlighten, a page in a glorious personal history to be written, and a lunch appointment to be kept.

There has been a fashion for a while to call some military meetings 'boards' – even quite martial aspects like 'targeting boards' or patronage-related events like 'promotion boards'. There was probably some hope that this nomenclature would convey a sense of gravitas, in the way that the Board of British Petroleum is a serious place occupied by people with massive brains and the judgement of Solomon. Might it be thought that 'board' conveyed the utterly misleading impression that anyone other than the senior officer present could pipe up with an opinion which would be listened to with something approaching interest? Hah! Many have tried to make such a dash for independence of thought and decision. The 30-something major, fresh from Staff College and hitched to a massively pregnant partner stridently encouraging rapid advancement from a tiny married quarter with broken heating to a bigger one seems especially prone to this. But all (in my once elevated experience) end up cast down on the floor like broken matchsticks by the ebullient brilliance of the senior officer present. Matchsticks can cry.

The meeting hobby in the commercial world as I have found it, is really quite different in important respects. First, a custom has taken hold since I last looked across a commercial floor (1977) that only a first name may be used in all discourse. This doesn't mean there is no hierarchy, because there clearly is, nor that all opinion is equally valued and valuable. Whilst the former is obviously to be encouraged (even I got that memo) the latter is clearly rubbish. Was this an infection from the telesales world – the 'can I call you [Insert first name here]' gambit intended to sprout into a sense of redundant matey friendship that soothes one through the fleeting business of being ripped off over insurances and credit cards? Of course they *can* use my first name, the issue is whether and why they think they *may*, without coming across as all sex-pest creepy – a judgement they invariably choose to get wrong.

Amongst all of these, we now all have just the one name and this offers people like me no clue at all as to what anyone actually does or their place in the galaxy. The armed forces are at the other end of the spectrum, with a splatter of badges transmitting surname, rank, and role. This reduces the chances of asking the soldier who does the pay accounting to mend a truck, whereas in the Afterlife I may quite innocently ask a Nobel-prize winning quantum physicist planning her holiday on Mars to get some photocopying sorted, and a cup of tea wouldn't go amiss.

Can you imagine how this enforced informality would have changed the course of twentieth century history? Would Mr Hitler have lasted so long if every time he encountered the guys from the Totenkopf Panzer Division, Heinz and Erich, they felt they could just sit down with Adolf to josh over their thoughts on that winter they just had in Russia? Would Pol Pot have been quite so successful in butchering 2 million of his own people if he had to stick to plain Saloth? Genocide demands a certain formality or people get too teary too soon. It is strange, but it seems that in civvy life today, you only get your second name back when you cross the threshold into mega-stardom: nobody could be impressed if one talked blithely about lunch with Mark, Bill, and Julia, but appending Zuckerberg, Clinton, and Roberts will certainly win points.

Name democracy has also encouraged cognitive attendance at meetings becoming entirely voluntary even if physical presence has been enforced. Before the Digital Age one could while away a dull session by studiously applying pen to paper, doodling genitals being an entirely accepted way of conveying sufficient interest. Now, however, it appears that it is perfectly in order to bring a laptop and phone to any meeting and continue the daily grind of emails, Googling exotic holidays and ordering dinner. The meeting continues to the tip-tap of the majority fully immersed in their own affairs, with a maximum of one ear monitoring for threats like an invitation to contribute more than an episodic grunt as proof of participation.

There is a generation gap here: those under thirty-five are immune to the burning rage that they endow in their elders by so obviously chinning off everybody in the room until and unless it is their turn to toss in some brilliance. The degree of offence taken is more obvious to the former military cohort, as for us listening to explanation and instructions is a proven valuable skill, key to self-preservation. There is real regret to be had from stepping on a mine because, whilst the instructor had pointed out the legion disadvantages of this, one was fully immersed in a fruity WhatsApp exchange. The whole chinning off thing was only made worse by the 2020-21 pandemic lockdown when everybody went home. As all meetings went online the range of excuses for dropping out of the video feed in order to play Call of Duty grew inexhaustibly. Zoom roulette for big events took root, where we all try to avoid being one of the nine participants kept visible on screen so we can safely concentrate on delousing the cat without causing offence or the risk of being fired. One sympathizes with the dear lady that toddled off to the loo in the middle of a Zoom, taking her laptop with her (commendably diligent) yet forgetting that she too was on camera, affording her many colleagues a treasured reminder of just what a massive lady-slash looks and sounds like.

At the heart of the discombobulation in World HQ about how *we*, serious lifelong military types, make our way (and – most important – our fortune) amongst *them*, the commercial and lifelong civvies the other side of the glass, is the chasm between *vocation* and *transaction*. When we started out in the navy, army, and air force we all went through the mill of basic officer training, popping out the other end with our heads and our hearts overflowing with the joyful determination to serve our country to our last breath.

We intended that this would involve many opportunities to crush the enemies of the Queen with that combo of martial skill and dashing elan for which all British officers are rightly treasured in the eyes of an adoring nation. Victory parades would be held at home and abroad in front of huge flag-waving crowds consumed by ecstasy and awe (literally throwing cash and their daughters at us as we marched by all steely-chinned). We would take our pick of the wine, women and sporting equipment of the newly dead and defeated, and eventually – with the stoic reluctance of one unaccustomed to accepting any reward greater than a shake of the hand at Queen level, succumb to the offer of a large estate within a hangover's distance of London, plus a Euromillions lottery-sized endowment with a free box for life at Twickenham, Wembley, Lords, and Wimbledon. Only some of this came to pass over the following thirty-forty years, but none of us lost, then or now, the sense that we were part of a something more than sweating for cash. We were, are, 'live to work' types not 'work to live'.

We know this vocational pull better as we look back than we did when we looked forward at the blank canvas of a working life in uniform. We saw no separation between work and private life, and this was more than because we lived in officers' messes or the depressingly titled 'Service Families' Accommodation'. It didn't really matter which, as nearly all of it was built in the 1930s, worn to a shabby husk by the 1960s, shabbier still by the 1990s when finally 100 million gallons of magnolia paint, plastic baths, and a reaming of the plumbing were allowed. The return of the armed forces from stations abroad over the last decade has seen a welcome splurge of Premier Inn style messes and new houses built to modern standards (cramped, fragile, no storage space) – but with working heating and plumbing and less lethal electrics. Across all this, our lifelong colleagues became, are, our lifelong friends. We lived in little wired-off cantonments in UK, or Germany or Cyprus or elsewhere, and we shared the same driving enthusiasm for our work and a common ethos for how we went about it.

Some of this is a bit mad – the practice of saluting for example is hard to explain rationally. It's not a symptom of automaton subjugation to the whims of a repressive and archaic military hierarchy, it's just the way that military people say hello and goodbye. It can, of course, be taken to extremes: the saluting of cars known or likely to be filled by senior officers is fraught with challenge and nonsense, as one example. For one particularly tall brigadier in a BAOR Garrison of the late 1980s, a Guards officer for whom marching about as much as possible and a great deal of right leg 'bend and drive' (the raising of a thigh parallel to the ground, followed by the violent spine-jarring stamp of foot to floor, generally as a prelude to leaving the office of a superior) was deeply ingrained and culturally pivotal. Saluting was a matter of life or death.

Life was permitted to continue for those who spotted the single star nailed to the front of his staff car as it clipped past, immediately ceasing whatever they were doing to fling up a really champion salute. Right arm, longest way up, shortest way down, a little waggle permitted at the top for a pause of a count of precisely two-three, fingers fully extended, hand and arm in perfectly straight alignment, back straight, legs together, feet set at 30 degrees, body square on to the salute – this is not simple stuff. Especially when surprised.

Death was the certain fate of anyone who failed to spot the moment. As the staff car of the day was a Vauxhall Cavalier, the kind of thing issued to travelling sales representatives in the extruded plastics business, there was just not much warning that the local Big Cheese was approaching. The car was black, of course, though a black Vauxhall Cavalier is more sad than sinister, and from the outside it was impossible to know if it had air conditioning – the main combat indicator that it must be a brigadier or better. As a potential saluter under pressure you can't work on the basis of heat or smell travelling at you at speed.

The Big Cheese, be in no doubt, was on the hunt: nothing pleased him more than catching out another witless specimen of military inadequacy, unacceptably unable to identify a hugely senior officer crouched in the back of cheap car as it shot past. The pleasure was sometimes enhanced if the offender was from one of the smarter regiments, a cavalry trooper, or – joy of joys – a Gunner of the Royal Horse Artillery, as this would provide the meat of an immensely pleasurable (for him) telephone conversation with the offender's commanding officer ('more in sorrow than in anger, old boy, but REALLY your chaps need to buck up you know..'). The recipient commanding officer would of course murmur back the required heartfelt, grovelling apologies expressing essential shock, disappointment, and determination to eradicate all such behaviour with speed and unlimited prejudice. The recipient commanding officer would also be thinking 'why does he think I give a fuck about this', but generally refrained from letting his mouth loose in this way, unless they were actually brothers.

The brigadier's joy would be far, far greater should the offender turn out to be from one of the more artisan bits of the army: a Signaller say, or from the Royal Electrical and Mechanical Engineers, or best of all from what is now known as the Royal Logistic Corps. Back then it was the Royal Army Ordnance Corps, but throughout history, then as now, it absorbs the men and women who are good at counting, stacking, pumping, humping, and dumping, with a tweak of glamour allowed from things like bomb disposal. This is all essential stuff, but not what a Guardsman feels at home with. Very happy to be kept in bullets and new boots, not so keen to see you for dinner.

Trapping a logistician created the additional joy of being able to exude condescension as well as disappointment to the miscreant's commanding officer. Obviously not on the telephone, that would be like calling your dry cleaner for a chat about religion, instead a tersely-worded memorandum expressing disappointment and offering lessons in the relevant foot drill from the neighbouring Guards Battalion would be written by the staff. It would be received with all due humility and regret, and pretty much ensure that on the next long exercise an administrative blunder would cause the brigadier to find his ration packs for three weeks were exclusively Gurkha curries and his sleeping bag was accidentally burned to a boiled nylon goo in transit – and a replacement would take many cold nights to procure through 'the system'.

It would have been easier if the brigadier had sat in the front passenger seat, but the form was that as HM The Queen probably sits back-left so should Her Majesty's representatives further down the food chain. The little star was a decent clue, so long as one was looking and generally nobody was. In the 1980s there was no longer the money to equip every brigadier with a marching corps of fife and drum and/or motorcycle outriders for his journeys between brigade headquarters (knackered offices with a flag outside) and Residence. This was the biggest house in the garrison by miles, originally built for a 1930s German general with lots of space for Schnapps-based leather-coated revelry, but now sporting a broken oven and a fuse box built from coat-hangers by Mrs Brigadier, who is convinced the place is haunted by Herr Goebbels and is therefore reluctant to be there alone in the dark.

The best staff car clue, if looking closely enough, was the eyes of the driver – who was also a Guardsman, usually one proven to be too dangerous to his comrades to trust with a rifle. He would be able to drive with the verve needed by his leader, for whom speed limits applied only to mortals, and also agreeably amenable to walking dogs and mowing grass as required. He would also be highly skilled in the art of polishing shoes to the glossy state a Guardsman needs to wear to feel complete as a person. Anyway, when driving, this man's eyes would widen like saucers in order to silently convey a warning to others of what lurked on the pleblon behind him, in standing fear of what was almost certainly about to happen. And what was almost certainly about to happen was that the car would pass an unsuspecting uniformed victim. The victim would be proceeding innocuously about his or her duties in fending off the prospect of Soviet invasion, which possibly included journeying on foot across the garrison to an exchange of boot-legged video tapes of extraordinary carnal activity in German. (*Ja! Ja! Und jetzt mit der pumpernickel liebling…*)

The car would pass, no salute was offered. Maybe worse, something desultory was shambled-up, a vague wave to the head – the equivalent of a millennial 'sup' without raising gaze from Call of Duty. The brigadier would immediately bellow-harrumph, order car to halt and driver to alight and apprehend. Part of the thinking behind getting the driver to alight rather than the brigadier in his magnificent person was to avoid the distress of a very large man in a big army hat unfurling himself in haste from the compressed setting of a Vauxhall Cavalier's back seat. Mostly it was to reduce the opportunity for the poor apprehended to really go for broke and knee the brigadier in the bollocks and make a run for it.

The driver was therefore instructed to seize the failed saluter, convey to him/her the full horror of what had transpired, pass on the full force of the brigadier's horror and regret at this astonishing and insulting lapse of good order and military discipline, and acquire in writing the offender's name and unit so that a report would be made. No doubt stiff action with major and deleterious consequences would follow, all bundled up in tonnes of righteous anger, profound sorrow at the collapse of the fundamentals of military civilisation, and great enthusiasm for retributive justice.

For the failed saluter, 'crestfallen' does not do justice to the feelings now coursing through their body. For some, especially the younger or more vulnerable (i.e. those actually carrying a full weekend's-worth of Pumpernickel Porn and not keen for this to become a matter of record) the best description would be 'shit-scared'. For others more seasoned, a weary resignation at the prospect of another interview involving neither chair nor coffee, conducted at 150 decibels by the regimental sergeant major would quickly take hold. The most quick-thinking would confidently name themselves as the leading actor from any film or TV programme the driver was unlikely to be familiar with, or a top-flight footballer, or if nothing else sprang to mind would write with a flourish 'Private U R Adicksor', a resident of whatever unit was next door.

However, the best course of action on seeing a black Vauxhall Cavalier screech to a halt was then, as now, to flee on foot as fast as possible, taking the odds that a staff car driver containing a lot of Gurkha curry was unlikely to be as quick as a soldier in danger of being caught carrying illegal videos. The driver knew the form if this happened, which was to give spirited chase, hide as soon as out of sight, and offer a cheery farewell wave to the fugitive. Then maybe some jogging on the spot to work up a bit of a sweat, though not so vigorously as to endanger the gloss on his lovingly tended shoes, black, driver/orderly.

The perils of a saluting culture notwithstanding, my point is that for all its quirks and oddities, the *vocational* nature of military service makes its mark on all who join up. Few other occupations invest quite so much in getting inside the head of their employees, smashing the furniture up, and installing a whole new way of looking at, understanding, and acting in this life. This is genuinely essential to equip people to do what is necessary, in close cooperation with their colleagues, to survive and win on the field (including sea and sky) of combat. This is how ordinary people are helped to do extraordinary things, bound by a common ethos whether they serve for four years or forty. It is also not something that is just shoved in at the start, this way of thinking and working is reinforced every day in the language, ways of working, and expectations of behaviour, and echoed in all sorts of myths, symbols, and rituals.

It is extraordinarily powerful when done well, and extraordinarily dangerous or hilarious when abused or done badly.

The symbology includes how every service person can work out the history and provenance of another just by glancing at their port-side upper chest when dressed up in the smarter forms of uniform. Medals, whether awarded for time served away on various campaigns, or acts of particular bravery, or for membership of Orders (Bath or Empire mainly), tell a life story so far at a glance. The beauty of gongs is that they cost buttons and yet incentivize far more powerfully than cash. The jostling to be amongst the first to be sent on a new operation is intense if after a reasonable period of time away it will earn a new medal. If this is ninety days, the jostling to get back home once day ninety-one comes around can be no less intense, unless that is things are particularly entertaining and the chance of being flown home stone cold and wrapped in waterproof plastic remains modest. Campaigns that go on for ages, like Northern Ireland 1969-2006 and Bosnia (roughly 1992-2006) carry different weight. There comes a point when they have been underway so long that if you are not wearing the medal you are to be suspected of being a war-dodger, even if the work has become almost entirely benign.

Most UK military campaigns of any size since the Cold War started in a blaze of excitement, surprise, chaos, and self-inflicted disaster; eased confidently into the cruise around year two with plenty to do but very little chance of anything decisive happening – certainly not quickly; started to get really dull after ten years or so; and then dribbled out with draw-downs and 'training missions' sometime after that. Throughout this cycle there are always brave and clever things being done, the personal tragedy of deaths and injuries, and a constant search for a silver bullet to get it all done and dusted by Christmas.

In our new commercial world, there is nothing like this. Staring at someone's chest for clues is nugatory and generally frowned upon. Many people seem to silently hold up how much they get paid as the mark of a life being successfully spent, in absolute and comparative terms, and yet no one is meant to talk about how much this is. If they do, here in the City the figure can safely be halved to get closer to the truth. I suppose bonuses are a sort of medal substitute? The idea of a bonus is alien to military folk, for whom wringing-out a refund for expenses from the MoD is an epic triumph. Requiring the Archbishop of Canterbury and Cliff Richard to certify all travel claims above 35p certainly raises the bar. I gather proper city boys wear their bonuses in Porsches, penthouses and polo ponies, but I still think a bit of tin that silently conveys that the wearer made it to Afghanistan and back counts for something more tangible.

One of the fundamental differences between a vocational life and a transactional one is in how dispensable people are. Paradoxically, military folk are very uncompromising with each other when facing shot and shell, but arguably far too gentle when not at war. Few military people are ejected from service for being incompetent in administration – just as well as the army would be emptied in some quarters – and people are generally helped to a niche they can manage in order to stay in. On the contrary, here in the City it seems that employment hangs by a thread and any day can surprise with a plastic crate, a P45, and an early train home – albeit with a thumping great cheque in some cases. Yet the massive financial rewards for many seem to rely mostly on just being present a lot and staying lucky?

The transactional aspect, though, is mostly in how people relate to each other. In the military, a vocation, it all feels personal. In the City, nothing is personal and everything is based on a bottom line. This doesn't mean people are rude and disobliging, in fact everybody around World HQ seems unfailingly pleasant, but it is also basically ruthless: everyone knows that they are there for as long as they add to the bottom line in some way, and will be heading for an early bath the day that is not so, without rancour. It feels quite liberating once understood, but also explains why so many former military either don't make or don't enjoy the transition. As seen from World HQ, it does mean that although we can't kill with our bare hands any more we can certainly still make a killing with them, so long as we learn to campaign to different rules.

Chapter 7

Iraq 2003

My Dear M,

A dank January in 2003 found me forming myself up at the 'Joint Services Command and Staff College' near Swindon. The College, relatively newly built in the contemporary Tesco style but with better pictures and fewer addicts taking a snort in the loos, is located near Swindon – a nod to the greater egalitarianism rightly today infecting the officer classes. It was created in the early 1990s in order to close the Staff Colleges that the Royal Navy, Army, and Royal Air Force had each happily run as individual fiefdoms for decades. This separateness had generously helped to underpin the notion that each of the other Services was basically a nuisance to the other, a feckless obstacle to acquiring all the riches necessary from the taxpayer for the essential development of one's chosen colour of Armed Force.

Building a single College was not just about saving cash, though this was *really* important to the bean counters. It was more about recognizing the lessons of military disasters over hundreds of years (and some successes) and trying harder not to get massacred again in future. The import of history is that making war well needs navies, armies and air forces to be joined up seamlessly rather than fighting each other like cats in a bag before they turn exhausted on the actual enemy of the day.

The new enterprise had been designed down to the last plug socket by Tim Granville-Chapman (who later became a 'General Sir' and the Vice Chief of Defence Staff) in an epic performance of wisdom relentlessly applied to the last and weeniest detail. As legend has it, he even decided against putting WiFi in the bedrooms because that would tempt officers out of the library in the evenings. As at least 25 per cent of the internet is already dedicated to pornography, he also saw no great imperative to nudge that figure up a couple of points on weekday evenings in Wiltshire.

Anyway, I was looking forward to a winter mostly indoors as I joined the very select ranks of the Higher Command and Staff Course (HCSC). This was a big moment in my little life: HCSC is acknowledged as the glittery path to the stars for British officers, the essential filter to the best command and staff appointments in UK Defence. I realized that this would mean quite a lot of brain-squeezing for four months, a pretty much full-on effort to establish in the eyes of the mighty that I was less of an idiot than the other idiots. It would mean writing some stuff that could not all be ripped off Wikipedia, coming up with razor-sharp questions without being accused of trying too hard, and doing my very best to master PowerPoint – at which I remain fundamentally piss-poor to this day, although I have learned how to beg others to do this for money. It would also mean visits to some of the more vibrant as well as comatose bits of the UK military and NATO, all in the name of horizon-broadening outings. These would be leavened by free issues of curly sandwiches and stale crisps, with some evenings to be spent out on the town – in my case hoping the competition on the course would be caught in a wheelie bin rogering a prostitute, just to even things up on the career front a little.

The highlight on the outing front was the ten days in France on a 'staff ride', an assertively guided tour of battlefields from Waterloo to D-Day. One of the great advantages of France is the very wide range of occasions on which this proximate neighbour to the UK has had its ass kicked by so many other nations transiting hither and thither across it with their armies on full rampage. Not only is a visit geographically convenient, any inspection is accompanied by fair cooking and affordable vino collapso – despite the grumpy waiters, who all richly deserve a good kicking at the end of each evening for their traditional customer-baiting bollocks. Half the challenge of the staff ride was about demonstrating intellectual magnificence about, say, D-Day standing in a hailstorm on Omaha Beach and half was about doing so whilst very thick of head and bloated of belly.

Notwithstanding my joy at four months in carefree student mode, I knew that at the end of it I would be resuming my duties as chief of staff of HQ 3 (UK) Mechanized Division and very likely then heading out to Iraq. This was because every man and his dog knew that in around April 2003 the US and selected friends would head to Baghdad at tank speed. We were in that dodgy phase of any military intervention when the politicians don't want to say that they're going to war when they know they will, and their militaries need to get properly organized for this and have a huge shopping in mind but are not allowed to call Amazon. Getting 177,194 troops in the right place in the Middle East with all their luggage and other gear (like tonnes and tonnes of ammunition) is a bit more complicated than, say, organizing a hen party in Estonia. (I accept that a military invasion may be quieter and definitely involves less throwing up into a stranger's handbag).

I knew I was safe in completing HCSC as the first to go from the British Army would be the 1st (UK) Armoured Division, at that time still billeted in Germany whilst the unpicking of the geography of the Cold War ran its gentle course. The 1st Division was already busy hoovering up as much stuff as possible to make its tanks, artillery guns and other armoured vehicles actually work, in full anticipation of a slow boat to the Gulf and then a long wait in Kuwait for the Big Off. Spending New Year in a surprisingly nippy desert hoping that one of Saddam's SCUD missiles didn't drop by struck me as less appealing than staying indoors just outside Swindon, trying to spell Clausewitz in big purple font on a slide.

The list of stuff that an army finds it needs when invited to go and fight will always be prodigiously long. All the things that soldiers make do without at leisure in peacetime suddenly become urgent and necessary, like body armour for absolutely everybody and extra tank air filters for dusty desert manoeuvres. Equally suddenly, the politicians see the need to find the cash, as they visualize without too much prompting the alternative of career-ending headlines in the *Daily Mail*. Yet they still also want this stuff bought from industry without anybody noticing almost until kick-off. This tends to mean agreeing to everything just a bit too late – especially when the time to shift it from a factory in Birmingham to a grid reference in the middle of a desert is factored into the equation. This is why quite a lot of the 1st Armoured Division went to war with the labels still hanging off their kit and bubble wrap blowing all over the desert.

In the case of this particular war with Iraq, the whiff of Mr Saddam Hussein's chemical weapons was enough to make everybody most enthusiastic about having a gas mask that worked and a plentiful supply of the ghastly charcoal-infused suits that go with them. Normally, wearing all this stuff is hot, sweaty, grimy and, even as military looks go, phenomenally uncool – so most soldiers do all that they can to give it a miss. However, when faced with the actual prospect of nerve agent appearing out of the sky attached to a SCUD missile, enthusiasm ramps up pretty quickly. The alacrity with which even the most sedentary officer embraced anew the skills involved in blotting every inch of themselves with Fuller's earth powder in pursuit of effective decontamination illustrates just what a motivator fear can be.

It seemed to me that if the 1st Division was dispatched into Iraq by no later than April, then the earliest I might be invited to follow them (so they could come home for a summer of victory parades) would be maybe June. One of the reasons I didn't mind not rushing out to the front was that my little body was still somewhat in recovery mode from the previous year's sojourn in Afghanistan. I wasn't as afflicted as some, but the waterworks still needed rehabilitation and the rest of my magnificence was due some concentrated investment involving time in the gym and taking my jogging trousers for regular outings. This would occur at speeds an Olympic runner might not find especially threatening, but frankly still quite impressive I thought.

I also reckoned that if the 1st Division was not too badly knocked about by the attentions of the Iraqi army and its colleagues in their air force, it might make it through to an early autumn handover in Basra. That said, the soldiery would unanimously take the view that the day they left home a clock started ticking that could run for six months max, especially if a lot of that six months involved desert living and some lumpy encounters with the Iraqi army. One of the other big factors that would tilt when the handover occurred would be the weather. This is not really such a big deal in Europe, but an Iraqi winter outdoors can be surprisingly damp and cool from time to time and after about April it is definitely and relentlessly ball-crackingly hot – way, way too hot for much running about even for the locals, let alone any fighting.

As history records, after quite a lot of faffing about Iraq was invaded on 19 March 2003 involving around 45,000 British soldiers and (let's not forget) the 130,000 from the US who led the way. By around 1 May the invasion stuff was pretty much done, and although Saddam Hussein would not be captured until 13 December, the intervention had quickly swung into occupation mode. World history does not record that I finished HCSC with a decent shove in terms of career prospects, and the day I left the College the 3rd Division was warned for duty in Iraq.

In a novel twist, this didn't include having an in situ Divisional Commander, as there was to be an interregnum between the same Major General McColl who had triumphed in Afghanistan the year before and the arrival of the new 'General Officer Commanding' (=Boss), Major General Graeme Lamb. The latter had been pretty busy crunching about Iraq for much of 2003 already, in his niche capacity as the nation's leading Special Forces-type cheese wirer of the Queen's enemies. He was due some time off to wash his socks (although he is actually a sock refusenik, even in a suit, which is a bit of a thing for the cheese wirers – but still most unusual for someone originally from a posh Scottish battalion). He would also need to rekindle his enthusiasm for multinational soldiering, although he was well versed in leading the US military from behind. (This is not the place to debate UK's 245 plus years of maintaining 'strategic overwatch' of our former colonies, a concept about which some US officers are quite strident in their objection.) When I say 'rekindle', I mean summon the will to lead a polyglot European division through all the post-invasion excitement that was being so comprehensively left to chance. He would join us in Basra, so between April and July I could just make stuff up again.

In the usual military way, the months before deploying to Iraq would need to be expended on a comprehensive, exhausting, and mostly futile training programme. This is quite a thing to get right, starting with the most basic skills needed to function effectively in the heat, dust, and tantrums of post-invasion southern Iraq. Beyond the obvious things like shooting very straight when required and not shooting at all when not required, there were some things to understand about soldiering in this environment. First amongst these, even if left generally unspoken, was the daily requirement to avoid spontaneous combustion of one's trousers in the heat. The most common and greatest threat to us all was not that an incensed representative of one or other of the burgeoning Jihadi-minded militia would apply shot or bomb to our good selves, but that we would be fatally wounded by our own exploding grollies. The standard British military crutch is built for temperate climes and responds badly to being steamed.

It was quickly established that the problem of overheating would extend to far more than our nether regions. From about April to at least October it could be so boiling hot that *every* crevice, especially those insulated by body armour and extremely exercised by having to run at a fair clip in the service of Her Majesty – either at or away from peril – was in great jeopardy. Exactly as in Afghanistan, without rigorous daily attention to military grade crevice management, very bad things would swiftly occur in places no soldier wishes to present to the medical services, let alone expose to their family.

Much worse than this, and without doubt the source of real tragedy for some, was the daily danger of the combination of temperature and exertion exceeding the capacity of a British body's thermostat to manage without resulting in untimely death. We were all basically used to the idea of being killed by cold, that comes with learning one's trade in the damp and freezing misery of Wales, Scotland, and Salisbury Plain. But the idea of boiling to death was a novelty, a novelty we were all very keen to avoid experiencing at first hand.

The obvious pre-emptive treatment for heat-induced death is to remain indoors, at least in daylight hours, wrapped around an air-conditioner. The locals were pretty wise to this and generally kept out of the sun in the middle of the day. Unfortunately, the tricky business of trying to maintain a sense of security, order and progress in southern Iraq in the summer of 2003 was not amenable to everyone having a lie down until the autumn. Worse, given the limitations of having arrived uninvited by tank in March and then having to adjust swiftly to what was legally an occupation (but always referred to as something a bit more jolly), the circumstances were getting trickier and the availability of the air-conditioners exceedingly poor. Amongst the saddest deaths amongst our number were those who got overcooked in their work. Often, by the time they arrived in a medical facility which was actually cooled their bodily thermostat had totally lost control and they were slipping inexorably away as their vital organs just packed up. My worst recollection is of a good man being found dead in a portaloo, to which he had adjourned just feeling a bit off from the heat of a recent foot patrol, never to reappear. Nobody wants to die in that tragic way, an urgent and timely reminder to us all to head to the nearest doctor when something is definitely not right.

This was all still a bit remote as we sat in Bulford in April 2003, working out how we would build a multi-national division and get it to Iraq in around July in order to let the 1st Division come home, literally for tea and medals. Given the task that lay ahead for us, it was more than a little tiresome that our ability to train was taking second-place to the requirement to put fires out in the UK whilst the members of the Fire Brigades Union were engaged in a brisk industrial dispute. The brigade that would be at the heart of our effort, 19 Mechanized Brigade, had been committed to underwriting putting fires out and as a result was not releasable for much of the training it needed to do in good time for its stint in southern Iraq. My suggestion that the Fire Brigades Union could start training for six months in Iraq, rather than just sit outside their place of work moaning for more pay than our soldiers ever saw, never made it all the way up the M3 to Downing Street.

The result was not so poor that we sent everyone a map with a cross on it showing Iraq's position on the planet, a bottle of water to get started with and advice to pack plenty of talcum powder. But it didn't feel very much better. Of course, there is always some capacity to sort things out when you have arrived at the war and can see the challenges at first hand, but it's not unlimited – as Napoleon and Hitler found when winter surprised them in Russia. We would in any case be conducting a 'relief in place', military-speak for taking on the work that was already in hand from the incumbents. But it was also true that running complex military interventions abroad as a come-as-you-are party bears some unnecessary risk.

The relief in place aspect was complicated by the requirement to exchange what had been essentially an all-British effort in southern Iraq with a multinational design. We had charge of four provinces: Al Muthanna, Maysan, Basra, and Dhi Qar, with contingents from nine countries to fill them with, and we would be subordinate to the American leadership in Baghdad (within the limits of coalition good manners).

Amongst our first challenges was to establish which nation would operate where in our patch and be willing to do what. Exactly as in Afghanistan the year before, it would be lovely if all we had to do was write one single good plan of campaign and then issue instructions to everyone who would then willingly and ably conform to it. Given that this is not how multinational coalitions work, everybody who wants to play a part likes to decide in their own sweet way what that party is going to be, the horse trading between capitals and between military contingents was as usual a protracted and sometimes awkward affair.

We had in our own mix 19 Mechanized Brigade from Catterick in Yorkshire, which would take the lead in Basra city and its environs and also in the rural, and contentious Maysan province. Their engineers, 38 Engineer Regiment, would be supported by a Norwegian company with similar skills and nicer trucks. There was also a forty-strong New Zealand band of engineers, which is really quite a big contribution from a smallish market town miles off to the right of Australia. The effort in Maysan was supplemented by a Danish battle group of around 450 good soldiers, struggling to communicate in any known language with a thirty-strong Lithuanian detachment taken under their wing. Al Muthanna province was the Dutch parish, operated by an 1,100 strong Dutch battle group. As this was miles from the sea, the obvious choice for the job were the excellent Dutch marines. It was just one of those things, but their start was made far harder by a massive outbreak of some sort of ghastly diarrhoea-like infection that floored pretty much all of them and required the deployment of quite a large medical team to fix them up. Death by ass-based dehydration in the heat was staring at them all, really quite scary stuff. An Italian Mechanized Brigade of 2,800 took stylish charge of our role in Dhi Qar province, supported by a Romanian mechanized battalion and a military police company – so another 500 soldiers – plus a 130-strong security force company from the Portuguese National Guard to do policing. All of this lot had to find its way together by offering up their idiosyncratic versions of English, written and oral, in daily communication – and all of them utterly baffled if anyone with a hint of Scottish tried to speak to them.

As usual in these adventures, how the US operated in Iraq and how most of the constituents in our multi-national division – South-East intended to go about their business were quite different. There was some cause to imagine that this difference was appropriate, given that the south was largely Shia and had been most egregiously treated by Saddam Hussein and the Sunni Iraqis, whereas the rest of the country was either Sunni and so not much enthused by seeing their leader pushed out, or Kurdish and determined that this moment in history would include their liberation from Arab domination. It was always a mix that could breed excitement.

This thought, that down in the south we would be the best of friends with the residents, was dissipating rapidly as widespread disappointment set in that we were not providing at a sprint the quality of life to which the inhabitants (numbering a few million) aspired in terms of comfort and prosperity. Some of this aspiration was really quite modest: to have a source of constant clean water, a regular supply of electricity or failing that the petrol to run the gazillion generators around the place. The need for water was self-evident, but without electricity there was no cooling in daily summer temperatures north of 100°F.

It was also true that even if we had strapped ice packs to every citizen, we would still have been seen by many as occupiers who should basically fuck off or, even worse, alien Christian crusaders who were going to stick around to steal all the oil, despoil womenfolk, and evangelize. Worse, even though we explained that we were as keen to go as they were to see us out, the level of trust was low: all the messaging, money and organization flowing across the border from Iran was bent on causing us maximum misery and instilling alarm amongst the population.

We were banned from saying 'I told you so', but any of us who had experience of popping into other people's countries uninvited had been saying for months that an invasion of Iraq would mean picking up some responsibility for its welfare and improvement, unless the plan was just to turn round and drive out as soon as the last agent of Saddam Hussein was done over. It is too crude just to say, 'if you break it you own it', but it's not that far from the mark – especially if you go to all the trouble after arriving uninvited to dismantle the local and national organs of government, ban many political parties, and send home whatever was left of the army and police. Basra was a city of 1 million people, at the time of our arrival a city of 1 million cross and hot people, even if they were genuinely relieved to be shot of Mr Hussein. Our capability as soldiers to establish complete order and prosperity was obviously a tad limited.

We all knew that there had been a conscious decision in the US not to plan for what happened after the invasion, because the plan was just to leave. When leaving quickly didn't look like a brilliant wheeze, the machinery that was created to act in lieu of a functioning Iraqi government was 'a bit thin'. In fact, I thought then and I think now that it was a complete crock of shite. As an example, a good man was eventually dispatched to run Basra as the Coalition Provisional Authority, a distinguished former British diplomat no less, but he arrived equipped with pretty much what he could carry. His first act on assuming his role was to head to the bazaar to buy a bed.

I have seen this kind of thing happen many times in the Balkans, Afghanistan, Iraq, and bits of Africa. The task of substituting for an entire system of government administration in the wake of a military intervention, or in the face of the collapse of existing institutions under the weight of their own uselessness, is assumed by a tiny number of dedicated, highly enthusiastic foreigners. Great intentions and a jaunty disposition are rarely enough to do the trick.

These folk often have some local knowledge or language, they certainly have no shortage of commitment nor lack of will to assert their newly endowed authority with integrity and wisdom. But so often enthusiasm does not equal talent and certainly not the capacity in numbers or breadth of expertise to be effective. I am certainly not making an argument for the military to become the civil administration, although that had to be done at the outset in Basra for a while. This included, for example, converting a reserve officer who had been deployed as a staff watchkeeper to become the paymaster for the whole of government in Basra, because he knew stuff about accounting and we had found a container literally stuffed with cash with which to pay local employees. It is an argument for thinking through all the dimensions of an intervention and resourcing them well enough, and for long enough, in order to deliver sufficient stability and success to be able to leave well. Otherwise, it can feel like we are simply turning our backs on the smouldering ashes of the place we have just trashed physically, politically, economically, and socially.

The day came, 12 July 2003 in fact, when the 1st (UK) Division was relieved and headed home. This found us (the 3rd Division) established in a terminal building at Basra airport, which had the advantage of being a big and modern construction (never actually used as an airport) at a safe yet convenient distance outside the city. Having a runway close by is always a good thing for expediting entry and exit. We also found it was such a sufficiently large target that even an unskilled Iraqi militiaman could prop a rocket on some bricks and point it in our rough direction with a reasonable chance of success. These bloody things may be small, generally 107mm in diameter, and wildly inaccurate, but if you are unlucky enough to be the recipient of it – even if more by accident than design – the consequences are frequently unpleasant. From quite early on we became practised at keeping helmet and body armour close at hand even indoors and adjourning at speed to the floor on hearing the alarm. Some of my more memorable meetings at Basra airport, especially later on in the campaign, were conducted whilst prone on the floor under a table and carried on in that British way as if entirely normal.

Home for me for the next few months would be the Departures floor of the terminal building. It could be worse, I thought, because it provided a big and open space with a roof that kept the sun off. There was enough room to set out the staff of a couple of hundred people in a suitably military way, our own little Tower of Babel found from the contributing nations. Military headquarters in the Western world have evolved around nine principal staff branches, each with a designated function. So J1 (where J stands for Joint, the shotgun union of all three services) is the HR department, J2 is intelligence, J3 is current operations, J4 for logistics, J5 is planning, and so on. There is also then a range of functional areas, such as my own sport of artillery – or 'fires' in modern parlance, engineers, and military police. The sum of all this is that big military headquarters exist as a sort of village under one roof, with all the ups and downs of village life – certainly a mass of gossip, perhaps the illicit sex quota generally a bit down on suburbia. And perhaps not.

At the centre of all this was the chief of staff, me as a thrusting colonel. Aside from having a general overview of the headquarters, I lead specifically on intelligence, operations, and planning. My counterpart, the deputy chief of staff, managed all the personnel and logistic aspects. I am doctrinally obliged to say at this point how very important logistics are, obviously nothing happens without the stuff to make it happen, and in this sort of campaign getting the logistics right was really the most fundamental thing we had to do. Without enough bottles of water, for example, we would be done in by lunchtime. On the other hand, unless one is born to it (and some really are) 'logistics' is basically a bit grubby and dull when compared to the vibrant, far more glamorous pointy end of the stick such as intelligence and operations.

I found I was to manage my empire from the well-selected purview of what was once intended to be the duty-free shop. This had the virtue of being a space with a glass wall around it, conferring the same status as any glass bubble does in any hateful 'open plan' office. It provided a modicum of refuge from the hubbub of the staff as they chuntered away solving the issues of the moment. As the duty-free shop, it also had a little storeroom behind in which to conceal military jumble like helmets and to which I might retreat when a thorough scratch of my invariably overcooked recesses was required.

Given the unrelenting demands for my attention that this role incurred, I was particularly keen to find somewhere to sleep that would not be intruded upon by the nightly respiratory torment of brother officers with too much army catering lodged along the length of their torso. The answer was a storeroom somewhere in the bowels of the building. This had the great advantage of being suitable for solo occupancy, but also completely windowless and reliant on a trickle of air from a vent in the wall. It was at least somewhere I could get silently horizontal for a few hours.

The major disadvantage of the terminal building was not that it afforded zero protection from intrusion by hostile shelling, at this time there wasn't so much of that anyway, but its propensity to bake its occupants. In the heat of a Basra summer providing cooling was going to be pretty vital to sustaining output. The good news was that this building came equipped with massive blower devices in the ceiling, all connected to some seriously industrial cooling plant. The bad news was that it needed a tonne of electricity to work and electricity was a rare and wonderful commodity.

Of course, we did have our own generators, otherwise how could we make so much noise that nobody for half a mile around would sleep properly? But our generators were not equipped to turn over an airport's cooling plant, that needed the full might of Basra's power grid. And Basra's power grid was the industrial equivalent of a car crash. Some of this was due to the depredations of war, some due to the poor performance of Saddam Hussein when it came to supporting the south (which is where most of his money came from, yet his ill-treatment of the Shia population was still horrid and prolific), and quite a lot the result of just shabby engineering. I struggle to put a shelf up that is in any way level or likely to defy gravity for more than ten minutes, but some of the electricity infrastructure in Iraq could have been built by someone like me – and that someone had not bothered to read the instructions.

More annoying than the eternally crap grid, was the local enthusiasm for dismantling the powerlines that we did repair. Sometimes this was just to be egregiously obstructive to us and anybody else they didn't fancy; more often it was to thieve the copper. No matter how often messages were circulated that if one must steal the electricity cable do make sure the supply is turned off before setting to work with the cutters, it just didn't seem to penetrate the copper-robber fraternity. We regularly encountered the frazzled earthly remains of a copper thief still attached to his work. Removing the body brought the same on/off dilemma for the authorities, who generally and often wisely elected just to leave things as they were if it was a bit out of sight – partly as a local health and safety advisory to anybody else who was attracted to a career in copper recycling.

The harsh reality of the shortfall in electricity was that for the duration of my stay the temperature of my magnificence and all its nooks and crannies was to be directly dependent upon how well Basra's power grid worked. When it did, all was literally sweetness and light. When it failed, which is often, all was literally pungent and gloomy. When we lost the grid and relied on our own generators, we knew we would at least have enough air to keep us from boiling over, but not a drop more. It was a bit like a sci-fi film in which all is proceeding according to plan until there is a sudden stillness as the air supply to the space station fails and doom is immediately on the cards. In our case, when the air supply went silent we knew it would be about four hours before things really steamed up and about three days on average before we would cease non-stop filtering of bottled water through every pore.

Basra had the additional treat in store of balancing mad heat with total humidity on those very special days in July and August when the wind came up from the sea to the south. I thought I already had pretty full experience of heat and cold, from the misery of Scottish mountains in January to the ass-cracking heat of a Balkan summer, but Basra took things to a new level. On the most special days the air temperature would hit 53 degrees Centigrade and the humidity stick at 100 per cent. I don't think any European body has this within its performance envelope, because the brain's instruction to all areas to sweat at full tilt is futile when the air has no capacity to absorb it. And 100 per cent humidity was inevitably more than the electricity supply could handle without fusing itself in one giant fizzing cluster of molten wiring.

I recall presiding over the morning brief on one of these days, standing in the half gloom of Departures with a circle of increasingly moist staff officers. When I had finished my (no doubt) sterling peroration, I looked down at my boots to find I was standing in a puddle of my own making as a great deal of water simply flushed out of my ankles. This was one of the rare occasions when I could see panic in people's eyes as they wondered if they would ever cool down or if it was to be their turn for the terminal body thermostat meltdown experience.

I found I couldn't devote every waking hour to wondering about the state of my feet and all the other areas suffering in the fetid darkness beneath Her Majesty's uniform. There was quite a lot of stuff I needed to get on with as the chief of staff. Top of my list was establishing what the new boss, Major General Graeme Lamb, was minded to pursue with his increasingly well-established train-set across the four provinces. He was no stranger to this part of the world, though one sensed that much of his previous acquaintance had been formed exclusively in the dark whilst strangling the most pernicious and objectionable opponents of truth and light. He was clearly at his happiest when embarked on matters most martial, barely repressing his enthusiasm for taking personal charge of lawful and essential slaughter even when discharging some of the other, wimpier aspects of senior command.

This included the imperative to feign empathy and tolerance whilst being lectured by the stream of twenty-something representatives of the world's self-appointed humanitarian agencies who swished uninvited through our headquarters. Their deeply-held purpose was to instruct us in the beastliness of our presence and the imperative that we atone. They thought elevating the entire population of Iraq to comfortable middle-class standards, including villas and swimming pools for all by the following week, was the mark. Having informed us of this duty, they would offer to sacrifice a day away from climbing the greasy pole of professional grief junkery to conduct a workshop on a subject of their own choosing.

My choice was to see how deep an imprint an army desert boot can leave in the ass of expensive denim when assisting departure, but theirs would be to explore, in a non-judgemental way, the morality of dental flossing with a dozen gummy Iraqi ladies corralled into a room on the promise of an hour with an air-conditioner and free soft biscuits. Graeme Lamb's personal technique for sustaining his attentiveness during all such encounters was to withdraw a clearly illegally-large clasp knife from his pocket and whittle menacingly away at a piece of wood, transforming this with real feeling from small lump to very sharp stiletto. I sometimes wonder whether he gave these away to his interlocutors as a reminder not to come back, or just wrote their name on them, storing a rapidly growing collection in a drawer ready for awarding squarely between the shoulder blades on some future dark night.

As I have noted already, it became evident that there might be a difference of view over how to restore Iraq to some semblance of security, stability and prosperity between our European-found division in the south and the American-dominated rest of the (very much larger) force to our north. On taking over from the First Division, my out-going counterpart (a very charming and competent cavalry officer called Patrick Marriot) had made it plain that if we hadn't left by Christmas (2003) we would be toast. He couldn't see how we would sustain sufficient consent amongst the local population to our presence for much longer than that, unless we were ladling tonnes of cash at them and had rebuilt everything. This we were unlikely to do.

There are many good records of what took place in Iraq at this time that explain well why it was 'so challenging'. The story includes: the failed assumption that we would be welcomed as liberators with rose petals and fireworks; that the enthusiasm for all Iraqi citizens to immediately bind together in peace and harmony would be all-conquering; that the potential perils of not having a plan for the day after the regime fell would not manifest; and that amplifying everything that was already hard by disbanding the existing government, police, and armed forces was a cool idea – even when there was really nothing to take its place and we simply did not have the capacity to do so. The latter move, of course, ejected some of the better-trained and more capable Arabs, some of whom had profited mightily under Saddam Hussein, out from being at the heart of things to the wilderness of being extremely and assertively cross at their loss, and thereby very well motivated to stir up insurgency and terrorism.

By the end of July 2003 we were saying to our leaders in Baghdad and London that unless we moved swiftly and effectively to do some relatively basic things, such as provide a decent flow of electricity and clean water whilst also describing cogently how we were going to restart effective governance, security and economy, we would very quickly find 1 million people in Basra expressing their disapproval through the medium of throwing rocks at us – or worse. Probably the only thing that united this population would be disaffection with us, because in almost every other respect they were inclined to tear chunks out of each other in the jostle to fill a political and social vacuum, seizing a slice of whatever pie existed. Corruption and violence were no strangers to this part of the world even before we turned up with our own supply of the latter. And as is always the case in situations like this, the absence of enough government and security to instil the rule of law is very quickly exploited by criminality of all flavours. Hungry people with no job or prospect of one will do what they feel they have to do to survive and protect their families.

Imminent disaster was not the view of many on the US political side in Baghdad or Washington (where victory had already been well trumpeted). They had a plan for creating some sort of Iraqi government out of the ashes and were disinclined to think that civil disorder and insurgency beyond extinguishing the embers of the previous regime would be coming our way. This difference of view was quite memorably exposed when Baghdad sent us our first (and, as it turned out, our last) 'CODEL' or Congressional Delegation.

This was a new one on me. I was certainly well used to small gangs of British MPs turning up in the name of the House of Commons Armed Forces Committee, which meant us following the instructions from the Ministry of Defence to tell them everything short of anything useful and certainly nothing new or controversial. I was already practised in ignoring this instruction, finding one way or another of sending them off with something genuinely meaningful to assist us with once back in Westminster. I was equally well used to nothing happening as a result of such visits, because in the UK system the government of the day understands that 'separation of powers' means 'chin Parliament off as much as possible'.

Not so, it seems with a CODEL. In the US system these visits really matter because Congress really can be very painful for the administration. Congress is constitutionally and personally charged with administering whackings that hurt on policy, operations, and (especially) money. Nonetheless, it did seem a bit odd that these US representatives of the Senate and the House would trouble themselves with coming our way: we couldn't vote for them, we didn't pay them any taxes, and we understood very well that our political asses were owned by London and the other capitals contributing to multi-national division South East (MND-SE – covering four provinces in southern Iraq). I said as much in cheerfully welcoming them to the terminal for their thorough briefing from me on what we were up to in the south, Graeme Lamb having wisely elected to be at the far end of our patch on the day.

However, and it turned out to be a massive and hairy 'however', these coves had already spent some time in Baghdad being briefed by our US senior leadership on how the campaign was going swimmingly well and the certain path to even greater glory was clear. At this time, the Provisional Coalition Administrator of Iraq was Paul Bremer, who saw himself – not without some justification – as the most powerful American official abroad since Douglas

MacArthur ran Japan at the end of the unpleasantness in the 1940s. Bremer reported to the US Secretary of Defense, Donald Rumsfeld, an arrangement which was itself a comment on how the occupation was viewed as a military exercise. Anyway, this CODEL had apparently arrived from the US harbouring some small suspicions that the adventure in Iraq was not going entirely well, causing Mr Bremer and his team to go to great lengths to dispel any such doubts. All was well and all was to be well.

Not only had this memo failed to reach me, it was also a memo that so far as we could see failed the Multinational Division South East hollow-laugh test, given the circumstances in which we found ourselves in late July 2003. Brigadier Bill Moore commanded the UK's 19 Brigade (including Basra) and he and our mainly European counterparts were cracking on with establishing a sense of security and a direction of travel to better times as best they could, basically reliant on the consent of the majority of the population to swing with us. There was no way harmony could be imposed by bullet. There were many both the locally and specifically aggrieved and the geography-agnostic and generally aggrieved spun-up by Iranian money and instructions to be objectionable, for whom our presence in no way met their definition of 'desirable'. In their view we deserved to be forcibly ejected. But the greater problem as we saw it at this time, was that we were losing the patience of the common man on the Basra omnibus.

One of the main reasons for this was that some four months after our unsolicited arrival most of the basic means of life were still broadly in tatters. The disgruntlement that this provoked was more than a little aggravated by the making of almost everybody who worked for the previous government unemployed. This was something that Mr Bremer was keen on, seeing no residual virtue in the instruments of state that Saddam Hussein had maintained. It meant a lot of people who once had a job were now feeling the pinch. Worse, they were being pinched in temperatures that were daily nudging around 50 degrees Centigrade. In these conditions having an intermittent supply of water, with mains electricity still something of a novelty, and – despite the oodles of it in the ground – petrol and diesel in very short supply was being taken all very personally. We were dealing with a cocktail of grief: there wasn't enough electricity to run the refineries that made the petrol that ran the generators that kept people's houses cooler and lit. As a military organization we could do many things, particularly industrial-scale violence, but mending battered refineries and electricity grids was not part of our lexicon. We did infrastructure band-aid when what was required was open-heart surgery.

This is pretty much the message that I handed to the CODEL: we were losing the consent of the public in southern Iraq to our presence and unless we provided material improvements within about the next eight weeks there was more than a fighting chance that we would be back to fighting – only this time it would be an insurgency/terrorism combo on a scale we should be pretty nervous about. Dealing with a problem like this could not be suitably addressed by the use of so much high explosive that the aggrieved population would be either destroyed or shoved out as refugees. It would have to be met within the sensible limitations on the use of force that required numbers on the ground to prevail – and some different equipment – that we simply didn't have..

So the CODEL, led it turned out by the combative Senator John McCain, took this message back to Baghdad and offered it to Mr Bremer in some fashion that appears to have registered. He was, apparently, beside himself with anguish. By that evening instructions were coming our way from Baghdad that Major General Lamb was to be sent home, along with that lying idiot of a bastard chief of staff. It pretty quickly was made clear in gentle response (from London) that, being British rather than American, the sacking business was a tad more complicated than might be the case within the US-only firmament. Basically, if we felt there really was a risk of glory turning to a complete crock of shite we were at some liberty to point this out to visiting politicians (though obviously not to the press, who did this perfectly well for themselves). The upshot was that we didn't get sent home, and General Lamb just continued to learn how to roller-blade on the runway out of hours in his usual spirit of lethal equanimity. He probably made a couple more named additions to his collection of well-whittled wooden stilettos. And, funnily enough, we never saw another CODEL in the remainder of our tenure.

A long hot summer then did turn out as we feared. By mid-August 19 Brigade was facing some quite large riots by an angry host of very hot and very bothered Basra citizens. We were on the slippery slope to more shootings and bombings being directed at us. This quickly led to a very complicated and expensive process of re-equipping a force that had turned up for a rapid invasion-and-then-home job, into a counter-insurgency/terrorism force likely to stick around for some years as we started to resurrect an Iraqi army and police to fill our shoes.

When transition to counter-insurgency happens, and it is hardly rare, it provokes all sorts of issues around fundamental questions such as how to construct and apply the rule of law. Whose law for a start? It was also hardly surprising that if we were partnered with Iraqi politicians at all levels whom many of the population regarded as thieving scumbags, then we were bound to be coloured in the same way. By failing to mobilize the resources that Europe plainly has (that certainly seems clear if you are a hungry Iraqi citizen with no job or prospects, looking at the pictures of London on your TV and phone) we were either guilty of incompetence or oppression. We found we could easily amplify the sense of inadequacy by creating local mini proto-governments ourselves, staffed by tiny numbers of enthusiasts combed-out from the stock of 'hard to employ but adventurous' at a loose end in UK. The tea and sympathy they could provide also illuminated our impotence.

My particular tussle as chief of staff with rule of law was around the rules for the use of force and the business of managing detainees. The first of these ought to be a fairly simple proposition: since we were not at war with anybody, it should be rare that lethal force was required, and if it was it should be in accordance with UK law (which was in any case a deal more restrictive than Iraqi law). The problem was that as the shooting and bombing of us became more prevalent, so the reasonable requirement of soldiers to fire back asserted itself. It was inevitable that when shots were fired, the recipients of our bullets would be readily aggrieved, and if also consequently dead their family and supporters – and anyone with an axe to grind against us – would be no less unhappy. The firer of the shots, usually a fairly junior soldier, was entitled to fire if he or she felt the life or the life of those to be protected was in jeopardy. If this seems straightforward, it really is not in the heat of the moment and quite often in the dark. If ROE regimes like this (as set by ministers) result in soldiers failing to fire when they really should poor outcomes accrue – and it is equally poor if they shoot when they should not.

We adopted an approach whereby following shots being fired resulting in death, the commanding officer of the firer was required to look into the circumstances and judge whether a military police investigation was merited. He at least understood the conditions in which the event had taken place, although whether his view then aligned with a military lawyer was always an interesting question. We could certainly be sure that there would be somebody privy to an incident (often a party some miles away and safely tucked up in bed at the time, sometimes in England) who was determined to see it as an outrageous crime, whatever the evidence. It wasn't long before some UK-based lawyers found a living as well as a cause in teaming up with Iraqis who, whether for good reason or just opportunistic malicious intent, wanted to press a claim. We certainly didn't help ourselves here by incidents of abuse and worse that were proven to be committed by some British soldiers. That did us real harm. War is a foul business and it's not made any better by succumbing to the temptation to do plainly illegal things just because you think nobody is looking or bothered. Because it is really, really hot is no defence either. Every such lapse is a self-inflicted wound that needed to be investigated and resolved.

When it came to the thorny issue of detentions (arresting people) we were also caught between a rock and a hard place. As our intelligence improved, we got a better handle on the armed opposition, including some pretty hard-core groups who were great enthusiasts for bombing and shooting us. This intelligence, actually a very structured and methodical process, could never be 100 per cent. It was often better on who was batting for the other side rather than telling us where to find them at any given time. On the other hand, it was often the case that following a firefight the soldiers on the ground would succeed in detaining the opposition before they had the chance to leg-it. Not everyone merited a bullet. The net result was that we ended up with a growing number of Iraqis in our detention facilities on the basis of the information we had established about them.

Some cases were more clear-cut than others, but it was our responsibility to make sure that we didn't hang on to anybody either wrongly or for longer than was necessary. So the first recourse was to look to hand over our prisoners to the Iraqi authorities once they had reconstituted themselves sufficiently, so our detainees could have a proper Iraqi criminal trial. This made lots of theoretical sense, but in practice the difference between intelligence and evidence is pretty significant: we might be certain from information we had that we knew somebody was out to kill us, but *proving* that short of catching them red-handed was a higher bar. We soon found that people whom we knew to be very intent on doing us a mischief were passed to an Iraqi court, where the lack of concrete evidence resulted in their immediate release and their swift return to armed malevolence. Even where we thought the evidence was rock solid, sometimes the Iraqi judge was minded to think otherwise and set them loose. Possibly more vexing, some offenders were actually convicted and jailed, only for them to be very swiftly released. This was the either the result of money changing hands or the prison staff receiving very assertive advice about their own personal mortality if they didn't let so-and-so out lickety-spit.

I sometimes found in my role as one of the reviewers of the people we had detained, assiduously advised by an army lawyer, that the written evidence on why someone had been taken off the street was less than fulsome. This, generally, was the result of an altercation in the dark leading to a young soldier detaining an Iraqi citizen for reasons he found pretty compelling (typically: 'the fucker shot at me'). For all sorts of reasons (mostly to do with being a bit rubbish with a pen) some soldiers failed to commit details to paper in any detail. So, unless there was additional intelligence to hand about an individual beyond a single and unilluminating detention report, the grounds for reasonably hanging onto somebody for very long did not exist. In the eyes of the soldier on the ground this put me in the same bucket as the Iraqi judge, who really was having a laugh at us, by releasing citizens known to be antithetical to our health and success. We were both seen as putting wrong'uns prematurely back on the street.

Imagine being that soldier who sees someone back on the streets with whom shots were exchanged just days before with great ferocity, a soldier who had taken some considerable personal risk to make an arrest (rather than just bumping the opposition off in the heat of the moment). He or she may explicably become disinclined to be so brave in doing the right thing the next time. Whether this results in ignoring coming across serious armed opposition (thereby deflecting the mortal risk to other soldiers on another occasion) or whether the choice between shoot or detain descends to a 'bang bang – hands-up' approach, the overall outcome is 'less than optimal'. War is this feral thing and the demands on (the mainly) young people who take part in it are tough to balance.

The same sort of argument unfolds about detained senior players in the latter stages of campaigns such as in Iraq, when the international force is shaping up to leave and the relatively newly installed domestic government is taking back the reins of power. The international military will usually have in their charge some very senior figures who lead the armed opposition. The interests of sealing the nascent peace deal will generally call for early release of these leadership figures, whereas the security of the international force and many others would see them banged up until the last planes are leaving forever. This was playing out when I served in Baghdad as a major general in 2008-9, a story for another day.

I am pleased to report that my 2003 sojourn in Iraq ended a little prematurely on the happy news that I was to be promoted to brigadier and dispatched to command 39 Infantry Brigade in Northern Ireland, spanning eventually across Belfast and South Armagh ('bandit country'). This was a bold move on the part of the mighty. The brigade had never been commanded before by anyone who was not from the infantry, a Gunner was an outrageous choice, or indeed by anyone (like me) with no residential tour experience in the Province.

It was certainly going to be interesting going from a campaign where everybody talked down the seriousness of the significant violence that remained and wondered when it would end, to a campaign where everybody talked up what little violence actually remained and assumed it would never end. More prosaically, I was leaving an operational theatre where the sun beat down for a theatre where the rain hardly stops. After seeing through a Basra summer, as I left in late October 2003 I resolved to never complain about the rain in Northern Ireland. Well before 2003 was out I realized that was a resolution no sane man could possibly keep.

Chapter 8

Technology and War

I have always been a follower of the Clausewitzian view that the nature of war never changes, but its character – the way it's actually conducted – changes all the time with thinking and technology. I know there are plenty of academics and psychologists who argue that fighting is not an inalienable or unreformable aspect of human make-up and that we really ought now to be able to civilize our way out of clubbing each other to a pulp. I hope they are right, yet judging by my own exposure to people's propensity to want *very much indeed* to cut out the heart of their enemy with a dessert spoon, this civilizing has some way to go. And even if you could get the 'stop killing' message to every adult now alive, you would only have to look at playground squabbling amongst toddlers to see that the bloodlust over who gets to ride the tractor first at playtime is part of the toolkit that evolution (or the deity of your choice) confers upon us.

War in all its many guises has the common and enduring feature of being horrid. No matter if it should be launched for what are truly held to be the best of reasons (and there is bound to be an argument about this), once let off the lead it just isn't like anything else in the catalogue of available behaviours for mankind. War has always been, and I will take considerable persuading to think it won't always be, this terrible thing where people die and stuff gets broken. I guess Europe has been pretty lucky since about 1945 in that only a relatively small number of its inhabitants have encountered this at first hand.

The look in the eye of the non-Serbs trudging past me on a freezing day in Bosnia, having been ejected from their homes not many hours before, revealed a combination of shock, terror, anger, and disbelief that somehow everything they had known had suddenly been ripped from them. For the benefit of balance, this look was replicated exactly in the Serbs who found themselves in the same position at other times and places in the battles for parts of Croatia and Bosnia and Herzegovina. The common feature is that war doesn't naturally do boundaries or rules, despite centuries of trying to limit it with laws and conventions. These are good things to persist with, but war as a phenomenon is just naturally a feral bastard.

The speed with which the fabric of civilisations stretching back hundreds of years is completely trashed by violence and the sense that there are no limits in how fast or how far this goes is completely shocking to anyone subject to it. It is one of the most vivid illustrations that humanity is always this struggle between emotions grounded in evolution and pre-history, institutions fashioned hundreds of years ago, and technology which people use without any understanding of how it works.

Technology in war, my subject for you today, is of course a massive part of how we fight and no less so today as we set about applying the wisdom and expertise found in the Digital Age to unlocking new ways of causing harm from pinpoint specific to industrial-scale carnage. I often wonder whether when Mr Gates and his peers were knocking out the first computers, mobile phones, and daft games in various attics and garages across America, did it ever occur to them that they would be equipping the navies, armies and air forces of their dotage with some brilliant stuff that is far better at the ripping out of hearts than at any time in history? I guess not.

They're not to blame for this, of course, what they built was for the entirely pleasurable purpose of enabling teenagers to make videos of themselves clomping around their bedrooms clad insufficiently and impractically, gyrating enthusiastically to the banging 'tunes du jour'. This keeps them distracted as their parents send fuzzy photographs of their genitals to colleagues and acquaintances, having exhausted Netflix's entire canon. Yet nobody should really be surprised if the technology of today changes how we fight as well as how we live, work, and play. It has always been thus. As soon as someone invented the sail, most oar-based navies felt at great disadvantage, at least when it was a bit windy. Gunpowder literally blew away archers and castles, and it only took about fifteen years to go from the Wright brothers getting off the ground to the first machine guns being successfully fired from an aircraft without also shooting off the propeller.

My own military career charts how technology has profoundly altered the business of soldiering, and my new sortie into the jungles of commercial life reveals just the same reliance on having groovy kit to get an edge. Both callings share a certain romantic attachment to the power of the widget, the notion that this new thing will be so much better than the old thing that victory/great riches will ensue. For some in both walks of life, it is enough that the new thing is so full of wizardry, usually expressed as many knobs and flashing lights, that whether or not it is any use is entirely irrelevant. So long as it drips enough technological sex we are happy.

I am just about senior enough to be able to describe today to a 21 year-old how the British Army was equipped in 1980 and guarantee to win a look of faint and patronizing amusement in response. I will be talking about a time before the personal computer, the mobile phone, even before waterproof trousers that didn't soak the wearer in sweat faster than any storm could manage. There was no global positioning system to convey from space exactly where one was on the planet to within a metre or two, so the young officer of the time relied on skill with a paper map and a prismatic compass in order to be comprehensively lost on the fringes of Salisbury Plain in the middle of the night. This is beyond Generation Z's imagination. (This was certainly *not* beyond the imagination of the residents of Urchfont on the North of the Plain in the summer of 1981, to whom I introduced a complete battery of six ten-tonne artillery guns and their twenty-tonne trucks at 02.00 hours, motoring manfully up a weeny one-way street until fully wedged-in, followed by two hours of not very silent – quite a lot of 'fucks' being thrown – reversing. For which, I apologize.)

This is not to say that when I was starting out as a soldier the implements to hand were entirely medieval. As an artillery officer I was expected to be a bit technical, as well as consummately dashing and hard. We did have a computer, called appropriately enough the Field Artillery Computing Equipment (FACE), which was essentially a pretty dim pocket calculator squeezed into a giant green box to which the British defence industry had glued a set of flashing lights and buttons big enough to bash with Gunner hands more used to heaving 96lb of shell about.

For those of us fortunate enough to be serving with the BAOR, this thing was cabled into the back of a 1960s armoured vehicle, a bit like an entry-level transit van with tracks instead of wheels. It had taken some time to arrange the ergonomics so that any user not imbued with dwarfism found their spine surrendering to permanent curvature after a couple of hours. In the UK, in the interests of lightness and dashing about with elan, exactly the same machinery was screwed into the back of a wheezing Land Rover – the same Land Rover that was required to carry three very large and very antiquated radio sets, hoping that at any one time one of them might work. Actually, one of them was so traumatic to use that pressing transmit instantly killed the rest of the vehicle's electrics and brought everything to a shuddering and inopportune halt.

Firing artillery is not the most difficult challenge to solve for mathematics, chemistry, and physics conjoined with some metal-based engineering. We prided ourselves on the ability to fire a shell in enough of the right direction based on a map, a compass, a set of 'firing tables' and some fairly simple sums. One just had to remember the order in which some sums had to be done. This manual process did not allow much for things like the weather, the rotation of the Earth or having a precise enough clue about where one was on the planet, so confidence about where the shell would actually land could be a bit limited – which is not great if there is anything to care about in roughly the same parish. If at the other end there were only the bestial representatives of the Soviet Union, then all would be well one way or another.

So having FACE was a useful complement to the basic skills and drills of firing artillery, really quite a cool blend of knob-pressing and military shouting. Of course, nobody was prepared to abandon the march of progress, so I was pretty quickly exposed to examples of technology being thrust into service regardless of whether it was either ready or really a good thing. The early 1980s did give us a thing, a thing called the Position Azimuth and Direction System (PADS). This was another large green box, containing some of the front end of a Harrier jet in the form of a jumble of whirling wheels and gimbals glued to some more flashing lights. Basically, what told a Harrier jump jet pilot where he was at 400 knots in the sky with his eyes screwed shut was certain to be good enough to tell a Gunner where he was on the Earth at 30mph. The sky, of course, is generally pretty smooth compared with the lumps, bumps, and ruts of ground-based warfare, so it wasn't an entirely straightforward technological transposition.

The game here was that a bright soldier, carefully selected for his (there were no hers at this time) ability to be within 6 feet of something hugely expensive and electric without breaking it, would inform the machine in great detail of where it apparently was. Ideally, this news came from a very carefully and precisely surveyed 'known point'. Less ideally, the news was drawn from standing on a spot that pretty much exactly reflected what was on the map and sticking a thumb on it. The soldier, with PADS bubbling along in the back of the Land Rover that is almost completely filled with metal boxwork, would then drive extremely carefully from the known point to wherever his battery of guns (usually six of them) was thought to be.

This was the first flaw in the scheme. Wherever the guns were thought to be was often not where they actually were, partly because they didn't have PADS to tell them this. The soldier with the PADS was not such a magician that he could work out where they were if they were not where they said they were, even if he knew exactly where he was. Nonetheless, sometimes in the dark, the PADS would arrive having followed every twist and turn of the route. This enabled it to decide after barely thirty minutes of mechanically wibbling away where the centre of the battery position really was, and also to assert with extreme confidence where north was.

There then followed some more wizardry involving a sort of compass-enhanced theodolite, more sums and quite a lot more military shouting, to get each artillery gun pointing not only in the same direction with immense confidence but also definitely parallel. PADS became one of those bits of technology that one hated for its infuriating idiosyncrasies, especially the propensity to stop working at the critical moment, yet it was also indispensable. In my new life, I find this is pretty much how people feel about their printers and Mr Apple's fondness for updating the operating system of his exquisitely designed computers with a flourish of unnecessary graphics – and random cocking-up of things like the email search that had previously worked perfectly well.

Today, of course, our lives are enhanced and cosseted in every way by technology. The basic stuff, like fridges and central heating, doesn't really change much even if the packaging does. But the explosion in social media and the app-tastic world count as something far more transformative. Some of this really is indispensable to the way we choose to live, it's hard to see how we would want to manage without Google search, Wikipedia, and many internet-based wonders. Other aspects are less essential: just because it is possible to make an app to do something doesn't mean that something is either a useful or valuable addition to the sum of human knowledge and happiness. Indeed, some technology brings as much disquiet and misery as benefit.

For every joyful teenager demonstrating by video the latest way to dismember an eyebrow, there are several more asserting in anonymous response that the eyebrow is quite cool but the face to which it is attached is that of a total minger. A further silent majority observing this troll-based interaction is then angst-ridden about the criminality of their own eyebrow and convinced they too are benchmark mingers. This is not the way to thrive as a teenager: I thought spots, a preternaturally hairy lip, and having to manoeuvre in disco mode in flared trousers were struggle enough.

Back in the military line, the most personal experience of unnecessary and upsetting technology in my own case arrived in the early 1990s in the hateful form of a glittering lie called the Battlefield Artillery Engagement System (BATES). This thing was born out of the cracking idea that given the massive advantage in artillery numbers of the Soviet Union (which had cracked up and gone home before BATES was even issued), what a huge wheeze it would be if every British gun within range could be swiftly and silently pointed at the same target at the same time in order to deliver a commendably decisive whack – and then move on swiftly with digitally-enhanced aplomb to do the same elsewhere.

This was held to be well within the compass of computer science in the early 1990s, all it needed was some slightly more complicated sums to be done in a bit more of a rigorous electronic way, and for everything to be connected to everything by some working radios. The people who previously did all the sums and shouting would henceforth only need to sit back, sipping the hot beverage of their choice, watching lights flash as the Gunners at each artillery piece toiled ceaselessly to stuff ammunition into them according to the instructions now appearing by magic on a tiny screen.

Nobody could fault the logic behind this. Everybody understood that it would take some training to make it work to maximum effect. Nobody imagined, at all, that this fucking thing would be so incomprehensibly, inconceivably, unnecessarily, and irredeemably crap that no collection of soldiers could ever make it work for real. It probably worked in a laboratory, perhaps even once in a classroom at the Royal School of Artillery; it might even have been understood by the people who screwed it together, but in the hands of people like me and my excellent soldiers, there was not a snowball in fiery Hell's chance of getting it to perform.

Some of the longest and most miserable weeks of my military career were spent in a classroom whilst a learned warrant officer, at least two pages ahead of us in the manual, explained over and over again what we were meant to do to summon the magic from BATES. We swiftly established that communicating with the spirits inside this machine required mastering a language none of us spoke. It was the equivalent of being told to reach interpreter standard in Finnish in four weeks, taught by someone who was only quite good at Norwegian. Perhaps most infuriatingly of all, when the thing didn't produce the answer anybody wanted or expected – which was all the time – it simply blinked at us. There was none of Mr Microsoft's helpful clues or error codes, no menu to turn to, just a sodding machine blinking patiently (silently suggesting we were all morons) whilst absolutely nothing happened, ever.

As a measure of our frustration, before BATES we prided ourselves on getting a shell in the air inside two minutes without any notice – even sometimes whilst driving along when the call to action came. With BATES, the simplest task remained resolutely unaccomplished after half an hour of vigorous swearing at it. The dream that this thing would take charge of every artillery gun in the army and point it with inhuman speed and precision at the critical part of the massed ranks of the advancing (and now defunct) Soviet Union remained unrealized in perpetuity. This is not just because the Soviet Union had evaporated but mostly because the damn thing called BATES was a crock of shite. After all that money and all that effort, what we did usefully have was a basic text messaging system, so all was not lost. We could now order up lunch from our cooks (conventionally they would be secreted in a wood close by in order to conceal the steam from our stew from passing nuclear bombers) all the more reliably and securely.

What we also had, however, was an actual handheld calculator which did the same job as the giant FACE had done but without the back injuries, if supported by a modicum of pencil work on a map. Instead of tiny screens directing half a dozen toiling Gunners in the service of their gun we were quickly back to shouting at them down telephone lines, and very pleased to be so.

This whole experience was a lesson in why it is important to master technology and not let it become the master. We ended up with something that was good enough, fast enough, and reliable enough for our business of flinging high explosive (with some essential accuracy) across several miles at the enemies of the Queen. BATES had involved many hundreds of thousands of pounds being spent trying to make something that was completely cake and arse. No doubt we could always continue to try and make artillery business more complicated, but we might not end up any more proficient at our job. A pencil writes in the rain, it doesn't need to be electric.

Now in the Afterlife, I see quite a lot of the same challenge from start-ups and big enterprises. It seems to be an aspect of human nature that we are so inquisitive and mercurial that we just love retreating into our sheds, even million-pound sheds, to make something that is new, even if it is of no great value or purpose. To be frank, it does seem to be a bit of a man thing as many of us on this side of the street are an absolute sucker for a gadget. Even in a multi-sex world, the lady division seems less in thrall of a gizmo. And for the benefit of my two daughters: I realize that's not just because ladies are consumed by the search for the perfect quiche. That's very old-fashioned thinking.

This is about more than the back pages of the Sunday papers offering us new and exciting ways of saving time, labour, and expense, prolific and important though that work is. I think one of the by-products of human creativity is that we are easily led into creating stuff for its own sake. Even as a four-star general I found that I had to regularly discourage very capable people from investing time and effort (and taxpayer's money) to knock up some wonder from scratch when it already existed somewhere else, just made by somebody else. It's not just Special Forces operators who much prefer to make something out of old bits of carpet, reading glasses, a smashed-up chair, and a lot of gaffer tape in order to see a squirrel on the moon from Wales, even when there is a perfectly good giant telescope next door.

Working as I do in the arena of defence and security technology, I see a stream of bright-eyed *wunderkinder* with an idea for new wizardry. These days this often involves conjuring up magic from data (which has to be in the cloud to count as sexy), artificial intelligence, and a special soupçon of software that will make a big difference to how conquering nations and instilling a just global peace are to be achieved. It helps if *wunderkinder* can claim to be directly connected to the CIA and the Israeli Armed Forces, and they all seem to be funded by somebody who can afford a house in Silicon Valley. Most often it really is quite clever stuff, but also usually neither unique nor easily connectable to the stuff that already exists. This can come as quite a shock to the wunderkind (and their investors), but new and brilliant doesn't necessarily mean useful, useable, or relevant.

There is, however, another dilemma important to our time in history: there are some really clever ideas out there, but often they just can't seem to penetrate the skull of the people in authority who really need them and could afford to buy them. Authority in this case generally refers to the politicians and civil servants responsible for making important things in our lives work well. These are people who are not technologists, but they are subject to immense public and media scrutiny for the way that they struggle for our benefit.

Both in and out of uniform I have observed very skilled technical experts try to explain to a normal human in a senior leadership position how a particular technological marvel will transform their business/function. The normal human listens intently, allowing their mind to swim gently over the references to maths, physics, chemistry and engineering that require far greater technical literacy than they will ever possess but pretty quickly anyway they gain a rough, intuitive sense of what is on offer. They then ask the expert how this thing that they're talking about will actually change the organization and function of fellow normal humans? The technical expert, who can't really be expected to have much of a clue about how the normal human passes their working day, then pretty much repeats a description of how the thing works and why that is wonderful. The normal human, still none the wiser about the technical detail or its application, retreats at this point for fear of being outed as technologically retarded. This extinguishes the spark of genius that could have become a blaze of transformative wonder in action.

This gap between the technically gifted and the rest of us is just part of the reason we seem destined to wrestle unsuccessfully for eternity with how technology can improve public services, at least in the UK. It is clearly easier in entrepreneurial life to make things happen quickly, indeed it has to be so in order to survive in the never-ending commercial scrap. It need not be so hard in public service. Yet there are multimillion-pound investments in giant IT systems that struggle to work, these are the medical, police, customs, and other equivalents of BATES. Google can handle more data in one day than even the US Pentagon uses in a whole year, whilst many public sector organizations still struggle to get an electric form connected to a clunky database.

Part of the explanation for this is that the commercial providers know what they're doing in the commercial space, this can certainly be at vast scale but is also often intrinsically less complicated than the delivery of things like healthcare, intelligence, customs, and immigration. There can be a basic problem of translation in applying something that worked well in commercial settings to a public sector task. On the other hand, the redoubtable public servants who will be the beneficiary of the new tech are often pretty convinced that they know their job and remain unshakably convinced that it is the function of technology to bend to their will and habit. After all, they are the customer and therefore right (though not really a paying-the-bill customer, as this falls to the taxpayer, whose opinion is rarely sought).

The 'customer'-based approach causes the commercial wizard to take what works pretty well and bastardize the hell out of it in order to accommodate the whims and peccadilloes of public service. This introduces such unwarranted and unique complexity that should the system be made to work (which is rare) it can never ever be updated in the lifetime of the people using it. Possibly worse, in asserting that there is only one way to do their job, the public sector user has eschewed any opportunity to transform either their organization or way of working. They merely wish to embellish well established, even ancient form with some hideously expensive and often inoperable technological accessory.

Another interesting aspect of the public-sector technological stumbling that is still playing out is whether having an incredibly complicated and generally mostly duff system makes for an easier or harder cyber target. Some experts argue that a tangled jumble of electric knitting of an IT system means that there are myriad ways in which any cyber enemy (spy, criminal or competitor) can penetrate and wander around undetected, as if they were strolling about a shopping centre helping themselves to whatever they fancy for free. Other experts claim that an entirely accidental and obviously undesirable IT mess makes penetration, let alone wandering around, very much harder.

Perhaps both sides have a point, but I recall quite a significant part of the UK MoD's core information system having a major wobbly requiring several weeks of really skilful attention to fix. It was far from clear for some time whether this was the result of Mr Putin taking an electronic journey through our basic level secrets, or whether unquestionably ancient machinery surviving on the digital equivalent of massive doses of Viagra had simply decided to throw in the towel. On balance, it was the latter – only marginally reassuring in the circumstances.

The dance with technology that is shared between my military life and my subsequent commercial wandering includes the search for, and belief in, the silver bullet that will trump all other things and deliver total victory/untold riches as applicable. In the military arena the idea that a wonder weapon will render all others obsolete and provide the holder with the means to conquer without limit has been around for as long as people have fought with more than their fists.

There is a bit of a cycle to this. First, a new thing appears in some ropey early form and attracts fanatical disciples who seize upon it and comprehensively overstate its magic and potential revolutionary powers. Much scoffing then ensues, especially from the established order dominating the current state of affairs. However, the disciples of the new thing, being disciples, are not easily deflected and continue to thrash around developing whatever it is into a state where it becomes a bit more genuinely useful and a lot less dangerous to the user. Ideally, at this point some sort of war turns up which gives the new thing a shove. As more of the established order convert to the idea that the new thing is more than a trinket it begins to earn its keep. At this point opinion gets carried away and the new thing becomes seen as the only thing, destined to sweep away all the outmoded nonsense that until very recently was dominant.

Somebody will then announce this is a revolution in military affairs, the like of which we have never seen before and which probably brings to an end the need to think any more about war could be or different in the future. Once acres of trees have been felled to print the pamphlets that explain why this is so, it becomes evident that whilst it is marvellous it is more of an important addition to the 'orchestra of war' than a replacement for all of it. A shift in balance will have occurred, important of course but certainly not meeting the definition of an all-conquering silver bullet. We are now at the end of the cycle, marked by how vigorously the disciples defend what was the new thing against the arrival, inevitably, of an even newer thing.

You can see this cycle playing out in big military shifts such as the arrival of gunpowder and cannon (and all that meant for people heavily invested in castle tech); the invention of the aeroplane (a very big deal eventually for navies and armies, and certainly for the air forces that it has spawned over the last 100 years); and today we see the same in how missiles and cyber are going to find a place in a Digital Age orchestra of war.

I suppose because cyber touches civil society, government and the military alike it is the new thing that most people have felt inclined to argue is going to make all other forms of fighting redundant. This is clearly wrong: nobody is being assaulted by laptops in many of today's struggle but they are being shot. It's also not entirely wrong, cyber-attack and they need to be resilient to it has now become a common and enduring feature of how war is fought.

It is much harder to whip up the same degree of interest shown in cyber in how technology, much of it developed for entirely civil purposes in places like Boston and California, has led to a new cycle of missile technology that is going to dominate the orchestra for quite a while ahead. In flinging broadband from space and producing regularly updated imagery of the world at about 1m accuracy on our personal computers, I doubt very much that Mr Musk and Mr Pichai were focused on how their tech makes the world transparent when states choose to fight.

The technology that gets satellites into orbit and tourists to the moon is the same technology that sends a missile bearing a great deal of nuclear or high-explosive bang across the world in about forty minutes. As the hypersonic missiles just coming into service shift at between five and twenty times the speed of sound, which is way too fast for the average human frame to withstand so there will be no question of strapping a pilot to future weapons like this. The same GPS that keeps farmers ploughing in a straight line when they have overdone the sherry at lunchtime is the GPS that delivers a ballistic or cruise missile through the window of one's choice anywhere on the planet.

When I started out as a soldier the prevailing dogma was that technological advance was led by military necessity, and this was certainly the experience one could point to from the Second World War and onwards. By the time I left uniform behind, this was unequivocally only the case in niche areas like aircraft stealth technology and nuclear weapons. Pretty much all the massive progress in the foothills of the Digital Age was being driven by clever people in egregiously casual attire dotted around the world, including Big Tech in the US. There has been a bit of a lag whilst technology built around data, processing power, networks, algorithms, and the like substantially reshapes how we live, work, and play. Inevitably, and it is inevitable, that same technology is now substantially reshaping how we confront and fight.

Some of this is pretty obvious, military people are going to have mobile phones now as well as the super-duper radios for very military purposes that don't rely on the internet. If AI changes how people make decisions, organize their offices and operate more effectively and efficiently, it's pretty obvious that the same understanding will be applied to war. Other aspects take a bit more thought. For example, if Silicon Valley cracks how to make a driverless car that really can get from A to B without human intervention – especially without mowing down pedestrians or smashing into other vehicles in digital outrage for failure to observe the highway code – then driverless military capability will flourish. In fact, driverless military stuff will flourish faster at sea and in the air because the challenges of making the tech work there are a bit less. As fast as the Internet of Things grips our lives, so a military Internet of Things will build new shapes of navy, army, and air force.

People rightly wonder how to apportion blame when a driverless car kills a pedestrian as a result of autonomous decision-making grounded in its programming, so people will wonder – harder than they do now – about autonomous weapons. When asked, many people express some ambivalence about the prospect of being arrested at the shops by a machine that has identified through facial recognition that they have an outstanding court summons, therefore and without further ado proceeding to clamp them to the spot. We do like our laws implemented imperfectly and we prefer to take our chances of dodging a human officer of the law, who is much more likely – let's face it – to be tooling around in a car or filling in a spreadsheet in an office than hanging about the shops. Although we could build machines that would infallibly arrest every miscreant on sight and post these machines in all public places, most people are likely to conclude that this is simply not cricket.

By much the same token we have spirited debates about 'killing by drone', where the accusation of foul play is often levelled. Sometimes, and I have to say I always find this remarkable, the objection is that the drone pilot is sitting comfortably in a box in the US not toe-to-toe eyeballing his target. Treating the firing of a missile to polish off a terrorist in the cross-hairs of a drone as a risk-free outing is decried as unfair advantage. I have not met any drone pilots who share this view. The key point, it seems to me, is that whether the pilot is looking at a screen in a cockpit that happens to be hurtling through the sky many thousands of feet above a target or whether the same lady is looking at exactly the same picture in a cabin somewhere in the US makes no difference. What is important is that a human is pulling the trigger, having had a good look and thought about what they are going to do in the circumstances. That's not autonomy.

The point about autonomy is that as autonomous stuff like cars, delivery bots, and golf carts take themselves around their bit of the world, most states will build weapons systems that kill within the parameters of their programming, without further recourse to any human intervention once turned on. This raises stiff ethical questions, or at least it does for many people. There are some military users around the planet who are not bound by the norms, laws, or values that many states share under the Geneva Conventions.

I hear some people argue that the only thing to do is to not have autonomous military capability. This is unlikely to work as most modern militaries already have some autonomous weapons for things like last-ditch defence of their ships and bases, where dealing with an incoming projectile in time is beyond the capacity of a human to react to. In any case, as fast as the Internet of Things rolls out in our lives the cat will be ever further out of the bag and autonomy just can't be un-invented. Even those who would remove autonomous defensive capability from military platforms generally change their position if invited to deposit their own offspring on such a platform and make their survival and safe return home for Christmas dependent upon an autonomous gun doing its thing.

In the same way that we see robots augmenting humans in many walks of life such as construction, manufacturing, and health so we will see robots in many shapes and sizes augmenting military forces. There is some good news to this that most people can share in. Introducing robots at sea, on land, in the air, and in space means that fewer humans need to be hired or put in harm's way. Most taxpayers will rejoice at the thought that the shiny new robots in their armed forces don't need to be paid, housed, entertained, trained regularly at great expense, and certainly not provided with a care home and a pension in old age. The rub is the degree to which these robots can visit violence up to lethal force on people without *people* pulling the trigger.

Many people object to the idea that as they go about their business as criminals they can be detained by a machine, many more people object to the idea that a machine can ever kill a human. It is certainly now possible: if a robot that looks very much like a human can excel at dancing then there should be no problem fitting the same robot with a gun and pointing it in the direction of the enemy. The enemy will not be wildly enthusiastic about a robot coming their way that moves faster, sees further, shoots better, stops far less for tea, and literally does not know the meaning of fear. Why should we care? Yet for very human reasons, we struggle with the idea that such a robot acting on our behalf will dispatch our enemy without any further ado.

For example, the idea that a robot would be the first through the door when assaulting the compound of a known terrorist causes consternation in some circles. If that robot, making good use of data and facial recognition in milliseconds, is going to bump off every person that it encounters and identifies as hostile, then we are well along the road of lethal autonomy. Here again, opinion divides when confronted with the alternative that the son or daughter of the opinion holder should replace the robot in being the first in, to take their mortal chances against the human foe, a foe now alerted, armed, and very cross because a large hole has been blown in the exterior of their dwelling and they sense their own imminent demise.

This debate flashes up in my mind every time the latest videos of more agile robots appear; the advances in the dexterity and mobility of human and dog-shaped robots are extraordinary. It is inevitable that as quickly as robots are built that are capable of picking up our dirty laundry that same ability will be applied to military and even sinister purposes (and they're not the same). This surely needs a lot of thought, but I think the advances in biosciences are much more significant for us all.

We are certainly blessed that very talented scientists around the world are making huge strides in how we understand DNA and the basic biological structures that create and sustain life. My General Science O-level (1974) and an Honorary Doctorate of Science from Cranfield are not quite enough to get under the skin of this, even when combined, but it is clear that the ability to unpick the DNA sequencing of every one of us is a phenomenal development. The people who are clever enough to do this are also clever enough to see how its application will dramatically improve things like healthcare and environmental protection. It will be fabulous when medicines can be made that are bespoke to our individual make-up, doing away with things like vaccines that are generically good for most people but specifically tailored to none. Similarly, what if science could make bacteria or some other laboratory manufactured organizm that ate the plastic in the sea? Hurrah for all that.

What we are seeing here is the combining of modern science and technology to create the potential for great benefit. Bioscience research needs people who are pretty good at peering down microscopes and poking about in the weeniest bits of stuff that make up a DNA string. (This is a long way from my comfort zone of firing artillery you will sense.) Making full use of this investigation needs support from the application of carefully developed algorithms to speed up research and the capability to put tonnes of data in the cloud. The mass of data and AI to examine it is what makes it possible to draw conclusions from correlations. We are obviously not talking about causation here, that is just too difficult to get to so far, but pretty convincing and useful patterns can be identified and conclusions drawn from examining the DNA of millions of people. The ability to do this that modern computing power and data storage provide means that work that would once have taken ten years can be done in seconds. And quite a lot of discovery is only possible at all with digital technology.

There are (obviously) big commercial interests circling the science as it crosses quickly from academia into useful applications in our world. Big Pharma is already engaged, but there is just so much more opportunity coming down the road. If the analysis of our DNA can tell us by correlation about our genetic predisposition, then it will be possible to tailor all sorts of products and services to individuals. For example, if this correlation tells us things about our life expectancy, we can be sold pensions that either recognize we are going to drop dead the day after we cash it in at sixty-seven or strung out to keep us in beans and mittens until we peg out at 102. This brings real science to the adage that 'you can't take it with you'.

The science might also tell us that we should forget a career as a rocket scientist because DNA analysis suggests we are just a tiny bit thick – perhaps a career driving a tractor would play to our innate resilience, physical strength, and natural eye for a good cabbage? In the same way, my DNA might suggest that I should have been fast-tracked at age 10 to a top university in order to become a leading light in matters of great import to mankind. Or my DNA might reveal that my place at Oxford in 1977 was by all biological standards a bit of a surprise and no doubt a waste for everybody except me. I'm saying nothing at this point.

This is all obviously quite dodgy ground because no one wants to be told at school that their DNA dictates the life that they should pursue, quite apart from the virulent debate that will rightly ensue about the difference between nature and nurture. Nonetheless, I think my spell in the Afterlife will soon be tilted by commerce getting into how to read the DNA of every citizen and to use that data to sell us personalized services. It is very likely that many of these really will make our life easier or better, after all there must be advantages in buying things that are designed specifically for us rather than buying a product or service that has been put together to satisfy everybody.

This is the point at which I have to say: 'and on the other hand'. The clever scientists who remake how we lead our lives on the back of all their brilliance are very unlikely indeed to have much time or the will to think about the potential dark side of their endeavours. Nor should they be easily deflected from doing what they're doing by considerations of its potential manipulation for malevolent reasons. The goodness, it seems to me, is still of overriding importance. But the fact is that the sort of understanding this science reveals also opens up massive opportunities for things that we are likely to find pretty disagreeable.

We might encourage, for example, the state to create a database of the DNA of every citizen and to use that to promote much better healthcare, including how an ageing population is managed. This is something we would all benefit from. Yet that same database provides insight that could be manipulated in ways that are not so altruistic. At the lower level of questionable behaviour, might we see some citizens wanting to know more about the embryos that they could choose their children from?

The upsides could be significant reductions in the presence of genetically propelled painful disabilities and diseases. The downside could be parents demanding that the embryo that they select to develop to adulthood must be the one with a greater genetic dollop of being brilliant, beautiful, and tall. Might we on a whim see discrimination against not just the thick, ugly, and short, but also the ginger, big-nosed, and not entirely fair skinned? An abhorrent idea, and of course it would be against the interests of mankind to remove rich diversity from the gene pool so that eventually we inbreed ourselves to extinction. Even the middle ground where people discriminate in favour of only the characteristics that are favoured by YouTube influencers doesn't strike me as a good place to go. Worse, what if only the rich have the means to make these choices, does that mean the advances in bioscience lead to self-perpetuating elites of genetically manipulated super beings? How would this square with the finite capacity of Eton to educate all of them for their rightful place of cocking things up in the Cabinet of their chosen nation?

Even worse than this, I think, is that a state would be tempted to take charge of the construction of the future population. Might governments of a particular persuasion think that it would be wise to award parents on a compulsory basis with the embryo that contributes to a well-designed and balanced future society? This might lead to some difficult conversations around the difference between: 'congratulations Mr and Mrs Y, here is the embryo of the future rocket scientist we want you to deliver nine months from now' and: 'well, Mr and Mrs Y, we can't all do the space stuff and someone still has to clean the bogs at the station, so get cracking with this one'.

This sort of narrative is going to struggle to get traction in many parts of the world, I doubt it would have legs in most of the UK for a start – and those who are attracted to it might be happier living somewhere definitively autocratic. However, there are states around the world where the primary role of the citizen is to contribute to the good of society as a whole, states which are regulated by a government permanently untroubled by trial by ballot box. This dichotomy could mean that in future there are societies formed by large numbers of freethinking, liberal and quite often splendidly ginger citizens happily moaning at their government's inability to satisfy every whim, and societies formed by very large numbers of artfully constructed facsimile followers marching at us for the glory of their superstate. If so, how will we get along?

The potential downside of advancing bioscience also includes how it contributes to what we might term the 'surveillance state'. We need to think about how in the future it will be possible for the government to know the DNA of every citizen and therefore to be able to make some prediction about all sorts of our predispositions. So quite apart from a government understanding the ethnicity of every citizen at a biological level, it may also be able to identify where a tendency to criminality or terrorism might arise. That will be quite a thing to have on your state record even before you were born. It could certainly lead to a government paying particular attention to the development of citizens identified as potentially troublesome. This is grim territory.

Keeping track of these embryonic (literally) troublemakers will be made much easier by connecting the data with the rest of the potential of Digital Age technology to keep track of us. Except for the very tiny number of people who are content to live in a cave up a mountain surviving on only what local nature provides, our digital exhaust is such that it is almost impossible to remain out of sight. Even a cave-dwelling hermit is vulnerable to being spotted by satellite surveillance when they pop out for a berry, a rabbit, or a poo. The rest of us generally carry a mobile phone that reveals where we are all the time. It also sets out the digital face we would like the world to see of us in the form of our social media posts and general posing about on Instagram et al. This does a good job of showing the world how we would prefer to be seen and understood, but the phone does a rather better job of telling anybody who can poke about in our data what we are really like.

Our phones reveal who we actually communicate with, what we say 'privately' on messaging apps (that are encrypted except when one reads the messages at either end of their encrypted passage), what we search for, how much money we have, how we spend it, and where we actually go as opposed to where we tell people we go. Oddly, we are still very much happier giving a giant tech company all this data because we are happy about how they monetize it so brilliantly (and making a fortune without really contributing to the tax take) than we are telling the government which we do have a hand in electing and pay taxes to. I guess there will be quite big moves to redress this balance in the coming decade, but the technology isn't going to go away even if regulated differently.

Anyway, DNA sampling could tell the government about our genetic predisposition, and then our phones assisted by our bank cards, travel cards, and cars will establish where we are, what we are actually like, and what we are really doing. We might also assume that once we buy more things like fridges that are connected to the internet (so that Waitrose knows we have run out of humus before we get all weepy), our own domestic appliances can play a part in telling others about us. I'm not sure I want a fridge that tells the world about my obsession with a daily dose of mango yoghurt. I certainly don't want the Constabulary to know every time I open the fridge door.

In addition to being snitched on by our kitchens, televisions, and lighting, we will be spotted in many places by the ubiquity of cameras and other sensors. The CCTV camera that was put up to manage traffic on the High Street is the same camera that can connect to the database that has our DNA recorded in it, linking this to an image of our face. And it's no good thinking as an average-sized bloke that popping on a wig and a dress will fool a camera connected to enough data: it probably only needs a square centimetre of face to establish identity and our gait will increasingly be used as a means of unequivocal identification. In other words, if our digital exhaust doesn't already reveal where we are then cameras connected to data and managed by algorithms will find us in most places in the real world. Once spotted, and we will be, we then need to reflect (as above) on how it will feel to have our legs clamped to a lamppost by the neighbourhood robotic special constable.

Of course, for most of us most of the time this all doesn't really matter, in fact from the perspective of safety and the provision of services it will pretty much be a good thing most of the time. It would be good to know that if we fell off our bike in the street, an ambulance would appear knowing who we were, our medical history and able to tell the next of kin that we had been carted off to hospital to be stitched up. Knowing that Mr Bezos and his peers, together with the state security apparatus of several countries, are entirely familiar with every recess of our phones and computers need not provoke a hissy fit. After all, most of us have nothing much to hide that really matters and our little transgressions into bad behaviour do not warrant a spanking. Yet – a big yet – just knowing that others know so much all the time does not feel like a good place to be. This brave new world of connected Digital Age technology raises important questions about how we wish to be governed. It also means thinking about how we wish to treat other states that decide to take a quite different approach.

In thinking about all this, I am in a permanent state of surprise about how little traction it seems to get in government or in civil society. One might have thought that knowing how it will become possible to design a population or know pretty much all the time where everybody is, how they are behaving and what they are predisposed to do would be filling quite a lot of column inches and airtime. There are some folk who are all over this, like the 'Stop the Killer Robots' campaign, which is doing an excellent job of highlighting why lethal autonomous machines should never be permitted to reach the stage of becoming weapons of mass destruction. Hard to argue with that, but not much of this is really breaking through into the daily currency of public debate.

Perhaps the answer is to get the best storytellers we have, the ones who work in film and TV, to seize on all this and make it into a blistering film or box set? Who wouldn't watch a story of how a government built a database of all our DNA and used it to perpetuate an oligarchy, identify and shoot a minority, track down and whip anybody who moaned a lot, and ensured that the right people always had humus in their fridges?

Chapter 9

On Nearly Being a General 2004–08

My Dear M,

In 1921 the UK broke with most western armies by abandoning the rank of brigadier-general, on the not unreasonable grounds that it was no longer going to have brigades (a brigade being a roughly 5,000-strong collection of several infantry battalions in the starring 'certain death in the trenches role' and supporting cast like artillery, combat engineers, signals, and logistics). Brigades had been immensely popular in the First World War, but no one should underestimate the enthusiasm for armies to obsessively and randomly tinker with their organizations and uniforms when not committed to a really big fight. Being a brigadier general was no comfy sinecure either during that war 78 British and Dominion brigadier generals and above were killed, and 146 more were captured, wounded, or gassed.

This change, which was of course reversed in a subsequent tinkering, led to a parting of the ways in when one may count oneself 'a General' between the UK and much of the military world, certainly NATO nowadays. Today, on promotion from colonel to brigadier in the British Army one is elevated to NATO standard grade 'OF6' just like a German or Italian (though with a lot less fuss involving sparkly wine and teary speechifying), but unlike the rest the Brit is not entitled to be called 'Brigadier General' – and certainly not general.

This is even reflected in the badges, which today consist of no fewer than four bits and bobs (actually one crown and three stars, so quite a spangly adornment for a hardened killer), rather than the crossed sword and scabbard that previously marked ascendancy to 'General Officer' status. By contrast, in the US on promotion to brigadier general there is rightly a lot of hurrah and fanfare about achieving a general's first star and a pretty smart US flag to go with it. A proper degree of military obsequiousness is then duly afforded by those lower down the military food chain. So even though a British brigadier is called a 'one star', they still don't get to be called 'General' by anybody – except abroad of course.

So when I arrived to take charge of 39 Infantry Brigade in Northern Ireland in December 2003, it was my first day as a brigadier and my first day as a one star, but it only partially marked the start of my service as a general that would eventually run, in a litany of unrestrained incompetence, to 2016. I think it is worth recording my arrival in Belfast as it was definitely a fairly big step up the leadership ladder for me – a different blend of challenges to refuse and opportunities to miss.

For example, it was my first time as a commander of military forces that the numbers under my charge exceeded any pretence of trying to know everybody's name. Even with the numbers just nudging into the low thousands, the best one can do is try to remember the names of the more senior figures and not mix up their partners, plus one or two of the iconic senior soldiers, and of course the small but colourful list of leading-edge nuisances that feature in any military command. This latter group seem to find no misdeed too far or too bizarre, with alcohol-fuelled assault of their best friend with a beer glass and driving somebody else's car into a building amongst the prevailing favourites. This minority is why for centuries people have metaphorically and actually 'locked up their spoons and their daughters when the military approaches'.

Leadership at one-star level is the first real command opportunity that strides the complicated and often misunderstood seams between policy, strategy, and tactics – by accident or design. For me, whether it was winding down the presence of soldiers accompanying the Police Service of Northern Ireland on the streets of Belfast at night or the more classically military challenges of securing joint military-police bases in unequivocally and occasionally lethally rumbunctious areas such as the 'bandit country' of South Armagh, there was both micro detail to be on top of as well as internationally significant policy dimensions to observe. I didn't fancy being the man who smashed up the Good Friday Agreement that shapes Northern Ireland's present and future.

A great deal has been written about the 'strategic corporal', the very junior military commander who finds himself or herself at the centre of a very small tactical action where their decisions, character, conduct and expertise will be applied to an outcome that turns the success or failure of an entire campaign. In Northern Ireland, for example, one bullet fired in haste, or misplaced anger, or honestly but at the wrong target, could unravel community consent to a generations-long peace process.

The 'strategic corporal', so history records, can be the absolute star of the moment, acting in ways that are so intuitively insightful and appropriate that what could have been a campaign-level disaster is adroitly averted. Usually nobody notices that a bad thing hasn't happened of course. On the other hand, the same 'strategic corporal' may also be wittingly or unwittingly the catalyst for an absolute apocalypse – typically the result of doing exactly what they have been trained to do without a scintilla of common sense. When this happens everybody notices, some people even travelling hours to the scene to make sure they are noticed taking notice.

The consequences are not so dramatic, but I do now see much the same potential for good and evil in my commercial undertakings. This is usually at the level of the 'strategic customer relations staff', who find the way to either gild or trash the reputation of an entire corporation in how they respond to an expression of deep disquiet or unhappiness from 'Customer A'. There is, I know now, a rule that the 'Customer is Always Right' – even when they are without a shred of doubt a Premier League Asshole.

The forbearance deployed in calmly deflating the furious and unreasonable whining of a dim-witted and phenomenally uncouth complainant (who may or may not be 'connected') is every bit as important and skilful as that shown by the soldier who could shoot lawfully yet decides for whatever reason it's not the right or best thing to do. In fact, having witnessed an example of 'Outraged of Little Throbton-in-the-Marsh' heaping their displeasure at a minor shopping inconvenience upon the battle-hardened staff of the complaints office of a well-managed emporium, it is good that these desks are unarmed. Though no court in the land would convict them for giving the complainant both barrels and a reload in the circumstances.

I offered my police counterpart in Belfast that when he eventually waved me off at the docks at the completion of my two-year tenure it would mark the end of the British Army's support to policing in Northern Ireland that had started in the very different and very difficult circumstances of 1969 – when I was 10 years old. He scoffed, as only a large and unfeasibly ginger Northern Irish policeman can, because after so long in the metaphorical trenches, the prospect of there being enough security and inter-communal tranquillity just seemed implausible to him.

Anyone who has dealt with the extraordinary stubbornness of some folk on both sides of the dispute in Northern Ireland to countenance anything that doesn't feel like misery and stasis would know why he might feel that way. In the end, we were both equally wrong and right. I was very nearly the last and by the time I left there was no routine patrolling in Belfast and the chain of manned observation towers that had for so long dominated the skyline in South Armagh had been removed – in at least one case by pulling them over with a tractor rather than some careful brick-by-brick deconstruction bollocks. But even as I write today there are Northern Irish residents hurling petrol bombs at their own police service, bizarrely rotting up only their own neighbourhoods.

On the other hand too, just before I left, September 2005 saw some of the largest examples of public disorder (polite for actual rioting) seen in Belfast for some time – and I don't think seen at the same scale since. The perennial – and to any outsider astonishingly dim – argument about who should be able to march themselves about exactly where in Northern Ireland persists to this day. At the heart of it is the reluctance of one community to see 'the others' marching through or around 'their' areas, with flags flying and bands playing. They are still metaphorically and occasionally physically mooning at their long-standing neighbours over the need for the triumph of one loosely faith-based group over another.

Asserting the principle of the 'freedom to walk the Queen's highways' (and notwithstanding that one group disapproves of the Queen as their head of state anyway), the marching about conveys a good deal of ingrained cultural animosity. This is amplified by the annually rejuvenated enthusiasm of rugged teenage youth for a fight that establishes their credibility as the latest cadre of community warriors in the endless sectarian struggle. In England, we give Colours to distinguished school cricketers, which is a whole lot less damaging as an outlet for proving youthful promise. In Belfast there can still be plaudits for chucking a brick at a policeman.

Some of the violence in Northern Ireland really was just hooliganism and needed to be addressed as such, but some of it was a veneer for the migration of self-appointed and unenlightened sectarian self-defence into just criminal fiefdoms selling drugs and dodgy DVDs. This isn't, in my experience, unique to Northern Ireland: quite often when the freedom fighters find the battle is over, rather than surrender the glamour and power of the prominent role they have seized in their communities and lose their nobility, they elect to continue with the criminality that once fuelled the cause to fund their continued high standing and blingy tastes. Fat, black BMWs, dodgy handguns, tacky suits and the attention of hot women stylish enough to set their chewing gum aside before offering carnal pleasures do not come cheap anywhere in the world.

The community leadership of a paramilitary/hood combo is helped along by a staple capability for low-level violence, sometimes focused on putative rivals and opponents and sometimes applied as an instrument of discipline to keep their own herd in order. Both sides of the sectarian divide in Northern Ireland even today still resort to shooting members of their own constituency in the limbs for various shades of transgression. A minor irritation might receive a small bullet through the flesh of the calf (which hurts a lot but may not leave much of a limp), a repeat or major offender is likely to feel the effects of a larger bullet dismantling a kneecap or an ankle – thereby maimed for life. A really slow learner could be deprived of both knees and both ankles.

Supporting the Police Service of Northern Ireland to manage their public order season was a major feature of my tenure. This runs roughly April to

September as the winter is just too miserable for brick-throwing by anybody. I had not done much riot-handling before, but the serious disorder in Basra shortly before my posting to Belfast was a fairly graphic illustration that it is not to be taken lightly. It may not involve the exchange of many bullets, but a brick in the face is no less painful.

Every country has its own rules of the road for how it likes its disorder managed. I was particularly struck by the creative attitude of the excellent Indian police sent to Kosovo when I was serving there in 2000. For these gentlemen (they didn't do ladies) anything less than 30,000 howling rioters counted only as a limp bit of pub closing-time brawling, in which everyone present should be awarded a sharp slap with a whippy stick and sent home to sober up. But when handling tens of thousands of stone-chucking hooligans it was perfectly in order to encourage them to disperse by hurling live snakes into their midst. It was well known that these snakes didn't enjoy violent passage through the air, nor landing on top of a swirling mass of hot and bothered humanity. As they had been kept egregiously peckish with their employment as a serpentine missile in mind, finding themselves amongst a lot of heaving, moist flesh was cause for a lot of snapping and thrashing about. Time for everyone to go home.

Snakes were definitely not within the rules in Northern Ireland. In fact, although there was undoubtedly a very malign element that really wanted to hurt policeman, soldiers and 'the other' flavour of citizen, many participants were keen on only *quite* forcibly registering their concern and then getting home for a late film with a kebab, still very much in one piece. After decades of many long nights managing disorder, the Northern Ireland police were extremely good at calibrating their response – not quite a mutual sense of what the rules of the game were but not far off. The police had also invested sensibly in a great deal of protective kit and a brace of water cannon, and knew very well how to ensure they would never be out-manoeuvred (including by keeping large numbers of my soldiers to hand). This meant that on many occasions all that was required of them was to stand there and be insulted and spat at, with very little in the way of serious bricking to contend with. Not always though.

The most popular riots were well established by appointment, courtesy of the calendar for the Loyalist marching season. In almost all cases the date, the time, and place were as widely known as the FA Cup Final. So too, I found, was the general formula for the totemic clashes at venues such as the ever-popular Ardoyne shopfronts in Belfast. In the morning, a small and sober Loyalist procession would march along from north to south and be met by the well-practised scowls of a small number of Republican-minded citizens who had risen unusually early and spent some early beer money working themselves up to the required degree of froth.

In the late afternoon the same Loyalist gang would be heading north, this time their numbers swelled by the many who now felt the need to walk to and through a part of town in which they didn't live and had no need to visit. There would be many bands of questionable musical proficiency and a relaxed approach to what constitutes 'uniform'. There would also be a small cohort on both sides of really very unpleasant yobbery, the hard core determined by one means or another to establish the full extent of their manhood in the rumble that they had an appointment to participate in.

Marching behind them, actually really only shuffling along with no scope for staying in step as it required just too much power of concentration, would be a struggle of lumpen camp followers. They were not inclined to actually risk a thumping from either the opposition or the police, but felt the need to be able to say to their peers (and their mothers) that they were on the spot when it all kicked off. These coves were generally easy to spot by the battered carrier bag of cheap cider that accompanied them in case more courage was needed. (Worth noting that once empty these bags can also contain a fair old load of hot wee to be hurled like a sling-shot at the opposition, though not without some risk of an own goal if tying the essential knot in the top proves too hard.)

The reception committee for the return match past the shopfronts was, after decades of custom, invariably well thought out. No surprise here, this event had many of the features of an overly militant inter-village grudge cricket match. Amongst the well-marshalled ranks of assembled yobbery there would also be some carefully crafted media messaging going on, led by middle-aged local leaders and sympathizers, none of whom were going to get their chinos soiled in an actual fight. They had had their time on hurling duties.

The front rank would be the twenty-somethings of the local community, imbued with a zesty cultural and youthful enthusiasm for testing their manhood in this annual event – and a few cans of firewater to stoke it all up. Behind them would be some genuinely hard core 'dissidents', the tiny number who really would take advantage of the occasion to throw a handmade bomb or shoot a policeman – spoiling the day for almost everybody else. This always added genuine spice to what otherwise would have been mostly a sporting occasion conducted in the spirit of pointless intercommunity thuggery.

Between the two groups of protagonists at 'the shopfronts' (because there were shops there, with windows on the street) was a corridor created by a very large number of police officers, augmented where necessary by soldiers. Soldiers would in any case provide the essential reserve capacity, kept close at hand but out of sight. Both community groups felt at liberty to use the police as their protectors, whilst of course also lobbying a bottle or a stone at them if they felt moved to do so.

There would come a point when the Loyalist-minded march moved north through the corridor formed by the police and came alongside the main body of the Republican-minded community. The former was determined to exercise its 'right to walk' home whilst flicking Vs and snot at the latter. The latter was determined to exercise its right to object to the walkers, not much caring to be reminded that this is all about Protestants defeating Catholics in 1690 and all the ding-dong that has ensued ceaselessly ever since. There would be a moment as the two parties drew parallel when it was possible that nothing more than words would pass between them...but then, just as one thought it might be so, some little toerag on one side or other would throw the first bottle – better still one filled to the brim with piss – and that was the day gone.

For the next few hours, a lot of stuff was thrown at the police and soldiers, including bricks and stones brought in especially for the occasion. There would be paint bombs, which were incredibly annoying if they ruined a favourite pair of well worn-in boots. There would also be a liberal supply of petrol bombs later on, these too required considerable forethought given the modern-day preference for tins and plastic. The decline of the traditional milk bottle is a major irritation for the contemporary disorder enthusiast in Northern Ireland. For the most part, wine bottles would not be used, wine not being the preferred tipple in these parts – and no rioter putting their life on the line for the honour of their crummy estate wants to be accused of being louche and bourgeoisie.

The police took all this on with tremendous stoicism, I thought, although there would be some injuries. Unlike a soldier, a police officer really doesn't expect to get hurt at work and this might explain why one or two fell into such immense outrage as a result of their pinkie getting a bit bashed. Only the promise of much time off and some cash could assuage the pain. Others, it has to be said, really did get painful wounds – this is a basically tough affair.

As the afternoon wore on into pub opening time, the ranks of aggressive youth diminished as hunger and boredom set in. A foray or two from the water cannon might also reduce enthusiasm, especially if it was a typically cold and wet Belfast July day. By mid-evening it was time to blood the next generation and fathers led out sons of no more than 10 to 12 years old, handed them an age-specific stone and instructed them to go and hurl it at the nearest policeman in Robocop gear 'and no swearing you little fecker'. No real offence meant and none taken – this was a whole lot better than the bloodlust of the most difficult years of The Troubles. Finally, the majority would spot that it was nearly time for the local evening news on TV and as it would be a shame to miss themselves on the screen after so much effort, off they toddled home.

It was also true that there were some very nasty elements at play. There was also always someone looking to take advantage of the unrest to do some big robbing. The highlight for me was watching the imagery from the surveillance helicopter of a large yellow JCB making its way down a street in East Belfast late in the evening, knocking over the street lamps as it went. Odd that anyone would think that the army and police in Belfast had not cracked night vision kit after more than thirty years, but there is a clue in the word 'think' here. Having smashed up what was almost certainly their own high street, their objective was to use the digger to extract an ATM from the wall in order to liberate the cash. As this was not exactly a novel idea by 2005, we had on hand a very competent Royal Engineer corporal driving our armoured version of a digger. I had hoped it could take rather longer than it did, this is top telly after all, but the corporal lost no time in conducting his own version of robot-wars by swiftly taking hold of the yellow JCB and dumping it on its side.

Looking back now at my tenure in command in Northern Ireland, from a leadership perspective it was a big lesson in strategic patience. When 'The Troubles' broke into major hostilities in 1969 it was more or less the latest, bitter expression of difficulties going back 1,000 years. In the generation that followed a lot of terrible things were done and this has inevitably and indelibly left its mark on all parties. I could make a logical case until I was blue in the face for suggesting to everyone that they get over themselves and move on in the best interests of their children. I might also point out how much the protagonists were cushioned by an immense amount of English taxpayer's money that provided duplicated quality health, education, and housing support to a place with an economy that could get nowhere near affording it. I could certainly say to my police colleagues that on the basis of the violence I had seen in the Balkans, Afghanistan, and Iraq, the occasional shooting and home-made pipe bomb was nowhere near the scale that merited military support. To put it another way, if we weren't already in the province, there was nothing going on that would justify us coming now. It was evident that having such a robust police-military capability meant the two sides could squabble and scrap without fearing it would get so out of hand that ethnic-cleansing would ensue.

None of this was particularly helpful to raise, except where I detected there were some police officers who shied away from really tidying up the hard-core dissidents, partly because it would stir up some community antipathy and partly because if they weren't still dissidents the most interesting part of their job – and the justification for some hefty allowances – would quickly disappear. They really wanted 'normality', just not until their bungalow was finished.

The bigger point, however, is that in campaigns like this it is not possible to ignore the scars that run so deep or to wish away deeply regrettable events or the potential for progress to always erode or reverse in some way. One of the secrets of this particular campaign is that it was bored to death: the ring was held long enough for more peaceful alternatives to take root and this importantly included avoiding any overreactions that might re-open wounds that were beginning to heal or give grounds for another round of fighting. Some problems cannot be fixed without recourse to methods that would be either counter-productive in the long run or just unacceptable. There was never any question of deploying fighter aircraft, tanks, and artillery in Northern Ireland, nor of imposing mass population movements to shove entire communities over the border. These are things that have happened in similar circumstances elsewhere in the world, and not entirely successfully to say the least.

If a problem cannot be resolved at an acceptable price, then it will likely be necessary to hold the ring for as long as it takes for the ferment to decline and new ways forward to appear. In fact, as I also remarked on in the Balkans, one aspect of this is that the leaders of the violence in 'The Troubles' tended to be in their twenties and the experience fundamentally shaped their approach to their lives. It did take until they had buried enough of their friends to sense their own mortality, and in particular produce children of their own and begun to wonder what life they will bequeath them, before negotiation and compromise seemed like an alternative. Maybe this is why revolutions and insurgencies tend to have a lifespan of at least half a generation and then take at least the same again before things are really stable again. Most never really end, they just fizzle out when the heart for yet more, indecisive violence ebbs away.

The two years as a brigade commander flashed past, it really was uberfulfilling to have a charge of a few thousand good soldiers, regulars serving a two-year or more tour in Northern Ireland and the full-time locally recruited forces. The latter may not always have been the greatest enthusiasts for some of the usual exigencies of military service, like a lot of running or going easy on the daily sausage intake, but they knew their job inside out. When it came to teaching others how to manage civil disorder Northern Ireland-style they were the masters.

Senior leadership and command is a pivotal life experience as I guess any CEO finds. As the commander you are entrusted with not just formulating good strategy and plans but also making sure that all parts of the organization know what is expected of them and are resourced and helped to do it. It can be immensely fulfilling, especially if able to relax and enjoy bearing the responsibility. Of course this means to some extent we are all role-playing and one can overdo the smoke and mirrors: we the leader as omnipotent and omniscient and also incredibly cool and without doubt a top-ten lifetime shag is a hard image to maintain forever. Perhaps that's just me. But these roles do matter in making good history, people need to have good leaders to follow and leaders need good followers to lead well.

A lot of this comes down to trust and relationships, exactly as it does in every other walk of life. It also requires a careful eye on how people are developed to do the things their role demands, we all learn on the job – even a president or prime minister encounters things that have to be navigated with a prodigious dollop of bluff. A lieutenant colonel commanding an infantry battalion of 650 soldiers will still be learning as he goes, even if he has been a star player in his career so far to earn that appointment. Some humility is essential given the limits of any one person and the odds that events will supply a kick in the teeth from time to time, no matter how well we think we are doing. The more senior I became in the army, the more I realised that there is a direct correlation between senior leaders coming to believe that they are truly a legend in their own trousers and the rate at which they set course to make an ass of themselves.

Commanders, like CEOs, invariably find that they are dealing with people who work for them who are too keen to please and desperate not to disappoint. The dangers of people telling you only what they think you want to hear are omnipresent. There is also the equal danger of subordinates too comfortable or too sly trying to work out how far they can go with indolence or worse, without being called out for a spanking. I found, and I am not unique in this, that it was important to make people sense that there was very little that didn't catch my eye and that poor performance had personal consequences.

The ability to hold key subordinates to account, making plain to them where they have succeeded and the prizes that will accrue and where they have fallen short and were in jeopardy, is one of the indicators of competent leadership at all levels. In tightly knit and hierarchical, family-like organizations such as the military, I also found that not every leader has the moral courage to act appropriately when someone who may be a lifelong friend has crossed the line. This is always a mistake and almost always found out, compounding one mistake with another when almost inevitably the truth comes tumbling out.

As brigade commander, the day came after almost exactly two years in harness when it was time to hand over and go. There might be some small relief at the prospect of passing on such responsibilities, maybe a small glow from things that have gone well – and certainly a much, much bigger glow from parting from the things that were a catastrophe yet didn't come to much notice. It is nonetheless an odd feeling that one day you are master of all that surrounds you in your small corner of the universe and the next day you are as forgotten as last week's news and someone else is wearing the big hat. Nobody is indispensable, yet handing on a command that has been cherished 24/7 for two years is like finding someone else in your house, wearing your slippers, and with your wife and children looking at you and wondering why you are still hanging about. The only thing is to hand over and go away quickly.

Unfortunately, when this moment came in Belfast in December 2005, when I had handed over house, office, staff, all authority to command, and trumpeted all my (no doubt) useful concluding thoughts, the weather simply decided not to cooperate with my departure. This was not God suggesting to mankind that I could not possibly be replaced, it was just Irish winter weather doing its thing. I had a car full to the brim with kit and a huge new collection of farewell plaques, pictures, and glassware, but neither the ferry to Scotland to get on, nor anywhere to take myself off to until the wind and rain subsided. The good news was that my departure coincided with the end of a piece of work in South Armagh that had required the services of a very large helicopter, a CH-47 Chinook – essentially a flying ten-tonne truck operated by a small number of skilled RAF types firmly strapped to it in their customary heavily-badged flying-onesies and unnecessarily vast helmets.

The most obliging (and ultimately very senior) RAF commander in Northern Ireland was as keen to see me go as I was to leave and so very readily saw how the back of his nice helicopter was easily big enough for me and my car. The only downside was the requirement to wear a noxious full-body rubber suit, not apparently a social thing but a precaution in case the journey ended prematurely in the Irish Sea. (There is nothing to be gained in pointing out to any air force that the civilian aircraft that ply exactly the same route do not insist that their passengers wear head to toe latex. This is about risk being ALARP, As Low As Reasonably Practicable, including aiming off for something not being absolutely tip-top in the big oily engine plus giant whirling rotors department.)

As we transited at many thousands of feet towards the English coast it turned out that we would pass by the airfield where the RAF's Typhoon jets are made and mended. It also turned out that there is a cute arrangement between RAF pilots that when two shall meet in the same part of the sky it is open to them to agree to have a little practice at shooting each other down. In this case, a Typhoon capable of 1,000mph and armed with guns and missiles ought to make short work of a large helicopter travelling at about 130mph an hour armed only with the many hard-boiled eggs saved from a week of RAF packed lunches.

Our survival, apparently, relied on the helicopter driver keeping the nose pointing at the Typhoon as it ripped about the sky. I agree that this doesn't sound terribly convincing, and it was even less convincing in a helicopter that was carrying not only a large tank of extra fuel but also quite a large car with an enormous amount of luggage in it. We were declared destroyed after about a minute, and it only took that long because the Typhoon driver wanted to get his money's worth with some gratuitous rolling about in the clouds. The upside is that I am pretty sure that I owned the only Land Rover Freelander that has ever done air-to-air combat.

In the well-established way of most armed forces, a joyous spell in command (for the few who are so lucky) is generally followed by a 'staff appointment'. In my case, as a 'post-command Brigadier' this would be to the Headquarters of United Kingdom Land Command, then located at Wilton, near Salisbury. As is often the case with UK military establishments, the grandeur of the title was distinctly at odds with the ghastliness of the buildings. This was a site that was probably the peak of building perfection on the day that it opened in the late 1960s, but by January 2006 it might still be 'brutal modernism' but it was actually a total dump.

In addition to the crumbling fabric and the omnipresent foul plumbing whiff, the increase in the popularity of the personal motorcar over the last forty years (still apparently a surprise to many Quartermasters and their Book of Regulations) meant that getting in and out at certain times of the day was a beast. On the other hand, when I saw quite how many colleagues were determinedly making their exit for home bang on 16.00 hours most days, it occurred to me that shooting every other one in the head as they crawled through the gate would be a sound start to improving HQ efficiency.

Happily for me, the omnipresent risk from a burst heating pipe was well worth running for all the excitement that came with being the army's 'Operations Officer'. I had a slightly mad title, 'Assistant Chief of Staff Commitments', but this meant I was responsible for all the army's operational tasking, deciding which unit or formation would deploy when and where. I also supervised the army's support to UK national security and resilience, from the annual sandbagging hobby to stem floods to very specialist support to events like the Russian poisoning of Mr Litvinenko.

My arrival in this post coincided with the movement of the British military focus in Afghanistan from the north of the country down to take charge of Helmand province. The policy and the operational detail of this deployment was led by others, particularly the UK Permanent Joint Headquarters and the MoD. My dog in this fight was to identify who would go, make sure they were provided with the right training and send them off with as much of the right equipment and support as possible in the circumstances. Of course, I didn't know then that what we started in 2005 would wind through some turbulent times and not conclude as a combat operation until I wound it back down again as a lieutenant general in 2014. There is never any guaranteed script for these things, no matter how hard people demand to see one at kick-off.

I thought it would be a fairly stable period as a staff officer, with most days much like going to work in an office like any other commuter (albeit in big boots and combat pyjamas, to maintain the martial atmospherics). I imagined, and I certainly was not wrong, that quite a lot of my time would be spent wrestling the bureaucracy of a 2,000 strong HQ – where I sometimes felt that any space in the calendar not filled by a meeting was to be taken as a sinful dereliction of duty. In fact, I quickly established that one of the most useful things I could do was to keep the whole, interminable meeting hobby fully fuelled and thereby keep my fellow senior attendees so comprehensively preoccupied that they did not have an instant left with which to distract my heavily pressed staff from actually working. This is one experience that is readily transferable to the commercial Afterlife.

And we were really pressed. There had been a theory that the UK would finish its adventure in Iraq before considering whether to have another one at similar scale in Afghanistan. Most of the army had already enjoyed a couple more turns in Iraq since the big kick-off in 2003. We were now well into the larger battles with what had become quite a lumpy insurgency, taking the lives and limbs of good people on all sides. But bigger factors were in play in Afghanistan, notably that NATO was taking charge of what had become a nationwide effort to support the development of better government, security, and economy. Getting started in Helmand was also part of a much bigger scheme for NATO and its future, with a UK commander at the helm in Kabul. Saying we were still a tad preoccupied in Basra was not the answer.

The next two years were dominated by a sexy army-speak catchphrase of 'Double Medium Scale Enduring'. In English, this means that it became unavoidable to field a brigade (for the sake of argument 5,000 soldiers) concurrently in both Iraq and Afghanistan and keep this going for some time – at least three years. Taking the then accepted benchmark that any one soldier should serve for six months in either theatre of operations, and then have two years doing other things before deploying again, we would need five soldiers in rotation per task. That meant roughly the whole army minus the recruits, sick, lame, lazy, and war-dodgers.

It turned out to be much more complicated than taking the entire membership of the British Army and tipping it into a hopper that delivered five equally sized lumps of capability on two parallel production lines, one headed to Iraq and one to Afghanistan. For a start, the equipment needed for each was different, and in some cases so new that it was being issued pretty much as fast as it came out of the factory. Just as perplexing, it was relatively easy to find the soldiers to carry rifles, but it was much harder to find specialists in the many roles that support these deployments. For example, if there is no one qualified to operate a fuel dump then quite quickly nothing moves or flies. This meant that some very skilled and experienced people barely had time to wash their socks from one tour before they were pretty close to heading out on another, and there are only so many times you can ask a volunteer to do this before they or their family decide that civilian life has to be better.

It was not just how long people deployed overseas for that was a struggle. To get an individual, a unit, a complete brigade ready to do a good job required a cycle of training and preparation that was in some respects harder on people than the tour itself. The imperative to not send people who were not ready tends to drive enthusiasm for preparatory activity that would fill every waking moment if left unchecked. Some significant bits of training had anyway to be dragged out over a year so that the limited equipment available could be passed around. We learned to count NOOBs, Nights Out Of Bed, to try and manage and ration how much was expected of people between getting off the plane from one operational tour and getting back on another for the next. We also had to count plane seats because where the RAF aircraft had to be fitted with anti-missile defence systems in order to come and go with confidence the number of airframes available was finite. This meant that in managing the flow 'to theatre', it sometimes felt we were filtering a small lake through a drinking straw. It also meant that some people were heading back for their mid-tour break when they had only been away for six weeks of the six-month tour, but we could hardly be driven by aircraft seats to allow only a proportion to have time off with their families.

I know there are parallels with many other walks of life in which a limited quantity of people and stuff has to service activity at broadly maximum sustainable output. I had charts that proved that if we needed to make the deployments any bigger we would have to start mobilizing the Scouts, Guides, and Brownies. I guess one of the differences for an army is that we were sending volunteers into harm's way and some into conditions for which the word 'Spartan' is an understatement. Many others, of course, would inhabit large and relatively safe bases for the work that they did, so overcrowding, overfeeding, and boredom would prey on their minds more than risk of shot or shell. We actually got pretty good at making the system work, largely thanks to a small group of officers flogging themselves often seven days a week. Both of my principal deputies eventually became lieutenant generals and the officer who was the absolute master of the Spreadsheets from Hell rose to run the UK's defence exports in government. This sort of experience is why the military are really good at taking planning skills to other walks of life.

After a bit more than two years of juggling the entire British Army through the operations hopper, I was standing at one of those pivotal crossroads. One road would take me on a horizontal career plane as a brigadier for eternity, perhaps forever shuffling the details of defence or Army money and organization – or maybe some spells abroad ruining my heart and liver on the circuit as an Attaché. Not really my thing. Another way would be the career holding pattern of a bit more education, indeed I was slated to attend the Royal College of Defence Studies. Nobody has not enjoyed a year of that, some have subsequently risen to great heights, and others have plateaued. But the road ahead could also include the jump to major general, real big boy pants stuff. This meant I needed someone in one of those few slots to die, retire, fail or be promoted, and for this to happen at the right time (for me). It's just how it is.

Chapter 10

Leadership

My Dear M,

Someone asked me the other day whether being an army officer, by definition someone deliberately trained and presumably experienced in leadership, was a help or hindrance in the Afterlife commercial foray that I have launched myself at? This is, I think anyway, an interesting question – it raises issues I could bang on ceaselessly about: there is nothing like talking about leadership in or out of uniform for unlocking the frothiest load of bobbins. Everybody reckons something about 'leadership', we are all both a leader and a follower in one way or another as we go through life. After around forty years as an officer I really ought to know something of what leadership is/isn't, certainly enough to define it in some way. If I were to struggle to do that – and I do a bit – does that mean I have been serially and seriously just making stuff up for all these years? Quite possibly, but I will obviously need to deny that.

I have found there is a standing handicap for military folk when talking about leadership beyond their own circle, because so few people (at least in Europe) ever have any meaningful contact with their own armed forces. This is usually a good thing in human history: when most people in the world have contact with even their own armed forces it is an oppressive experience they neither relish nor wish to repeat. In the UK, where we frown on oppression as a rule, most people generally rely on clunky and often quite mad military stereotypes drawn from the world of entertainment when it comes to knowing their navy, army, and air force.

Sometimes, I am happy to admit, this stereotyping can actually be quite glamorous, but the glamour may also often involve a ghastly, premature, and dismembering death in the heat of some epic battle. It is even better for the glamour-count if the story includes the untimely and spectacular death of the hero *and* the sacrifice of the love of a good and definitely comely woman. A woman who will now forever mourn in dignified silence, not simply gaff off to the next bloke on her long list of potential suitors. If heroic death can be incurred at the hands of a demonic foe (Nazis are still favourite for this, perhaps due to their good eye for a natty black uniform) and/or include earning redemption for some disgusting lapse of conduct in earlier life, then the erstwhile leader is forever quids in, though still very firmly dead. All this glamour can transfer to the prevailing mythology about non-fictional military leaders (i.e. me), which is fine, but not if it is also assumed we are all desperate to die in a blaze of glory just as soon as possible.

Sometimes the duty stereotype is totally negative, the on-screen military leader is comprehensively over-acted as the source of all evil – customarily emitting a stream of profoundly malign, beastly, and generally deeply fascist content. If this dark portrayal includes an astonishing capacity for anally retentive behaviour and an obsessive interest in vigorous spanking so much the better – based on Netflix and other streamers of popular entertainment. I am irredeemably a two-headed baby-killer in the eyes of some who Google me, just because the interweb records me as having been present in combat pyjamas in various of the world's trouble-spots since 1977. I can't claim I receive the postbag of a teenage songster with a mad haircut and a gift for soulful vacuity, but I am still surprised that a few nutters do go to all the trouble of writing to me via the Military Secretary to express their fondest hope that I die slowly and – somewhat paradoxically – *very soon* from a thing that is painful and untreatable.

Most of the great British public generally understand their military through the medium of a combination of 1950s war films, 1980s comedy – especially the Blackadder genre, and the soldiers who rummaged handbags at the London 2012 Olympics by day and boosted the birth rate in East London by night. It's Blackadder that does people like me over. If the only general someone has ever registered is Stephen Fry's General Sir Anthony Cecil Hogmanay Melchett ('if nothing else works, a total pig-headed unwillingness to look facts in the face will see us through'), perhaps it's understandable that today's military leaders are starting from a low point in hoping to convey all their talent and beauty. Actually, I was always rather more taken with the brigadier who featured so smartly in 1970s episodes of Doctor Who, although I have subsequently agonized between admiring his splendid bearing under considerable Dalek-induced stress and the necessity of cultivating the sort of moustache otherwise only found in porn films. (Apparently.)

Nonetheless, could I have navigated the journey from second lieutenant to four-star general without really knowing with something close to certainty what good leadership is? No, that would be bollocks. If I had, I would be either an actual imposter or over-infused with an unhealthy dose of impostor syndrome, and I don't accept that either applies. And if I were not sure enough about what constitutes good (including military) leadership, how could I know what bits of this would transfer well to captain of industry stuff? I regularly assert out loud that a lot of what I see going completely and unnecessarily tits-up in the general cluster of commercial life can be pinned to the chest of rubbish leadership, so I am sticking my chin out here.

An easy place for us to start on an exploration of leadership is to agree that the point of an army officer at any level is to *lead*. Otherwise, how would one justify the hierarchical status that the greenest young officer – the proverbial Rupert, and these days Rachael too – is provisionally awarded on passing out from basic officer training? This privilege is based on the several hundred years of military history in which youthful officers, once drawn from the upper classes and kitted out in a glossy uniform bought on credit in Saville Row, are stood out front of the lower orders (dressed in government-issue sackcloth) in order to be instantly mown down as the opening futile gesture at any proper battle. The junior officers of today now earn their place for training as sacrificial cannon-fodder strictly on merit, not absence of chins, but they still are expected to lead from the front and by personal example.

Leadership is in fact the whole point of institutions like the Royal Military Academy Sandhurst, the place at which all British Army officer careers start and quite a few immediately reach their ceiling. Other officers do flourish further up the greasy poll of the rank structure and a tiny few succeed enough to accomplish great things in starring roles in the 'cauldron of battle'. Most people's understanding of military history is pretty sketchy and perhaps that accounts for why I find I can get black looks in some company if I muse about the herculean challenges faced by commanders in war. This seems to be taken – by some – as if I my revelling in the history of people who had become pre-eminent as warrior-chiefs was right up there alongside witchcraft and incest in the public's shitlist. Perhaps because of the misplaced sense of a world going 'post-conflict', when the Soviet Union imploded, I encounter people for whom the very idea that it is still necessary to have at least some capable people who know how to lead hard fighting well is out of step with modern times. This is balls.

Do many people really believe that because war is so horrid (yes it certainly is), that as we have managed a generation in the West without being seriously scared of invasion or civil war, somehow war will now forever give us a miss? I wish they were right, but it flies uncomprehendingly in the face of human history so far to believe this and – I think – ignores the relatively limited evolution of human ability to control of its own unfettered bastard emotions through the limited scope we have developed for pure rational thought. And if we can't just wish this requirement away, we are going to need more than General Melchett, with all his perspicacity and splendid face-fungus, to work out how to survive the experience of war biting us in the ass in future. Look at what is happening in Ukraine since 2022.

As I recorded in the introduction to this collection, Sandhurst did things to me that have shaped my entire adult life, for good or ill. The most obvious manifestations of this even today are obsessively polished shoes and an aversion to walking-out in public wearing trousers that do not bear a proper crease. Actually, an aversion to being out of bed in trousers not rigid with starch. As I lapse into the weakness that attends the Afterlife, though still only after deep emotional wrangling, I have relented on creases in denim jeans – but only because I know that wearing jeans in my seventh decade causes quite enough public nuisance *and* delivers acute embarrassment to my offspring. But as I am blessed with buns of steel that the devil's cloth captures and displays with such prolific grooviness, I insist to them they should be applauding not recoiling.

The impossibility of being late is, however, still non-negotiable, and the definition of being on time is being everywhere a minimum of five minutes before it is remotely necessary. Ten is much better. This is not just a military thing, I apparently share this trait with the world-famous motoring journalist turned gentleman-farmer Jeremy Clarkson, although we do differ in so far as for some years his stomach has arrived five minutes before his spine and mine arrives pretty much concurrently with my ripped abdomen.

I am pretty sure that Sandhurst did more to me, or for me, than just improve my punctuality. Having now had the opportunity to see many young officers straight from the Academy at work and play at different points over the last forty years, there really are some enduring and sensible features about how leadership in the military works that Sandhurst inculcates. First, there has to be a strong enough sense of committing to a vocation. Soldering can be quite hard work, often hideously dull between rare moments of buttock-clenching excitement, and almost invariably conducted at times and in places less comfortable and sociable than one might sensibly prefer.

To take just one example, the vocational tug applies to the British Army's Household Division, which provides all the various flavours of Guardsman to stand erect with a great deal of dead bear on their heads outside Royal palaces, along with their world-beating demonstrations of armed synchronized walking. This may appear more glamorous than standing in the mud and rain of some forgotten wind-blasted moor on the periphery of Europe, but apart from the tiny few who truly find that standing guard totally taxes all their mental and physical capacities to the limit, all Guardsmen very much prefer getting back to the business of slaughtering their country's oppressors in the mud and rain. You just can't be good at this unless really committed, the exigencies of the job will wear out anyone only along for the ride. (British soldiering is historically mostly about mud and rain, though obviously more recently opportunities have come up to give it a proper go in sunny countries, but the point stands.)

In just the same way, the Royal Navy knows that its job is to be rolling about in the north Atlantic, throwing up over each other as wind and swell very substantially deplete the attractiveness of their calling. The occasional sunset cocktail party on the flight deck of a frigate firmly tied up alongside in Portsmouth (likely for its own safety, they are frequently short of vital bits these days), with Royal Marines thrashing bugle and drum, may make up for weeks at sea, but the weeks at sea will keep coming.

At the core of their business, the Royal Air Force contends with long hours flying utterly lost in the dark whilst managing bladders swollen by government-endorsed fizzy pop to the size of basketballs. This requires dedication, commitment, and impressive self-control beyond a merely transactional level. There will be occasions when these pilots can relax with their miniature railway magazine collection before – and this is a deeply entrenched and unique RAF tradition – burning a piano, especially a piano that is not theirs to burn. But they still have to get back in the incontinence-intolerant sky time after time.

The point is that without a sense that serving in the military *matters* and that there is some nobility of purpose beyond merely (and generally reliably) topping up a wallet with never quite enough cash at the end of each month, then there will quickly come moments when noble purpose is trashed by the grimness of it all. Without a sense of service as a vocation, the commitment of the ambivalent will be crushed by geography, by being soaked, freezing or sweating to destruction in boiling heat, and always by being so knackered that another life as a freelance widget salesperson on an abandoned industrial park near a disused steelworks will beckon with urgent and convincing force.

For most young officers the idea of leading perhaps thirty soldiers (sailors/airmen/marines) is the thing that dominates. Most I guess will have had a go at being in charge of others on their passage through life to reach the gates of Sandhurst or Cranfield (RAF) or Dartmouth (RN). They might be the sporty types who have exercised their heart and lungs to bursting point in exhorting the rest of their team in hot pursuit of one form of ball or another. Maybe they were given a position at school or university which involved extracting their peers from bed to do something about which they had extreme ambivalence – which in the case of most young adults is the act of getting out of bed alone. These early trials do give an early glimmer of fire in the belly and the will to lead in battle, without excluding the rise of the truly narcissist megalomaniac. They mostly aim for politics though.

Some officers, I have no doubt, were either born with or developed a notion that they were simply destined to lead others, without there being any cause for thinking this was justified or in any way a promising thing. Some will slip through the net of selection and training to become the greatest of many potential liabilities to the success and survival of their appointed subordinates. As a result, battlefields throughout history have swallowed up those few leaders whose followers have firmly concluded that they are attached to a really risky prospect on the mad, dangerous, to comprehensively hopeless spectrum. The solution sometimes is to advance the demise of their toxic leader by taking assertive action, generally from behind and with a gun. The 'fragging' phenomenon observed in Vietnam, whereby a US officer considered to be more of a risk to his men than the Vietcong was treated to an all-American grenade, is not unique in military history. There is fragging in politics too, though rarely at the level of mortal danger and more about being metaphorically and multiply stabbed from all angles by loyal and smiley supporters. I haven't seen much evidence of fragging in commercial life, but it is early days.

Overall, most young officers in a navy, army, or air force are driven by the buzz of being placed at the head of a small group of people all prepared to do their thing in harm's way. This responsibility is not nine to five, it extends to total consideration of well-being, welfare, and development. This is clearly one of the major differences between the military vocation and most commercial roles. In the former there really can be no great separation between work and life in the way the participants think about their part, aided by the geographical reality that a great deal of military service means living miles away from the rest of civilisation. If you are committed to a life in which it may be necessary to instruct others whom you know well to do things which may very well lead to their serious injury or destruction, there has to be a bond of a special nature. Hope and curiosity only go so far.

I know there are also commendable and important vocational bonds and commitment in some commercial enterprises, from a start-up running on the adrenalin and life savings of the founders to huge companies doing things fundamental to the success of daily national life. But in all these cases the plan is that the workforce always gets to go home in one piece. Yes of course there is ruthlessness and rigour in having to fire people on the back of some 'poor numbers', but this is rarely a personal thing or accompanied by loss of life or limb. For many there is a difference between satisfactorily working to live at the office/factory/shop and the living to work vibe needed to enjoy and thrive in the military.

This leads me to a second observation about the idiocy of commonly held stereotypes of how modern militaries operate. No matter how many times I have set out to non-military audiences that military service functions on the basis of inspired cooperation by consent between leaders and followers, the belief sticks that military leadership is essentially about hierarchical shouting.

In fact, military leadership relies on a common ethos and understanding grounded in trust and example, and there is a massive, systemic investment in a way of delegating and empowering that has been forged in battle over decades known as 'Mission Command'. When I describe this to some commercial audiences, the very first observation in response is always (boringly) along the lines of: 'yes but aren't you all trained to function as automatons in a rigidly enforced hierarchy, so of course everybody does what they are told all the time'. Then, if they really, really want to be tagged for life in my eyes as Really Annoying the speaker will add '…whereas in the commercial world we have to think for ourselves…'. This remark is always best dispatched at me with a look of benign condescension. In a fair and decent world anybody above the rank of lance corporal or equivalent present on the spot would be empowered to take a shovel to the speaker's stupid face. Otherwise, I am totally relaxed about it.

I have tried to explain this to myself as a result of too many people spending too many wet Sunday afternoons watching ancient films about the Battle of Waterloo, First World War, or perhaps anything capturing for entertainment British military activity over the 1,000 years up to about 1950. The whole 'lions led by donkeys' thing refuses to go away quietly. Perhaps this is because there really have been some lions and some donkeys at any point in history, but the greater point is that this idea that British soldiers do what they're told in an unthinking and non-consensual way is mostly bollocks.

Where it is wonderfully and demonstratively not bollocks is in the way some soldiers/sailors/airmen/marines, sometimes very green and sometimes very seasoned, have responded in the heat of a very difficult moment to do something spectacularly brave and with great personal consequences. In my own service, reading the citations for medals for individuals who have responded to the demands of a fierce encounter in battle with a combination of instinct, character, and professional skill was a great privilege. Choosing which actions succeeded in being recognized was never easy, even though the bar for an award was always kept consistently high. No wonder all military people recognize what is conveyed by a little piece of cloth on the chest of another in uniform that denotes a Military Cross, or a Distinguished Flying Cross, or a Mention in Dispatches. The medals that go with serving time on tricky campaigns like Afghanistan and Iraq are also instantly recognizable by the military community as part of a biography of a man/woman with military substance.

The important thing that is also absolutely not bollocks is that getting people, even highly trained and highly motivated people, to do things that they can readily see means huge effort and serious personal risk never works on the basis of compulsion alone. The citizens who become soldiers, sailors, airmen, and marines don't leave their brains at the door, which is just as well as military service needs some thoughtful people.

Yes, of course, there is a requirement to accept it may be necessary to do things at great personal cost for the wider benefit of the mission in hand, and to do things when every instinct is to remain firmly fixed as tightly as possible to the floor until all the shooting has stopped. But the vast majority of military people act because they understand not only what they have to do but also *why* and *why it matters*. Nor do they want to be told *how* to do the things they know how to do perfectly well, like everybody else they prefer to be left to do their thing in the way they think best in order to deliver what is asked of them. This is Mission Command – delegation and empowerment for the fighting business. Or any business.

This means that leaders have to be good at explaining the *why* as well as the *what*. Sometimes this is easier than others, especially as some military activity requires enormous physical effort for quite limited but necessary potential gain. It's a small example, but if the necessary thing to do is to ask an infantry soldier to spend twenty-four uninterrupted hours digging a very big, very wet trench just in case the war turns sour in his direction, and as soon as it is dug to full magnificence it becomes necessary to move on without a shot being fired – or much, much worse to fill it in again – then gratitude will be in short supply. This is where the ingrained humour of the British soldier kicks in; as he or she shovels the earth back in, they know to the core of their being that they are led by muppets, but they are muppets who can be moaned at and who are still trying to do the right thing. There is never really a problem when a British serviceman is moaning, or taking the piss, but there is a very big problem if they are silent and sullen. A bit like having children, but with higher stakes – and in my experience less annoying.

The field of battle is a tumbling combination of what people try to do, how good they are at it, what the opposition is capable of, the factors that always make a difference like terrain and weather, and then just the sheer bloody luck of the draw. Step to the left and an anti-personnel mine concludes your mortal proceedings in an instant, step to the right and you get to die at home in bed of extreme old age, proverbially surrounded by an extended family protesting at how you banged their inheritance away on wine, women, and Call of Duty – and wilfully squandered the rest. There is no way of knowing at the time you walk down that path on just another day at the front what the outcome may be. I certainly never alighted from a helicopter that landed intact in places like Afghanistan without a sense of having got away with something.

The nearest commercial parallel to this that I can think of is the precariousness of some employment, where people come to work in the morning without a thought that by the end of the day they will have been fired, especially if they've been in that job for decades. That is clearly uncertainty that tells, but it's not quite the same as coming back from work stone cold dead. If being stone cold dead is a possible condition of employment, people are going to act only by understanding pretty clearly *why* they need to do the thing that they've been told to do, even if they know ultimately they have very little choice about it.

We should not think that the degree of choice for a soldier is defined by the possibility of refusal met by being shot by their own officers and NCOs, although that has certainly been a feature of wars in the past. The reason military people do highly risky things is because they know that the man or woman to their left or right, the people whom they serve alongside every day, really need and expect them to play their part. Most soldiers go forward into battle not for any God or country but for friends and colleagues, and none of them will do very much if they think the enterprise is foolish or wrong. An order to go forward based only on vanity or stupidity tends to result in engines breaking down, knees giving way and a great deal of getting lost in the dark en route.

The demand on military leaders to provide explanation, inspiration, example, and direction – and to manage expectations truthfully, has to take account of the reality that the people whom they lead are actually normal human beings, even when made fitter and issued with a lot of military luggage. The thirty or so soldiers (or sailors, or airmen, or marines) may indeed be absolute paragons of military capability and virtue, but it is a bit more likely that there are thirty or so individuals present who are all capable of conscious thought and no less immune to an emotional tug than the rest of the family that produced them. Each soldier has a personal bundle of skills, character, and experience to bring to the fight. Some of this, sometimes, includes a skill for being basically an idle little shite mostly determined to do as little work as possible for as long as possible, and definitely not keen on being the first to volunteer for Operation Certain Death. But even this character will have made it through military training and found a place in a military unit that has to be justified not just to the taxpayer but to the others around him or her. Nobody wants to find that their sleeping bag has disappeared on a long January night out in the woods because they have behaved like a selfish idiot.

The shopfloor of an army, navy, or air force can be a very broadly tolerant place in accommodating a range of congenital indolence, but not when the chips are really down. In fact, and not just in Hollywood, it often turns out that the platoon's leading reprobate blossoms under fire into the total Captain America and saves the day. Sometimes even in the real world this means they really are forever converted to upright military citizen, henceforth stalwart exemplars of their trade, in other cases as soon as the shooting abates their normal jogging as a lazy pain in the ass is resumed. It takes all sorts, within reason.

It is entirely the same mankind that populates all forms of commercial enterprise, from the marbled palaces of high finance dedicated to stuffing rubbish debts into whizzy derivatives to grubby workshops under the arches bodging wrecked cars back into sleazy life. Commercial as much as military life is a consumer of leadership one way or another and there simply cannot be one recipe for success that fits all. It is also true, I think, that the way leadership is needed changes with the growth of an enterprise or with different circumstances. The sparky, ever-mobile and supremely thick-skinned entrepreneur that gets things going in any sector just may not be the right person to scale things up well, when things like strategy, planning and carefully husbanded relationships with customers really do matter as much as a keen eye on for a price and the primacy of cash flow. As a soldier I obsessed about ammunition supply, in business I now feel the same about cash.

Perhaps it's easier to understand leadership from the other end. Instead of trying to pin down what works well it may be better to address what bad leadership looks like? Everybody knows bad leadership when they see it and there is just so much of it about. I don't exclude the military from this, to do so would fly in the face of quite a lot of defeat, chaos, and avoidable massacre, but right now from my perch in the Afterlife I am regularly struck by just how rubbish so much leadership is, even in the most glossy and cash-infested commercial enterprises and the most exalted corridors of the civil service.

Perhaps it is partly because in commercial life and occupations like the civil service there is much more of an air gap between an individual's private life and their work? Are the expectations of holistic leadership lower and the tolerance of venality and incompetence higher, in practice if not in theory? There is no end of leadership *theory* filling airport bookstands to groaning point nor codes or long lists of values to turn to, but it also seems there is quite a prolific supply of deceitful scheming shitbags wanting to be put in charge of things that matter.

There are many glorious examples where commercial leadership is of the highest order and extends well beyond making consistently high profit to include making consistently fulfilled people. But I would say that the average score for leadership is pretty low, sometimes and reasonably because there just has not been any opportunity to be instructed in or learn about how leadership works. Certainly not in the way that armed forces are so heavily invested in. There is something risky in the idea that an individual can be elevated to take charge of their peers because they have proven extremely proficient in a skill or a service, when in making that elevation they need to acquire important new leadership expertise which they only have had the chance to acquire by osmosis. Some people really do thrive in the face of this opportunity and others fail, but I keep my greatest regret for the many who *could* lead spectacularly if only they were given the training and the opportunity – and some tolerance whilst they found their feet and grew.

I certainly see examples where elevation is accompanied by ready acceptance of the blessings promotion confers – the plumper chair, a credit card to dine clients and perhaps an assistant on which to heap as much of life's dross as possible. These advantages are not always matched by the reciprocal enthusiasm for picking up the obligations that come with leadership. These obligations should certainly include illuminating for one's team what is to be done, by whom, and by when – rather than leaving this as a voyage of bewildering personal discovery for each employee that leads to avoidable tears and legitimate rage.

It certainly includes leading by personal example, especially when things get tense, massive additional effort is required or setbacks have to be accounted for. The last of these is one acid test for someone who claims lead: do they shoulder the blame for things the team may have got wrong for any reason, or do they reliably and shamelessly ensure that the poo cascades to the point of least resistance? As many have previously recorded: when looking down the ladder of life one sees only smiling faces, when looking up only assholes.

In my new status as aspirant captain of industry I wonder how the youth advance from the newly joined trainee filled with a rising sense of panic to one day reach the gilded portals of the Chief Executive's suite? How does one also get from being enticed with vouchers for free pizza to trousering piles of the company's stock worth millions and several hundred thousand pounds a year? I am all up for big rewards for big success, and I now speak as the proprietor of start-ups where there are no vouchers and the stock is worth less than a stamp, and as a grubby adviser hired in various ways to offer pearls of gravitas-encrusted wisdom to any throbbing enterprise. (These are pearls which the recipients inexplicably seem to feel at complete liberty to ignore and keep from any actual effect on their throbbing.)

As a consultant there is occasionally the condescension of a building pass to avoid having to queue at the door with the Deliveroo operative, but never really any doubt that one's proper place is to be back in the visitors' carpark as expeditiously as possible. I am still working out how in commercial life a keen and enthusiastic youngster is given the structured development to be ready to be CEO and as CEO justify more income than a whole town? There are some good degrees like MBAs and PhDs, but otherwise it seems to be mostly a personal crusade to acquire the acumen and record required, with a dash of luck and timing, and a little bit of standing on the backs of lesser mortals in the corporate melee.

There are similarities between the military and the commercial in the way they share the phenomenon of the triumphal passage of the self-designated Conqueror of the Universe. As a keen proponent of equality and diversity, let me make clear that although this is more often attributed in legend to the male of the species, there is no doubt that neither the public nor the private sector have any shortfall of ladies who are determined to mark their passage to the stars in bloody stiletto marks on the backs of anyone littering their path. It was also certainly true for a few hundred of the most recent years that the military was pretty much a sport just for boys, but this is not the case now any more than it was in ancient times. Anyway, the point is that in every walk of life a small percentage of people are crystal clear in their own mind that they are going to take charge and it's only a question of time and aggression before everybody else cooperates in this.

This approach actually works in many cases as a combination of some talent, a lot of confidence, a really thick skin and, above all, unshakeable determination to succeed – it really can be the winning recipe that secures a senior leadership role and thrives in it. This can often be to the greater benefit of everybody else, even if only accidentally. No doubt you and I can both point to people we know who fit this bill, they are well ensconced running a big chunk of public or commercial life – or indeed entire countries, even countries convinced they are constitutionally and culturally immune to allowing madness and unrestrained toss-pottery to take the helm.

In the military it has always been the case that a small number who joined as junior officers have carried with them for their entire service the solid conviction that they will be the greatest commander on the battlefield in the history of war. A few of these were comprehensively delusional and quite rapidly found that the practical aspects of realizing their ambition were entirely beyond their meagre powers. It is quite hard to convince those who do need convincing that you are ready to command an army if you are always the wheezy one at the back of the run, the one most likely to hit only fresh air or own foot when handed a rifle, and psychologically incapable of reading a map even in daylight. If to this winning combo are added a clear predisposition to commit genocide at the drop of a hat and unshakeable enthusiasm for hurling one's comrades against machine guns the other side of slow walk across a huge ploughed field, then the future will swiftly be brighter in another profession.

Some who share the dream of supreme command turn out to be filled only with immense youthful enthusiasm and little actual talent, though even this is worth more than leadership by hot air generators or vessels of densely packed shit. The enthusiasm does tend to diminish once in gritty contact with real life in uniform: the amount of work that is actually required to excel as a professional soldier; the requirement for tolerance of boredom and stupidity in some settings; and the misery of garrison life when posted to the end of the known world on a major's pay.

If the youthfully enthusiastic officer doesn't quite grasp the profound limitations of the last of these rapidly enough, their fragrant other half is generally not slow in pointing it out. That promise of a massive porticoed residence, smoothly serviced by ranks of liveried staff that featured quite prominently in the underpinnings of the marriage vows, is unfulfilled by a wide margin if home is actually a leaky, minging quarter in Bulford with a view of the tank workshops. This is the point at which the lady of the house explains how a glittering military future is to be sacrificed for the substantial prizes of duty manager work in a reasonably large branch of Waitrose.

But there are the others, the genuinely and unshakeably born to lead and incapable of moderating that with any shred of self-doubt, who will stay. Some prosper in junior officer training by being really, genuinely outstanding in every respect. They will out-polish, out-iron, out-march, out-run, out-shoot, out-shout, and out-bullshit everybody else – and likely also to make sure that it is they alone who successfully court, win and supply a high-decibel rogering to whomsoever is in the Sandhurst eye as the girl most sought-after for a seeing-to. So indomitable is their determination and spirit that not even the cruel drudgery of a Cold War – or far worse, no war – soldering can deflect their vaulting ambition.

Remarkably, at some point these thrusters almost invariably acquire a spouse who entirely subscribes to 'The Mission', a perfect union for storming through the thirty-year conquest of an army from within. This was particularly true in the days when an officer's wife was expected to accompany her husband to any far-flung post (indeed it was their calling so to do, as there was no question of an independent career) and expected to be the leader, teacher, social worker, and shop steward for the wives of the men her husband commanded. Any young officer who thought that the fragrant Mrs X didn't know Major X's precise location in the army list and had metaphorically biro'd this onto her own forehead was in grave danger of being fatally bayoneted by a glance over the pre-dinner snifters for failing to register that true greatness is at hand.

Even in the early days of my own service the seating of officers' ladies at formal occasions in the mess was more emotionally and politically charged than many national revolutions. Many husbands have spent the rest of the weekend after a Dinner Night locked in the cellar for failing to advance their (lawfully wedded) loved-one closer to the giant silver centrepiece that graphically reproduces the slaughter of the regiment at a vital point in its illustrious history. This icon marks the spot where profound and career-enhancing proximity to the commanding officer's ear is to be exploited over several glasses of Chateau Collapso. It doesn't seem very likely that spousal seating plans can cause quite so much turmoil in most commercial settings, although I bet there are some long-established city and legal institutions where the scope for unrest is still pretty big?

There is more common ground between the military and many civilian professions in the way the future most senior leadership is chosen from thirty years out, by drawing only on the pack of people who were selected at the start of their careers and chosen only for their abilities as a junior leader. There are of course many similarities at the core of leadership between the requirements at basic shopfloor level and the requirements of senior military command or in the boardroom of a major enterprise. Integrity, loyalty, the ability to think under pressure, belief in setting a personal example, selflessness, and courage – especially moral – would all seem to be pre-requisite at any level. On the other hand, there are also very many different qualities and skills needed at different levels, so selecting only for leadership of a platoon (thirty people) is not obviously the best filter for choosing a supreme commander (2 million).

In the military, a young man or woman fresh from university who is selected for a military commission has been chosen for their ability to lead a small group, perhaps thirty, and to thrive in their chosen environment at sea, on land, or in the air as a junior practitioner. In the army, for example, this means that they hopefully learn to be competent in the field doing all the things that come with soldiering. This includes being quite physically fit, basically waterproof, content to live off vile food for long periods, and able to learn and execute a fairly wide range of skills and drills at the head of their little command. So they need to: shoot reasonably straight; know what to do when shot at (which may well involve flattening themselves into the earth at lightning speed and digging frantically with their nipples); talk on the radio without coming across like a Dalek; be pretty good at first aid – especially in the face of really grisly traumatic injury; hold the map the right way up even when lost; and know how to work out and issue clear instructions to their band to expedite them towards a fiery death with the appropriate wash of military jargon.

Pretty much the same must be true of a newbie lawyer, accountant, surveyor, insurance broker, banker, baker, doctor etc, etc? Presumably, on entering these professions there are some things that you have to learn to do and some ways of behaving that set you up specifically to be a net contributor at entry level? I guess they may be a bit more narrowly cast, certainly not involving the unlimited liability of the armed forces, but no less important to establishing a junior leadership position. It seems to be common to all occupations that everybody is chosen for their competitive ability at shopfloor level and nobody is chosen because they will lead the whole thing in thirty years' time?

In many ways this makes tonnes of sense, everybody enters via the same route and has the opportunity to develop over time into a middle and then a senior leader. As they go along this journey, they acquire a combination of education, training and experience, the expertise and intuition they need to succeed at different levels. What emerges at the top will certainly have stamina, a great deal of experience and many great stories of learning by cock-up. On the other hand, what if the people who really would be ideal as senior leaders don't much fancy or can't pass the bar for a place as a junior leader?

What if the best potential senior leaders do make it in at the bottom but then find they are so unfulfilled by flogging around for years in the weeds that they give up and try their hand at something else which they think will unlock their talents more freely? My own sense of the military is that quite a lot of the top talent bails out in their late twenties or early thirties because they feel the need to mate, breed, and own property, whilst at the same time the novelty of a junior military career has worn a little thin or – just as difficult – they have hugely enjoyed crunching the heads of the Queen's enemies at sea, on land, or in the air and they don't much fancy being sent to command a desk for years where the only weapon to hand is a laptop. And let's face it, most military officers – there are exceptions – are better with pictures than words.

I wish to make it clear that I am not saying that the choice for the most senior military command appointments therefore defaults to the last remaining dunderhead still standing thirty years down the track, the last of the few just too thick to leave. Fortunately, and I'm going to cling to this thought quite tenaciously, throughout history there have always been enough really good people who are so fixated with military life that it never occurs to them that they should leave of their own accord, and this sentiment is reinforced by their being iteratively successful. Successful in this sense means that they succeeded in winning selection for promotion at maybe thirteen points in their career, won places on the coveted career courses at different levels, found their way by selection into the top posts for thrusting officers, got all the right top-flight recommendations in their annual appraisals, and managed to avoid getting caught for anything too regrettable of a professional, social, or personal nature along the way. Nonetheless, even having navigated all of this, there is no guarantee of a brilliant outcome for all once the winner is finally in the top seat.

One of the reasons for a mixed outcome in a military setting is that arrival in the most senior appointments is necessarily breaking new personal ground but also hostage to the unlocking of way too much ego. If we dip into military history here a bit and take the Second World War as an example, there were some exceptional leaders on all sides. To get appointed to command an entire navy, army or air force in a global conflict they had all shown great form and pointy elbows on the way up. But whilst on the way up, some of them had more than a sneaking suspicion that they were truly and absolutely destined for great things – sometimes concealing this thought and sometimes not. But once finally handed a major command as befitting their talents, some could not resist (or perhaps still distinguish) between what was the right thing to do and what was the right thing that brought them greater glory.

Just reading about the personal relationships between Montgomery, Eisenhower, Patton, Bradley and others as they led the forces of the 'free world' through France in 1944 illustrates how the decisions and operations that touched on the lives of literally millions of service men and women could be tilted by the personal ambition of a senior commander. They were without question great generals with great accomplishments, but they knew that only one of them would be ever the liberator of Paris or the conqueror of Berlin and whoever that was would have a better place in history than the ones that were stuck and forgotten in the woods outside. Of course, Charles de Gaulle made sure it looked as if he had liberated France single-handedly armed only with a pistol and a pout, and the Russians were in no doubt that only they were going to crush Berlin and they would do it in a style that atoned without mercy for the deaths of 20 million of their countrymen.

There is a particular thing about how the sort of 'alpha male' that is attracted to becoming a great military commander and finds himself atop a vast and obedient hierarchy succumbs to the temptation to assume the powers of omnipotence and omniscience. The degree to which this exists varies between different national military cultures, but I would judge that the bigger the armed forces and the further they are from having to actually fight, the greater the temptation of the senior leaders to get a massively big head and an ever more splendid, badge-festooned uniform. As a British 'Chief of Staff', I was 'compelled' to wear an aiguilette, a chunky bit of gold rope on my right shoulder with a thing on the end for attaching my horse to something solid.

Now that I reside in the Afterlife, one of the questions I ask myself periodically is whether the same fatal predisposition to ego-mania occurs amongst the leaders of very large companies? The answer, in short, is that of course it bloody does. It may not manifest itself in conquering entire nations at the cost of many lives and the destruction of the fabric of civilisation, but the risk of ego trumping the limits of role and reason is no less. This appears to manifest itself in the shape of bonuses demanded, debts leveraged, balance sheets emasculated, company jets misused, and mergers and acquisitions fantasized over. Just as an army is only loaned to its commander by the society that formed it, so a company belongs to its shareholders – and even if it's a private company or if it has supranational scale, it has responsibilities and obligations that are wider than merely filling the already bursting wallet of the bloke temporarily appointed to be in daily charge. I will remember this when I finally get a vast company to run.

Chapter 11

On Being a Major General

My Dear M,

After a testy couple of years spent bunging everybody in the army through Afghanistan and Iraq who had all the usual limbs intact (and a few who had parted with at least one but were still remarkably keen to get back into battle), I was in a very dangerous place in army career terms. The potential jump-up or not to major general would dictate quite a lot of what then happened to the rest of my life. Brigadiers are sometimes and not attractively labelled as the 'nearly men': the number of vacancies for the step up to two star rank was considerably smaller than the number of keen and talented candidates with their elbows stuck into each other's ribs. And by the time one reaches this point, the mid-forties or so, the opportunities to play rugby for England, strum guitar with Bruce Springsteen, or be the first to climb Everest backwards and naked were definitely thinning. I was extremely fortunate in that I had retained my full suite of Love God looks and physique, even though my time over 400m might be a tad longer than a couple of decades earlier.

So it was with immense, silent thanks and an ill-concealed dab of self-congratulation that I found myself stepping off a plane in Baghdad in June 2008 as a major general, the newly appointed deputy commanding general of Multi-National Corps Iraq (MNC(I)) – with the prospect of at least nine months 'doing the do' at the heart of an immense US-led military intervention. This was the height of what became known as 'the surge', the time when the US doubled down on the challenges after the 2003 invasion in order to establish some sort of working Iraq that could be left to fend for itself, neither slipping into interminable civil war nor falling under the hegemony of its grumpy and assertive neighbours.

For a British officer, joining a huge US force feels like moving from the worthy but incontrovertibly threadbare lower echelons of the UK's football league arrangements to join the senior management of Manchester United. The scale of things is essentially ten times greater than the present UK forces operate. Even if I thought I was pretty good at holding my own in British and European military circles, the size of what I was now joining was a whole new ball game.

That ball game required me to become a temporary honorary member of HQ XVIII Airborne Corps, which had arrived in Baghdad en masse a few weeks previously from Fort Bragg to assume the mantle of MNC(I). It had worked itself up into a proper froth of excitement over at least a year before deploying and expected to stay in Baghdad for fifteen months. Fifteen months in this role at the pace and complexity it proceeded at was a massive ask of commitment, physiology, and family. The HQ staff also knew that cracking the insurgency would determine to a very large extent the degree of success or failure of an iconic and clearly troubled campaign that dominated headlines for so much of the early years of this century.

That much I knew, this was a big deal, but what I had not really grasped was the reality of a headquarters some 3,000 people strong overseeing a force of around 150,000. I had certainly not grasped quite how different the approach to the work to be done was between US and European command styles. I was pretty much attuned to NATO-style rolling up for a spot of morning briefing (earnest staff pointing at a map) after a decent and leisurely breakfast. This might occasionally be preceded by some earlyish jerks/jogging to tune up the magnificence, but let's not overdo this. The briefing would be followed by a light programme of mostly visiting things 'on the battlefield' to cast a fatherly eye, dispense some wisdom whether needed or appreciated, and consume other people's biscuits. None of this would interfere with a sociable supper and then some moderate communing with rubbish films before nodding off in one's plastic containerized bedroom. This is, it became very clear, is not the American way of war.

My new US colleagues, highly able and immensely experienced without doubt, seemed to have an allergy to their own beds and a relationship with email that smacked of a psychotic fear of unanswered messages and a deep-seated fear of missing out. Their way was to drive the human physiology out to its limits and park there until they were finally allowed to go home. This partly explained why they liked to start the day before most Europeans even remotely considered easing themselves out from under the combat duvet, and this start simply has to involve grim jogging in circles of various sizes in the dark. Only then may they get back to the emails that they will have been curating only four hours before.

Any longer than five hours in bed would be considered illness or infer addiction to self-administered genital-based horizontal unpleasantness. For One Stars and above, food would be allowed but it must be delivered by an attentive assistant to the desk in a mess of congealed burger'n'fries. Time spent bimbling off to the vast dining facility (a vast cafeteria known as the DFAC, obviously) could be costed in messages not read or vital instructions neither received nor issued.

I did fear that I would have to conform to this nightmare, knowing full well that it would be misery. I was therefore delighted to find that as the only British general in the headquarters it would be widely assumed by many on the staff that I was present purely as some sort of coalition trophy wife. So long as I turned up to the major set pieces, there would be an awful lot of US-only stuff for which I carried the wrong passport and operated the wrong spelling to participate in. Amen to that.

On the other hand, the inner circle at the headquarters, led by the hugely able, charismatic and physically immense Lieutenant General Lloyd Austin (at the time of writing serving as the US Secretary of Defense), really did have things they wanted me to do where I might conceivably add something useful. They didn't have to do this, lesser men would have parked me in a gilded corner of the Al-Faw Palace with responsibility only for consuming more Ben & Jerry's than previously considered humanly possible, unless summoned to exhibit coalition warmth. I genuinely felt privileged and on notice to perform.

The thing they most wanted me to do was to be the senior bridge between a vast American force in the field and an equally large and active Iraqi army and police. The US side felt very much in charge of proceedings and held a simply huge amount of cash to keep things going. They were honestly imbued with the ambition that the Iraqi army could one day step up to take over the lead, and mostly convinced that that day was about a century off. On the other side of the arrangement, the Iraqi leadership felt that they had already taken back charge of the security of their own country and yet the Americans hung about and just kept cocking things up in their inimitable way. At least the US military had pots of money that could be stolen without much fuss. The Iraqis were cheerfully imbued with the ambition to see the Americans mostly confined to barracks or gone, having first handed over all their equipment, the money, and anything else that might be useful. The whiff of a family visa for life in California would always be popular, so best keep things cordial.

On the one hand, I would participate in the incredibly well resourced and comprehensively over-organized process that characterizes a huge US military machine in action. An unstoppable tidal wave of PowerPoint slides, each wrought to detailed perfection by expert font artistes, is applied to matters great and small. As this inexorably lights the way to truth and wisdom, I sometimes felt my last-minute interjections that there might be 'another way' (sometimes misconstrued as me hinting that the proposal under scrutiny was a crock of poo) were not much welcomed by the many who had toiled without pause for weeks to get to the nirvana of the golden 'recommendations' slide. Our common objective was that, after all this detailed analysis, decisions would be taken that US commanders in the field would then follow, asserting them to their Iraqi counterparts as the one true path.

On the other hand, around 300 yards away in the new Iraqi Ground Forces Command HQ, Lloyd Austin's counterpart, Lieutenant General Ali Ghaidan Majid – a man entirely and, I occasionally felt unreasonably, unencumbered by self-doubt – would stare at a (US-provided) map with a large number of Iraqi officers to see who knew the most families in the area under present consideration for Operation SECURE SOMETHING. This conversation was conducted in a sweaty fug of dodgy cigarettes and fuelled by tea laced with an arm's artery worth of sugar.

These gentlemen were schooled in the military ways of the Soviet Union, which requires that plans should only be lists of desirable outcomes, the units to be engaged, and all the stuff the US taxpayer must now, immediately and without question give to them. They would then head off to the area of operations to do what they always did in the way they always did it, despite an accompaniment of steely US advisers waving doctrine pamphlets and PowerPoint at them. The Iraqi generals made their own mind up about what was going to happen, passing this as instructions to their commanders to press on their American counterparts as the definitive expression of what was really going to happen next.

Sometimes the US and Iraqi plans coincided pretty well, sometimes both sides thought they were following the same instructions when actually they were massively different, and most often, each did what they felt they needed to do anyway and broadly things more or less worked out. This was just as well, some of the larger events I found myself in some sort of charge of required the work of upwards of 50,000 soldiers on the ground, facing some pretty resolute and gritty Al Qaeda-type opposition. With 150,000 US troops plus about the same in Iraqi soldiers spread across their own ten divisions covering the whole country, it was bound to be a bit chaotic anyway.

War is mostly chaos infused with brief moments of terror and long intervals of utter boredom, but Iraq at this time was far from straightforward. There was a serious dispute between the US and the many Iraqis who were not fond of being occupied, even though many did not mourn the passing of Saddam Hussein and his regime. Almost a working majority of the Sunni Arabs did realize that the best way to get their lives back was to help drive down the insurgency, an insurgency mostly fuelled by fellow Sunni Arabs who were still deeply aggrieved at events post-2003. The majority view was helpful.

The hardest nut to crack here was Al Qaeda, who had benefited greatly in terms of spleen and know-how by absorbing many of the former very able officers of Saddam Hussein's army summarily ejected from their careers and income in 2003. This was not helpful at all. Leading the charge against them, were the Shia Arabs – mostly from the south – who were thrilled now to be in the ascendancy in government. Although they knew that a stable future required a fair sharing of power with their Sunni brothers, they really struggled with finding the will to get on with this after so long feeling, not unreasonably, very left out and oppressed. The lack of will to share power was very unhelpful.

There were many other Shia who were far from interested in an accommodation with the Sunna and implacably opposed to the US being in their midst (mostly but not exclusively for faith-based objections, with a dash of habit). They were in the closest of arrangements with their activist neighbours in Iran, for whom the US and the UK were respectively Satan Major and Minor incarnate. This was really unhelpful.

In the middle of all of this were the Iraqi Kurds, as hostile to the insurgency as they were ambitious about carving out an independent Kurdish state, which all flavours of Arab and most of the neighbouring countries, were determined never to permit. This played out in a country with a wrecked economy and some deep scars from recent and ancient historical events, so it was no great surprise that there was still a lot of death and destruction every day. It didn't feel like a global market for holiday homes was about to burst out in Iraq.

In the Iraqi army (to which I provided daily marriage guidance in their constantly fraying relationship with the US military) there were some divisions and brigades that were distinctly Sunni, some firmly Shia and some almost completely Kurdish. They all vaguely subscribed to the idea of 'Iraq', but with very different conceptions of how the detail would work. Nor was it always clear where the boundaries were really drawn. Some of my brother Iraqi generals would spend much of the working week railing at the awkwardness of their Kurdish comrades and then head off for the weekend to the cooler, calmer setting of their weekend house in the Kurdish regional capital, Erbil.

The one thing that did seem to be a common thread was the ingrained enthusiasm for official corruption. Well out of sight of our understanding of how things really worked, a massive web existed of jobs being sold and exploited for the positional authority and control over resources that they conferred. Some of this meant ripping off mostly the US taxpayer, which was more than just theoretically unreasonable as this money was sustaining the entire ship of state. Some of this, to which I objected personally far more, involved Iraqi commanders thieving the money that was meant to provide decent food and blankets for their own soldiers. That should get a chap shunned in the officers' mess forever.

This period coincided, as work like this often does, with another round of trying to establish a decent electoral cycle. In this case it was the Iraqi provincial elections that were on the radar. Having previously been party to similar exercises in Bosnia, Kosovo and Afghanistan, I was correct to anticipate that there would be an obsessive focus on running the polling day, when what was really needed was a robust process that starts with candidate and voter registration and ends with the installation of the leaders and officials who have legitimately won the ballot. This is about nine months of hard labour, not a couple of busy days ferrying tamper-free ballot boxes about. It could hardly be a surprise that politics at this time in Iraq was dominated by identity rather than issues, so voting would be mostly about entrenching sectarian fault-lines. This is not to say that people were not aggrieved by the state of crumbling and weak government services all undermined by endemic corruption, as well as the heat and the flies, but there was just no confidence to let go of faith, tribe, geography, and family in order to coalesce differently around fixing these kinds of issues.

No one was in any doubt that if the election could be stolen it would be, so the attention to detail in arranging a fair and transparent process was assiduous – a total balls-ache in fact. Our particular part was to provide security for polling and to transport completed ballots to the counting venues. This ought to be pretty straightforward given the numbers of police and soldiers available, but the agony over the precise arrangements in contested areas was profound.

It really mattered which sort of police stood closest to the polling building and which flavour of military formed the next and successive rings: the detail underpinned how the ballot could either be stolen (prolific stuffing of boxes with forged votes being the fave) or maintained as free and fair. Most factions favoured establishing their own stuffing arrangements, only grudgingly exceeding to a neutral outcome if they couldn't get away with it. Tension was particularly sharp where Kurd met Arab on the complicated territorial fault-lines between these communities. The hours and hours of negotiation at senior general level about who would stand precisely where, armed with what, and with exactly what provision for food and beverages, remains with me now as one of the low points of what was otherwise a very stimulating chapter from a professional point of view.

Having arrived in June I was able to repeat in full the joys of an Iraqi summer, this time in the drier heat of central Iraq – exchanging the 2003 misery of humidity in Basra for the 2008 occasional orifice-filling doses of huge dust storms in Baghdad. It was always baking hot, so much so that walking about outside in the heat of August was frankly best avoided. This was not because I was a wuss, my principal Iraqi interlocutors in the Ministry of Defence downtown in the Green Zone needed no advice on the virtues of avoiding outdoor activity in the middle of the day. They were masters of assuming a horizontal position somewhere cool and dark until the worst had passed. Weeks might pass.

It transpired that an important mark of seniority and power was to have in one's office an air conditioning unit so powerful it could cool Hell. It was essential to run these things at maximum output and to be seated right next to it. This indicated one had truly arrived in Iraqi military circles. I found transiting from 50 degrees Centigrade in the shade outside to −15 degrees centigrade in their offices presented a major dressing conundrum, quite apart from the toll on the health of my loveliness. I think it took about three months to establish such good personal relationships that I could ask them cordially to 'turn the fucking thing off' without impugning their manhood. By this time, I was being charmingly referred to as 'Abu Naji', a long-standing nickname for the British in Iraq. It refers to the name of the driver of the Iraqi monarch, Ghazi bin Faisal, who had allegedly murdered his master and faked a car accident. From such a low base even I hoped to prosper.

There were some days when it was so hot that on arriving back in the optimistically named Camp Victory from either being roasted in a helicopter or fried in an armoured vehicle (even there always clad in enough helmet and body armour to defeat utterly Mr Toyota's finest air conditioning), the best thing to do was to remove boots and walk otherwise clothed into the shower. I should point out that as the British Deputy Commanding General I was gloriously quartered in a villa by the artificial lake that graced the Al-Faw Palace complex, so my showering exigencies were not communal. War with an en suite shithouse is pretty cool actually.

I was never sure what the previous purpose of the villa had been, although it still had some of the furniture and features associated with Arab-style social excess. There was quite a lot of scummy fake gold trimming and the beds could accommodate half a platoon of willing participants resolutely unlocking the secrets of the crowd-based chapters of the Kama Sutra. It was at least quiet and cool, although when we discovered that the entire electricity supply was earthed only to a nail in an outside wall, my suspicions were re-affirmed that the workmanship Saddam Hussein had presumably paid for in whippings and free mud was not top notch. I was grateful not to be electrocuted by my own shower, a fate which did actually befall some US servicemen in facilities elsewhere.

Having a hand on a military operation of this scale and intensity was without doubt one of the highlights of my service, and of course very different indeed from the life I now lead in the commercial world. I know where my heart is, but nothing lasts forever. I am clearer from a degree of retrospection about the lessons of this experience, even quite basic things like not conflating activity (personal or institutional) with substance, and the imperative for leaders to sustain themselves for as long as it takes to win. There are few prizes just for effort or covering half the course. Like other campaigns, one of the repeat lessons was that there are some things that cannot be solved quickly no matter how much force, money, or hope is applied, they just have to be managed until they bore themselves to a conclusion.

My American comrades were extraordinarily able and tough soldiers, but their punishing regime drained creativity and ambition as months of sleepless routine wore them out. This never meant that they could not rise to the occasion, and there were certainly some occasions to rise to. There was nonetheless a growing resistance as the weeks passed to unpick an exhaustively complex plan when the circumstances changed or to consider a different strategic angle. This could be ascribed in part at least to being permanently knackered. This is a good illustration of why any CEO should get more sleep and time free of dross than anyone else in the firm.

I undoubtedly learned most from Lloyd Austin himself. He bore the full weight of an enormous command with the seriousness it demanded without ever seeming burdened. Never losing sight of the bigger picture either in Iraq or at home in the US was a big win. As an A-grade veteran American airborne warrior he had seen enough blood and shooting to intuitively know what really mattered. It is also quite a skill to be able to tolerate and not be deflected by all the fluff that comes with the span of authority he held. Unlike many very senior military leaders and commercial equivalents, he was particularly good at working out what decisions he personally needed to take and when he needed to take them, leaving as much of the rest as possible to others – and kicking their ass if they didn't fill their part. He wouldn't be rushed into premature action or decision just to clear his inbox or TDL. Most of all, even though XVIII Airborne Corps had invested well over a year in forming their master plan for how they would crack the problem of Iraq, as their time in Baghdad wore on and things changed, he did see that the whole vast enterprise would have to adjust with it. The arrival of President Obama on the scene was also quite a big clue.

As an outsider, I was extraordinarily well-absorbed by this huge American machine, and as an outsider I was also in a privileged position to see how relationships between very senior American leaders were managed without being 'on the pitch' in career terms. It was inevitable that American division level commanders, the two-star generals responsible for very large and difficult parts of the country, would have their own thoughtful views of what needed to be done and the priorities that this required. It would have been a miracle, and a miracle that rarely occurred, if these views had coincided exactly with the position of the Corps Headquarters set over them. It meant that there would be some very robust debates between senior leaders and sometimes some very firm instructions were issued that were far from welcomed by the recipient.

It was also very clear that the US Army and the US Marine Corps take quite different views of how the world works and the relative importance that each should play in it. This is a debate that has run, cat v dog, for generations and will never end. Mostly that is a good thing, a bit of institutional competitive rivalry is healthy – the visceral hatred rather less so.

In Iraq, the disputes about priorities, actions and resources would sometimes result in quite a lot of chuntering at me by my two-star divisional commander peers. As a neutral, non-US figure in the Corps headquarters I could be an escape valve for steam or a discreet conduit for a re-engage, but never to the extent that decisions made and communicated were not faithfully enacted even when unwelcome. How different this is to what I sometimes observe in parts of UK government and commerce, where instructions are simply ignored if the recipient doesn't think that they are the right ones or they just can't be arsed. It also illustrated how there is no law that says you have to like the people that you work with, but you do have to work with them to the best of one's ability.

By the time I left Baghdad in around April 2009, I knew that my next billet as a major general would be in Germany as chief of staff of the headquarters of the Allied Rapid Reaction Corps (ARRC), which is still today one of the major contributions that the UK makes to NATO's high readiness forces. UK provides the HQ framework and support, some fourteen other nations produce members of staff, the whole thing then being located in the Cold War relic of the British joint headquarters near Mönchengladbach. This was built on a swamp in 1952 by West Germany as the Cold War was warming up nicely, with the idea that it might last twenty-five years.

Fifty years later the buildings were excusably past their best, but still housing quite a vibrant British-led community with post offices, schools, and a NAAFI shop selling marmite. The NAAFI understood its mission to be to take the very best that UK supermarkets can offer, throw it all away and stick the remaining lowest common denominators on the shelf at a healthy mark-up. On the other hand, it did provide service families with the kind of stuff that made them feel at home, and avoided them having to brave German supermarkets with their complicated approach to sausages and obsessive addiction to asparagus. The IRA had gone to the trouble of bombing the Rheindahlen Camp NAAFI twice (in 1973 and 1987), even without the provocation of shopping there very much themselves.

My interest in the ARRC's geography in 2009 was rather limited because I knew that one of my major tasks was to move the whole thing out of Germany to a new home near Gloucester, which is where it is now. I thought I would be in Germany for a year, followed by perhaps two years in lovely Gloucestershire. This was a very pleasant prospect indeed, a job like this is very largely devoted to the proper business of soldiering in NATO with pleasingly large fantasy forces to manoeuvre around big maps. The ARRC was mostly, but not exclusively, focused on Russia being beastly on the fringes of NATO, although there had been major excursions in the 1990s to Bosnia and then Kosovo, and in 2005 an epic tour in Kabul. With a bit of luck, in my view, something catastrophic would happen in the world and we would be off again.

In the absence of catastrophe, there would certainly be a pretty dry series of large military exercises and other forms of training to work through, none of which involved any actual death other than through cirrhosis of the liver. Indeed, the greater risks would come from occasionally losing a bit of sleep and – much more frequently – pigging-out on the catering that seems to come with any large NATO enterprise. This all sounded right up my street, an impression more than endorsed on arrival by my first interactions with a lively and thoughtful international body of officers. A week studying the Second World War campaign in Italy in the warm spring sunshine of the Amalfi coast seemed to me to be heaps better than more boiling in my own juices in Baghdad.

So it was with total confidence that one sunny afternoon in September, having been in Germany for hardly three months, I was sitting in the garden of the rather nice house in Wegberg that came with the job, clad in my cycling attire with sporty bicycle ready to go close by. I was waiting for the call from the Military Secretary that would affirm, as fully expected, that any idea that had been floated somewhere that I should immediately stop what I was doing and proceed in haste to Kabul and a completely different job was clearly ridiculous. I had been away in Iraq for about nine months, packed for Germany the day I got back and then arrived as Chief of Staff HQ ARRC about a month after that. The ARRC was a big deal for NATO, changing chief of staff again so quickly would play badly, and the move to UK was a major development. Continuity was key. Thirty minutes later I was on the way to Afghanistan via something of a panic handover to my successor starting in the Departures lounge in Heathrow Terminal Five, another rushed exit from UK to join HQ ISAF once more.

The same Graeme Lamb who had commanded the 3rd Division during the excitement of Iraq in the latter half of 2003 was now a recently retired lieutenant general contracted in a personal conspiracy with General Stan McChrystal of the US, the new commander in Afghanistan, to work out how to ease the Taliban out of fighting. This was essentially a reprise in different trousers of the 'Sunni Awakening' that they had engineered in Baghdad to separate (successfully) the many more moderate Sunni Arabs from Al Qaeda. I was apparently not just the man for the job in the Afghan version of this box set, but also the only possible man for the job – clearly flattering, but essentially cobblers.

To be honest, this was the first and only time that I arrived in an operational theatre pretty much wishing that I was not. Baghdad had been quite hard work and the four months in Germany had been fun, so the prospect of perhaps a year of more military compound life was not immediately appealing. Having travelled for something like thirty-six hours to get from RAF Brize Norton to Kabul, I arrived in the middle of a chilly early winter night. I was not at my most generous of spirit; it was three in the morning and the good people of Kabul were either asleep or still burning excrement. As I walked into the plastic container that would be home for the duration, the floor shifted under the considerable weight of me and all my clobber, thereby causing the shitty glass on the shelf above the clearly well-used grotty little sink to drop into it and break into a zillion pieces – each needing to be hand-picked out. That just about summed things up at the time.

I was clearly not the first leader to be dispatched to do something at a time when they would prefer not, and in the military the doctrine of 'unlimited liability' applies from day one. So this comes with the territory. None of my personal reluctance to be doing this job at that time could infect either the task at hand or the team that was slowly forming up, but I didn't do a perfect job of remaining calm when getting started was handicapped by so many daft obstacles. 'Forming up' turned out to be quite a grand description of the tiny band that was present at the start: the local enthusiasm for launching this adventure had run well ahead of NATO's will and bureaucracy to resource.

As no doubt many others have encountered in their own endeavours, once a big bureaucracy has finally lined up all its paperclips, getting things like telephones and chairs is so much easier than in my new life in commercial start-up land, where every penny counts. But if that big bureaucracy is still at the 'Who The Fuck Are You' (WTFAY) stage, then every single thing is difficult. I found in Kabul that we were still some way from achieving WTFAY status. WTFAY status would be big progress. So my new role kicked off with stealing unattended furniture from around the camp, kidnapping spare laptops and begging for phones from the local Special Forces types. They didn't seem to need to account for these things in triplicate, each signed with the blood of a newly sacrificed child flown in specially for that purpose by a NATO accredited supplier of 'sacrificial children, document assurance for the use of'.

The job, it turned out, was to establish the Force Reintegration Cell (FRIC) to fulfil the not entirely straightforward proposition of constructing such an attractive offer that many of the junior Taliban cohort would pack in the shooting in exchange for many dollars and some wives and go back to subsistence farming for pennies in their home villages. In return, they would have to give us at least one of their more care-worn weapons (the good ones of course would be buried somewhere close to hand) in return for the prospect of training, a job, somewhere to live, regular money, and a quite important undertaking that their neighbours would not slaughter them in their new beds over all the recent unpleasantness. It presupposed that departure could be accomplished in such a way that those Taliban who still wanted to fight (and there were really loads of them) could accommodate the departure of their erstwhile comrades and not shoot them in the face at the farewell drinks.

The good news was that there was money to buy this, perhaps $5 billion from Japan. The less good news was first, none of the aforementioned attractions – the training/job/houses/money/security – yet existed. Second, nor was there any sign that giving up was seen as a brilliant wheeze in the ranks of the Taliban. Third, even if some Taliban really did want to jack it in, there were plenty of figures in the *international* effort across Afghanistan who thought this was basically all madness. This included some who would not rest until every last member of the Taliban had been publicly eviscerated with a rusty nail, such were their scars of war. Fourth, some powerful figures saw our scheme as an unwelcome and very premature intrusion into the business of making a tonne of cash out of perpetuating the conflict. Fifth, the well-established international habit of only very slowly and very badly implementing plans that might one day contribute to a peaceful outcome did not radiate much hope that we would be different.

So I found myself in loose charge of Stan McChrystal's side bet that a way could be found to end the fighting that did not mean either first engineering the military defeat of the Taliban (which was probably not possible without laying waste to a lot of northern Pakistan) or building up Afghan security forces so that they were completely ready to take on the fight (which would only be possible if the US taxpayer stumped up billions of dollars a year for eternity).

I also found myself resident once more in the camp that I had first built from scratch in 2001, when the original form of the ISAF was born. The camp that I had imagined would never need to harbour more than about 350 people on a less than glamorous extended military camping expedition for no more than six months. It was now home to about 2,000 souls in its eighth year of plumbing trauma. The tents were mostly gone and in their place was a city of plastic-cube buildings and some biggish sheds for things like eating and exercising. There really wasn't much more geography locally available, the place was busting at the seams.

In common with other extended NATO interventions, a 'village' of different 'National Support Elements' had been created by troop contributors to provide a home from home for their staff. These are a bit like embassies, regarded as sovereign turf with each applying their own view of what was sensible in terms of the availability of food and alcohol to offer. The food offered for sale was a welcome change to the comprehensive but dull menu in the main 'Dining Facility', but the booze was a source of constant friction.

My American colleagues are subject to General Order Number One from the moment they left US soil, which means no alcohol will touch their lips until they arrive back home. Actually, nothing other than US rations touches their lips as GO No1 appears to exclude all forms of amusement other than digital. My European colleagues did not think that serving overseas at great and imminent risk from rocket, mortar, bomb, shell and bullet need in any way cause them to go on the wagon for the duration. There were rules that intended moderation would apply, but these were on occasion interpreted with quite some elasticity, based on the number of people found from time to time face down in the camp streets completely shitfaced.

The UK approach to this, a recipe applied in most other similar settings, was the 'two can rule': one may have alcohol on certain occasions when 'standing down' was permitted, at the rate of no more than two cans of beer per person. Two cans that would be very carefully supervised in distribution to ensure that no one person became the repository of a lot of other people's cans as soon as outrageous sums of money changed hands.

It may sound daft, but things like different national views on a beer in settings like Kabul form part of the leadership challenge of keeping a coalition of many nations together. My own view, then and now, is that trying to please as many people as possible by allowing for variations and hoping for restraint does not sit well with the real exigencies of military service in difficult places. Far better to have a single, clear ruling that many people will not like but can acknowledge is clear and fair: no drinking in an operational theatre. In fact, it only took one very difficult evening in Kabul with a way less than satisfactory response to a very challenging operational situation from a few over-socialized staff to ensure that the rules were made considerably sharper and clearer.

As the FRIC work began, I found that the single greatest hope for the Taliban reintegration ambition was the appointment of Mohammed Masoom Stanekzai as the Afghan official responsible for the programme. He had four great virtues for this role: he was trusted by the president, he had no political base and so threatened nobody in the hierarchy, he was genuinely motivated by the desire to see Afghanistan emerge as a healthy unitary state, and he was very well versed in the sheer scumminess of politics in the region and the immense limitations of the international community, especially the UN, in making a tangible difference. He knew how hopeless people and institutions can be whilst also knowing full well that there was no alternative but to forge on with them. He had gathered around him a tiny team of people that he trusted, which was a pity because some were loyal but utterly useless and others made up for what they lacked in loyalty by taking uselessness to even greater heights of bewildering incompetence.

This is pretty much how all these gigs work. This is an Afghan problem which has an Afghan lead and has to be designed and executed in a way that Afghans will accept. However, the Afghan staff in the lead have almost none of the formal skills in things like planning and communication that would allow them to be effective, nor do they have a single bean with which to fund their ambitions. Worst, they will not be divorced from a tradition of government which essentially endorses that the duty of an appointment holder is to siphon off as much cash as possible for their own benefit. This usually starts with a black Mercedes and some very poor taste furniture at home.

Taking corruption to the next level requires travel to somewhere with many shops, like Dubai, in order to convert stolen cash into watches, man jewellery, and – for the spectacularly well-oiled – waterside apartments. In Afghanistan the cash funnels operated in stereo: entering stage left were the gushes of dollars from the expansive Afghan opium industry and from stage right came the tidal wave of cash from the international community in one form or another. Minister Stanekzai just didn't do any of this, but it was always apparent that we would both have to work hard to keep both Afghan and some UN staff fingers off our $5 billion, should we ever get to the point where we could start to draw down on it. A scorned woman has nothing on the fury of a war zone contractor whose snout is being kept out of the latest trough.

The other, more discreet, part of my role was to try to engender a conversation with the senior leadership of the Taliban, without whom this thing will never end. This is obviously a bigger and harder deal than trying to encourage youngsters to come out of the trenches and go home. It is a much harder deal indeed when these people really don't think that the fighting has run its course. Having a safe haven too is a bit of an insurgency match-winner, and the Taliban could retreat to the remoter parts of northern Pakistan, based in part on a fractious and uncertain relationship with Pakistan's intelligence service. The Taliban then and now could match the genuine popular support for improving Afghan authorities by pointing to the looming certainty that they will be abandoned by the US and its co-travellers sooner rather than later. Only the outsiders have deadlines.

The Taliban also knew very well that the international presence might change conditions and opinion in the more built-up parts of the country, but there were still a lot of people elsewhere who did not want their careers in opium interfered with. They were others who were genuinely, viscerally ill-disposed to the Afghan government which kept robbing them, their hatred made worse by the government being partnered with foreign military who not only harboured Christian intent to proselytize but also bombed wedding parties at the drop of a hat. These were not especially propitious conditions for a project aimed at talking about a peaceful resolution, even after ten years of this round of Afghan fighting. And at the time of writing, it is still the case that nobody under the age of forty-six in Afghanistan has lived in a country that was not at war in one way or another.

The tragedy always is that for as long as it takes the leadership of opposing factions in Afghanistan to find a path to the discussion that will result in accommodation and power-sharing, people on all sides will be hurt and killed. My own experience has been that where the lid comes off major tensions, such as in Northern Ireland, the Balkans, Iraq, and Afghanistan, even if it was thought at the start that the issue would be resolved by force quite quickly, about a generation will pass before something passing for peaceful normality returns. It is rarely brought about by force of arms, more likely by exhaustion, including exhaustion of the idea that there is a victory to be forced.

In these circumstances, quite a lot of my early tenure running the FRIC did seem to involve sitting on my ass in the grubby surroundings of HQ ISAF wrestling in one way or another with planning and resourcing the project. Although it was something that General McChrystal was personally invested in, many of his senior subordinates thought it was an utter waste of time. All they saw was an enemy that had plenty of fight left in it (and its leadership really was convinced that it would win in the end) and Afghan National Security Forces that were developing at what can best be described as a gentle pace, miles from being ready to stand alone as the international military left.

There was also some resistance to the idea that it is possible to fight with one hand whilst reaching out for negotiation with the other. There is certainly something here about how hard it is for the fighters to know that they are putting their lives on the line when others are trying to negotiate a way forward, but it is hardly unusual in the way that these things are managed. Very few fights end up as simple military victories. For all that I was pretty assertive in selling the potential of reintegration, I knew that I was met with polite scepticism and an inexhaustible capacity to consent and then evade anything that might have looked like helpful cooperation – with some noble exceptions.

By this time, late 2009, ISAF was very comprehensively underpinned by the US military. Although it was sheltered beneath a NATO label and very usefully augmented by substantial contributions from other NATO nations, the fact was that the US called the shots. This was to do with a lot more than the huge military effort, so much of everything else was propelled by US cash. Just across the road from HQ ISAF sat the large, new and very shiny US embassy that controlled the non-military bits of the campaign under some heavy hitting diplomatic leadership. It was possible that the US military view and the US civilian view might very usefully coincide but achieving this was – it seemed to me – quite elusive. On some occasions the loathing expressed by US soldiers for their own diplomats was only exceeded by their instinctive hatred for the US Marine Corps. The distaste and suspicion all seemed quite mutual anyway, and yet rarely got in the way of things once good manners prevailed – and instructions came from the White House.

After a while, there was quite a lot to be done outside the fence of HQ ISAF, either travelling around Afghanistan to speak to senior military leaders or in Kabul itself meeting with Afghans and other elements of the international presence in the city. Moving around Kabul had become far more painful and constrained than even moving around the central zone in Baghdad in 2003. It required a full close protection team (two armoured vehicles manned by very competent and heavily armed Royal Military Police close protection operators) to make astonishingly slow progress on the roads between the HQ and various embassies and ministries, due to the proliferation of armed checkpoints sometimes every 100 metres. It was often literally quicker to walk, but that was also thought to be too risky. There had been and still are frighteningly large bombs in the centre of Kabul from time to time courtesy of ISIS, Taliban, or other like-minded killers of random citizenry, despite all the security. So much so that by the time of my final visits in around 2016 even the driving had been banned in favour of the world's shortest (and most expensive) helicopter rides.

Each embassy reflected its own national characteristics and its own interpretation of how close they were to certain death at the hands of insurgents at any moment. Some I don't think ever left their compounds and this – unsurprisingly – could lead to some googly-eyed stares and odd behaviour after a few months. I was closely interested in where nations had invested in catering that merited the death-defying drive to sample. I am pleased to report that the best breakfast was *of course* provided by the British Embassy in the ambassador's residence, lunch in any Scandinavian shop would include a lot of small dead fish despite being 1,000 miles from the nearest sea, but there was no beating the Japanese embassy for a fabulous, authentic Japanese dinner. No wonder they never left the compound, everything outside would have been a comparative disappointment.

My opportunity to continue to sample the international cuisine of war-torn Kabul in between efforts to reconcile the apparently irreconcilable, was cut short by another of those unexpected demands that cannot be resisted to go and do something else. There were obvious advantages of maintaining patient continuity in the evolution of the FRIC in its slowly maturing partnership with an Afghan effort that really was gaining in credence, capability, and reputation. So after only about five months on the job my successor was being sought. It would be fair to record that such a clearly premature departure was not enthusiastically received by General McChrystal and even precipitated a sharp intake of breath from Mr Stanekzai, but this was another case of the paymaster deciding where the piper was going to play. It was also another reminder that without commitment and sufficient endurance in quite complex senior leadership positions, the risk of a drop in progress and confidence will generally manifest. Butterflies are lovely to look at but not great at getting heavy lifting done. My successor served for a full eighteen months and stuff really got done.

Anyway, it turned out that I was heading to London to take up the role of the Assistant Chief of the General Staff (ACGS). This was the *primus inter pares* position of all the major generals in the British Army, the only one with a seat on the army board, operating as the chief of staff to the head of the army and a sort of army general manager. In this case the urgency was a combination of the incumbent moving on and up (always a good sign) and the onset of a long-awaited major defence review following the arrival of the Conservative government in the May 2010 general election.

If there was one thing I felt pretty confident about it was my understanding of the strategic environment in which the UK now found itself and in the complex art and science of current campaigns. This was helpful, but on the other hand quite a lot of the ACGS's role was about the detailed construction of the army's people, equipment, activity and support in a massive work known colloquially as 'the programme'. There are some officers who very successfully make an entire career in managing 'the programme', and there are others – like me – who had very successfully avoided this sort of wrestling over the previous twenty-five years. My 'O' level in maths and the sound bites dimly remembered from my Master's in Defence Administration ten years before were going to be sorely tested.

Things got off to a flying start: I shot back from Afghanistan and pretty much went straight up to London to begin situating myself for this new role, which included finding somewhere to live close to the MoD in London. Happily, it turned out that really quite a large apartment came with the post, not just any apartment but an apartment tucked into St James's Palace – right on The Mall. My two daughters, then of university age, were quick to see how this would enhance their social standing – and I was quick to see how it might work as a platform to deliver them rather better husband prospects than their form to date had suggested was likely.

So one sunny morning in May I was taken round my splendid new London home. It was easy to imagine how despite it very evidently being in a state of graceful falling down, with medieval plumbing arrangements and heating that would cause Greta Thunberg to spontaneously combust in rage, we were going to have a fab time. After many years of camping in shit-holes on the Queen's business I would now be walking to work across St James's Park to an actual office with a door (glass) in the Ministry of Defence that I could call my own. Needless to say, that same afternoon the phone rang and I was informed that very senior bean counters in the ministry had decided it was all too much to bear. The following day I was looking for a one-bed weekly-boarder arrangement within cycling range of the MoD. Not for the first time my enthusiasm for a rapid return to shithole camping was being swiftly rekindled as the reality of London cease-fire life dawned on me.

Looking back, being the ACGS during the 2010 defence review was by a comfortable distance one of the most miserable experiences of my military life. Being ACGS was great of course, having a whole army to tinker maladroitly with could only ever be a joy. But wrestling with the effects of post-2008 financial crisis-induced austerity with a government that saw how defence just didn't register as an issue with voters was fated to be a toss experience.

After the complex struggles of the Iraq and Afghan campaigns, many voters were minded to put defence far from their minds, no matter how hard people like me pointed at the different, deeper, darker potential perils of Putin's Russia, resurgent China, and a planet wracked by climate change. On the one hand there was an army that had really sweated to manage the demands of recent years and saw the review as the opportunity – long overdue – to secure the resources it needed to do these things properly and sustainably. On the other hand, there was a new Tory government that needed to slash public spending and really didn't want its army to do Afghanistan better, it wanted its army not to do Afghanistan at all.

So what ensued was a miserable experience of arguing daily, in that reasonable, complicated, and often price-dominated yet value-destructive way that the Ministry of Defence works, about how much smaller, less well equipped, and hollowed out the army could be. As is always the case in these reviews, there is bound to be a struggle between urgent rhetorical ambition of all sorts (which tends to be politically attractive and nobly described) and money (which tends to be less and later than the ambition demands). In 2010 the winner was always going to be money and that just meant that the gap between ambition and resources that every review creates was going to be immense in this case.

When faced (very often since 1945 in the British Army's case) with demands for cuts, all armed forces will either consciously or unconsciously default to preserving structure (numbers of people and equipment) at the expense of real substance like ammunition, buildings, engineering, training, and conditions of service related to pay. This is partly to maintain long-run ambition about size and capability, partly to preserve the shop window for the better days that will surely come (but haven't for about thirty years), and partly because hollowing out is largely invisible until tested by the arrival of a war that doesn't seem imminent.

Part of the game in a review is to 'put everything on the table', not just so that everything gets the same scrutiny but also to raise the spectre of cuts that no government will sell to itself or its voters. In our case the investment in good soldiers to do 'public duties'(aka the actually quite skilful marching about in front of places like Buckingham Palace) would seem to be less important than preserving the fighting power of what is meant to be after all *an army*.

Of course it would be possible to hire a production company to deliver a carefully scrutinized contract that would muster students and other itinerants into pastiche uniforms, supported by some suitably-trained musicians, and get them to be HM The Queen's ceremonial guard. The police do the security anyway. In fact, plenty of other countries do use rather lesser mortals than professional soldiers for their state ceremonial, it seems there are people who really enjoy this sort of thing: stamping their feet in time to a drum is undertaken with great vim. On the other hand, finding a defence minister who is brave enough to drive down The Mall and tell Her Majesty that we are closing down the Household Division, horses and all, and handing the work over to G4S has always proved tricky. Still, we can go cheerfully round this buoy every four years or so.

The summer of 2010 was dominated by iterative discussions about what would go – people, equipment, activity, and allowances were all given a scrub. The lowest point, as usual in these things, occurs in around August when politicians take their divinely conferred long summer leave (to bring the harvest in on their country estates) and head to a beach to write bitchy novels about each other. This leaves officials to continue the wrangling over cuts unfettered by politics but definitely shackled to the Treasury's view of a spreadsheet. The discussion becomes unlatched from what is politically doable and so all manner of complete ass is tested. No cut is too deep or too mad if it makes the spreadsheet add up.

Seasoned programmers know that this will play out: once ministers have exited their budgie smugglers and made a triumphal return to the capital most measures will quickly fail the hollow-laugh test and be abandoned. I was not a seasoned programmer and I smelt real stupidity and catastrophe, so they were at least four occasions when I went home on Friday knowing that I would have to resign the next week if the particular 'daft measure du jour' was accepted into the emerging plan. It was a very very close run thing, and it certainly did the army serious harm as a fighting institution, some of which has still to be corrected.

As is traditional, one way of balancing the books is to play Fantasy Efficiency. This means positing that some new technology, some new way of working, or the thinning out of supporting cast like civil servants, industry and 'non-essential' regular forces will take the trick as 'productivity' drives ever upward. What this means in the short term is that cuts don't have to be taken or can be programmed for a couple of years hence, because these efficiency measures will be so successfully implemented by the time the funding hole needs to disappear.

Some efficiency is of course sensible and necessary, no one will argue that pressure to be efficient isn't an essential aspect of good government. But in the circumstances of the 2010 review closing the gap meant adopting some efficiency measures that reduced quite important aspects of what an army needs to go to war to tokens and holograms. The attention here is always on the pointy end, particularly the infantry and the regiments that have existed, often for a few hundred years, that will go to the wall or suffer extinction by serial amalgamation. Simply because there is less political and public attention, the cuts that are made in dull but important things like engineering and logistics seem to pass without a murmur – but the fact is this is just as essential to a fighting machine as a bloke with a rifle.

There were also sharp lessons for me here in how government really works in this sort of review. I had anticipated that the Whitehall machine would produce many tonnes of learned papers on every conceivable aspect of the UK's defence and security. There was no disappointment on this score. A thrillingly comprehensive menu was constructed across government and then in even more exciting detail within the Ministry of Defence – no stone would be left unturned in the search for things to cut and things to pretend to switch investment to. Written to exacting deadlines by authors plucked from their daily roles and having quite a big career moment in the sun, the compendium that resulted was an exhaustive review of the entire defence firmament and its associated truths, untruths, prejudices and ambitions.

In the name of impartiality it was felt in the MoD that the obvious thing to do was to get someone who was able but who had no knowledge of the particular matter to adjudicate it. Sometimes this worked, and sometimes it produced some piss-poor paddling in very shallow waters, not even a face-in-the-water level of a deep-dive. It is also inevitable that some authors were trying to square a genuinely objective look with the expectation that they must write the answer that they think the powers-that-be wanted to see. Anyway, in playing the game, part of my role was to ensure that the army contributed as well as it could to all this stuff – in the expectation that it would matter in framing the outcome.

The honest truth, however, as in every review that I have since encountered, is that these papers are read by the circle of officials that wrote them and pretty much nobody else. There are simply too many of them, certainly too many words and not enough pictures for there to be any realistic prospect of them being read by the ministers who take the really difficult decisions the night before the results are announced. In any case, at the top of government the outcome of a review is broadly ordained before it gets going and so most senior effort goes into shoehorning the facts that emerge into the ordained narrative that existed at the start.

In addition, I learned the bureaucratic trick of using a key meeting as the fulcrum for a bundle of major decisions, ensuring that the meeting is too short and too overloaded with material to digest for any serious debate to occur. The many recommendations in the papers are then taken as agreed whether they were even discussed or not. There is a timetable to keep to after all. For the 2010 review it didn't really matter what else needed to be talked about because the Defence Board discussions simply could not break out of endless wibble about aircraft carriers, especially whether they should have a catapult with which to fling jets into the sky or a curly ramp at the end to do much the same for a different sort of jet. (They went for curly after a lot of dithering.)

In the end, after months of work and a great deal of institutional heartache, in 2010 the army knew that it would get a bit of a slashing. It wouldn't have mattered if Russia had chosen 2010 to march around the Baltic states in tanks laying waste to all in its path. Given the obsession with fixing the public finances – my thanks to all those bankers selling duff loans to each other with vim and impunity – this was about taking hits to defence. The size of the cuts were subject to some rhetorical window-dressing to pretty-up the truth that these were not 'unavoidable' cuts but some sort of rational strategic adjustment.

On the night before publication when it came down to the final conversations in 10 Downing Street, what actually happened was the usual political horse trading between the money and what politics would bear, including backbench opinion. This is the moment when eyes and assholes are screwed up to the max in order to find a bearable way forward. In addition to Herculean levels of efficiency targets (still not delivered ten years later) a plan to bail out the reductions in regular numbers by improving the reserves over about five years (which did make some sense) was telescoped into making the reductions and lobbing the job at the reserves almost overnight. This made no sense, but the fuss would be lost on most of the electorate and would die down quickly in the public eye.

Perhaps my greatest personal struggle in this review business was between what I thought was my duty, to answer the question I had been set by government, and the opinion of many of my military peers who thought the questions so ridiculous that I should substitute answers to questions that I had not been asked but should have been. I know many in business will recognize the similarity here with producing a competitive bid that answers the exam question set by the customer. On the one hand, it is important to introduce genuine innovation and advantage, and on the other the question set has to be answered, not least because those who are marking the answers are often the same process termites that set the question and for whom doing different or better is not necessarily appreciated.

So when I was asked whether a reduction of the army to a certain size would still allow it to fulfil a prescribed set of tasks, the honest answer had to be yes, even though that prescribed set of tasks was nowhere near the same as the list of what the army actually did, nor reflected what sustaining an army as an institution required, nor was anywhere close to recognizing how the strategic environment around the likes of Russia was becoming much more difficult. This complexity and reality, I felt, was an unwelcome factor in getting the spreadsheet to tally up at the money people wanted to pay for defence in 2010, so just best ignored – the electorate was neither wiser nor much interested.

It would also be fair to say that the experience in 2010 was a stark reminder of how little the British political class, that is the span of people who are bold enough to submit to election to Parliament, know much about or are really even remotely interested in defence and security. This reflects in combination: a generation of freedom from 'existential peril' since the Cold War rather inconveniently ended; the pain felt from recent campaigns in Iraq and Afghanistan; and mostly the truth that there are just far greater electoral stakes in economic and social issues.

That is not a bad place for a democracy to be for as long as it does not simply ignore how the world is changing and how it could bite the country in the ass. I found that complex defence decisions were decided on by ministers and officials (and there are exceptions of course) with a minimal grasp of what was involved or the issues at stake. I also found that decisions could be decided on by single-issue fanaticism based on the knowledge of just the one thing filling an already crowded mind. For all these reasons, and maybe I was just rubbish as ACGS anyway, but the 2010 review that needed to be a reset of UK defence and security as the post-Cold War era ended and something much more menacing began to replace it, was actually only a steepening of the trajectory of post-Cold War military decline based on what the government chose to afford according to their reading of public opinion. This is how democracies operate, of course, but it carries substantial risks for a very bad day at some point in the (near) future.

Chapter 12

Senior Generalship

My Dear M,

I had been told by the mighty that I should expect three glorious years continuing as a major general appointed as ACGS. This would give me plenty of time to take a prominent role in implementing the cuts that I had so magnificently helped heap upon the army in 2010. To my total joy this was not to be, as we rolled into early 2011 I met with the greatest good fortune of being promoted to lieutenant general (which felt really adult) and moving one floor down in the Ministry of Defence to take up the mantle of the extensively titled Deputy Chief of Defence Staff (Military Strategy and Operations).

This job changes its name roughly every three years to catch the mood of the moment, and in this case the Chief of Defence Staff of the day had a thing about 'Strategy', so that was going in the name one way or another. (He also tried really hard to introduce the notion of strategy to Mr Cameron and his playmates, but they were having none of it: a box of stuff with which to try and avoid being overwhelmed by events was more their thing – and they did get to choose.)

What the job always involved was taking responsibility for all UK military operations and planning at MoD level, including integrating that into the wider work of the Whitehall machine and key allies. Honestly, for me, this was like giving a chocoholic the keys to a Cadbury factory. Having just dabbled in the misery of juggling 'the programme' through a penal review I did know a bit more about how to do that, but I certainly didn't care to do it any more then when I started. I had spent what seemed like forever between 2001 and 2010 on various military interventions around the world, so I reckoned I had a pretty decent grip of the operational side of the business. Enough to bluff my way for a couple of exciting years in London anyway.

The two years that ensued were easily amongst the most stimulating of my professional life, despite the wear and tear of being 'always on'. Except when formally handed over (for things like leave) I was on a four-hour string to respond to any and all alarms. Of course, there were some elements that were a bit of a balls-ache, particularly the twisting agony of concluding combat operations in Afghanistan by the 2014 deadline.

This wasn't so much because ending a war by appointment rather than success is bound to have its limitations: we were, after all, deciding to stop and leave the rest of the fighting to our Afghan colleagues pretty much whether they were ready or not to pick up the full load without us. It was mostly tiresome because the government of the day was convinced that the military was going to drag its feet over finishing off and coming home, much preferring to sustain the attractive work we had fashioned for ourselves out there and all its attendant resources than put it all down and head back to barracks and a life of polishing our buttons. This standing suspicion meant that the very serious and practical business of handing over sensibly to the Afghan military and withdrawing our people and our staff in good and secure order was constantly ambushed by accusations of foot-dragging and PM-level whippings to go faster.

My part in this was to lead the argument at senior official level in Whitehall, leaving my three-star counterpart, the Chief of Joint Operations – the diminutive and irredeemably Yorkshire Marine Lieutenant General Sir David Capewell – to actually make the plan and tough it out in execution. This was my principal inoculation into the joys of Whitehall committee work, whereby some truly very clever and committed people across both Home and Foreign service come together to share their independent views of what was going on and needed to be done in a seamlessly connected effort. This conversation having been completed, they each returned to their departments to generally please themselves about what they actually did, just so long as their own ministers were kept happy and well fed with Tweets.

This British way of 'collegiate campaigning' does have the strengths of diversity and some degree of equifinality (people will try to find their own separate way towards a common goal), but it is also hardly necessarily the most efficient or effective way. The notion of independence also didn't seem to apply quite so much to the military because everyone had a view about what we should do as it was the most public and most expensive aspect of government work in the security arena. I also detected an annoying whiff of condescension.

I guess some of my colleagues felt that one would have to be a bit of a dunderhead to commit one's adult life to the military when they were so many proper jobs to do that would make better use of a lapsed grasp of elementary Latin. Worse, anyone – like me – who had stuck it out for decades probably needed some help in the brain department and should on no account truly breach the inner circle in the Whitehall Palaces of the Mighty. It wasn't as if I supported the idea that the military should choose what wars they fought – we would be forever shooting up France if that were so – but I did think I knew enough about industrial-scale violence to be of some help. On the other hand, when government rejected our proposals about the pace of withdrawal from Afghanistan and the military then duly obliged by jogging faster it did feed the predisposition that whippings were necessary. But going faster didn't often mean we were also doing our Afghan partners any favours.

I also found that when there is not very much going on in UK defence and security matters (i.e. no war of national survival) the need to decide on almost anything rapidly ascends the government machinery. Sometimes this makes sense, for example if a decision is going to play out in public and in Parliament, then ministers are bound to want to have their hand on the tiller. In other circumstances, what were really very mundane things: the routine targeting of shopfloor terrorists, where some patrols went etc, seemed to demand the personal attention of the Archbishop of Canterbury, the Dalai Lama, and every civil servant within 500m of 10 Downing Street. These decisions were generally well within the compass of the lieutenant colonel commanding on the spot. I could never be sure whether a major shooting war breaking out would moderate this habit. Maybe the enemy would oblige by bumping off some of the layers of non-decision-makers in the opening rounds.

The Whitehall institutional urge to find consensus, most especially when there is a very wide range of competing opinions (only some of which really matter – though in the spirit of collegiate campaigning it is impolite to point this out) meant that almost everything needed a mass of jibber-jabber. The inability to find that consensus without a race to the lowest common denominator would generally result in as little as possible being done without another meeting. Everyone could agree on that.

We were wrestling at this time with the birthing phase of the National Security Council (NSC) in the UK. The NSC brought together all the ministers who had an interest in the country's defence and security, which is a good thing. But there was never enough time to talk about some important matters that the members were generally (and mostly forgivably) completely unfamiliar with, which is a bad thing. What this essentially meant, I found, was that the Prime Minister of the day would turn up with a pre-cooked solution for the issue of the moment in his hand and this would be trumpeted at the end of a meeting of no minds after an hour's rushed and often cock discussion. Over time, it did improve the level of understanding and debate very gently. Nonetheless, the practice of asking ministers to bang out an opinion of what needed to be done at the start of the NSC meeting and only asking the expert officials in attendance at the end for their advice, did seem to me to be one way of expediting the more random outcomes.

I arrived in this post shortly after action had been taken to apply bombs to Libya in order to inhibit Mr Gaddafi's enthusiasm for crushing the opposition to him. As is so often the case, what started out as an urgent response – in this case to prevent Benghazi being overrun – spawned an ambition to carry on the good work and remove Mr Gaddafi and his regime. Libya was unusual as these outings go because for the first time for a very long time the US had elected not to be in the driving seat. We shouldn't overstate what this meant because without the continuing US support with: command and control facilities; surveillance in the sky to produce targets for air attack; and a lot of air to air refuelling capacity, it pretty much wouldn't have worked at all. There is a lot more to US leadership than a big bloke with lots of stars on his uniform always being on the telly. Nonetheless, as the actual bombs were mostly being dropped by a come-if-you-feel-like-it selection of NATO partners and some Gulf allies, it did feel a bit like being let out of the house on your own for the first time without your dad.

Coming at the end of Afghan combat operations and with the history of hard pounding in Iraq still very much in mind, the campaign in Libya was conditioned from the off by the thought that, whatever the situation was, it was not going to need – ever – British or US soldiers on the ground. Whilst this was basically the same kind of 'discretionary' intervention as Iraq or Afghanistan, the societal and therefore political appetite for expending blood and treasure on such an enterprise had evaporated.

This sort of reticence to get embroiled has happened before in history, for obvious reasons, and when it does it spurs on demand for finding other ways of doing military things successfully. In this case, it was accompanied by the bizarre yet attractive thought that somehow a whole-of-mankind length chapter of military history had really finished: boots on the ground would never be needed again. It would henceforth be quite enough to just precision-bomb the crap out of the opposition, with a dab of cyber-tinkering for wider interest and a bunch of deniable Special Forces types on the ground to jolly things along and point bombs at better targets from time to time. As a sure-fire winning strategy this is as daft in conception as it is tiresome to manage if people really think it will produce decisive results in big, sweaty issues.

Given the pain of Iraq and Afghanistan, I guess this way of thinking will likely persist for quite a long time, probably until the next genuinely existential threat appears and causes a reset of the appetite and imperative to fight 'red in tooth and claw' again. The peril to achieving a successful outcome in Libya was amplified by the same thought that ambushed affairs in Iraq in 2003: when the regime was toppled, no matter how much china had been broken in the process, there would be no stabilization effort – at least not by the people who had done the china-smashing.

As usual, the (obvious) risks existed that the virtues of dumping on Mr Gaddafi would be lost in a whole world of pain once the many powerful factions in Libya went into squabble overdrive to try and impose what happened next. There was mitigation on hand in the fond hope that the UN would arrive to save the day. The UN does sometimes do this, but only when it has had about a year's notice, when nations cough up the troops that are good enough to impose peace and stability whilst politics takes root, and when a lot of other countries stump up a tonne of cash. This is not an entirely implausible way out, but we knew not to hold our breath. So far, the UN has indeed sent some intelligent opinion to help.

Much of the summer of 2011 was spent wrestling with how bombing things in Libya would fix the problem. When things seem to be moving slowly the 'obvious answer' was to bomb more things more often, thereby ratcheting up the cost of opposition. There were two major obstacles to this: first, quite a lot of things that would really hurt were also actually illegal in terms of being militarily necessary, discriminate, and proportionate targets. Bombing an oil refinery so that Gaddafi's tanks run out of diesel sounds cool, but less so if the same refinery supplies the generators that keep hospitals functioning. Second, the business of bombing is actually more complicated than having a pilot pop over a target in a jet, take a look over the side and jettison 1000lbs of high-grade explosive.

There was not much of a shortage of jets, though it was still disappointing that some NATO members decided this affair was not for them and others really weren't much good at hitting anything that needed more than city sized accuracy. What there was, however, was a shortage of flying tankers, for some reason modern jets have fuel tanks the size of thimbles. This is perfect for air shows, not much use for winging about over a continent the size of Africa. The problem would have been greater still if Libya operated the sort of air defence system that countries like Russia and China can put together, because the tankers would then have to stay so far away that the jets' thimble-sized tank would limit targets to about the first 200m of Libyan beach.

Fortunately, Libyan air defences were not negligible but also not unbeatable. The US very helpfully biffed the more threatening parts anyway. The bigger challenge was that in order to bomb something you first have to find it. Doing that from the air or space needs big and expensive satellites or reconnaissance aircraft (including drones) which can survive against most air defence missiles and provide really high-grade imagery. Not many countries have these, certainly not all the countries that were willing to stump up jets to do the bombing. So one of the major limitations of ramping up the bombing campaign was that we didn't have enough means of finding things to strike. It also rather gave the lie to the thought that the US was not playing a major role just because it wasn't taking substantive charge. The US obviously has more satellites, reconnaissance aircraft, and flying petrol stations than anybody else.

An additional difficulty was the division between those NATO members and others who had air forces that could only do bombing by appointment (take off, fly to a point known in advance, bomb it, fly back) and those who did bombing as speed dating (fly to Libya, hang about in the sky, be directed to a new or moving target, bomb it accurately, go home). We needed more of the latter the more the Libyan opposition to NATO shifted about.

From a military point of view, it was much harder to defeat the opposition when they stopped being offensive and went into defensive mode. They were probably not Premier League standard in the business of fighting at scale, but they certainly knew how to string together a coherent defensive position with layers of resistance and well concealed reserves including things like tanks. Our Libyan freedom-fighting partners had far less formal training, indeed their approach to attacking was sometimes limited to deciding which pub car park to meet in, encouraging everyone to bring at least one gun and some sandwiches, and decide on the spot in which general direction the gang would then head, hoping not to get annihilated. This ad hoc approach could be helped out a bit by the odd bomb from NATO thousands of feet up in the sky, but it was not an easy gig for anybody to follow.

Once the regime was on the defensive it was much harder to find them and they had sufficient military competence on the ground that no amount of wishing could deplete. The things we could do to break the log-jam all required us to do more on the ground, such as deploy artillery, but that fell foul of the 'no BOG' rule (no Boots on the Ground). By August I was running out of ways of explaining that doing just more of the same thing would result in the same stalemate. Happily for us, our luck turned and enough of Mr Gaddafi's erstwhile supporters saw the advantages of parting company with him to join whatever the future would be. The game was then up for the regime.

The end of Mr Gaddafi and the jubilation in Tripoli gave a few senior politicians from Europe the opportunity to join a genuinely happy throng, dancing trousers on. What happened subsequently, as history records, was the predicted and predictable meltdown of government and all that goes with it as the major factions turned on each other to contest for the spoils of victory. There is no joy in pointing out that this was as foreseen as it is still bloody and messy when it happens, but still worth recording that making war well generally means being prepared to see things through – even though it will take longer and cost more than was forecast at the start. Stepping in as we did to make a difference at a crucial juncture seemed to be important. Stepping out once our immediate objective had been achieved and leaving behind a seething mess may be rational from a European perspective, but it has done many others no good at all.

The winding down of the Libyan intervention coincided with the winding up of arrangements for the London Olympics in summer 2012. You might be forgiven for asking what this had to do with the British Armed Forces, indeed that was the prevailing thought amongst most of Whitehall as they began to roll out the plans for supporting the Games. This was a festival of sport, a joyous international occasion and an opportunity to showcase Britain as its vibrant and hospitable best. Hard to see how British prowess at inflicting violence on an industrial scale fits into this. I entirely agreed, although there were bound to be one or two specialist things that the armed forces would do (as they normally do), like providing high-end and very specialist capability for counter-terrorism. We could also, very unusually for London, provide local air defence against nut jobs in microlights or helicopters, or attempts to fling high-street drones at the Games venues.

The idea that the Olympics was not a military festival was not shared universally in the armed forces at the time, where there is an entrenched predisposition to do some major marching about with large bands at any prominent national occasion. This institutional FOMO was often asserted and became tiresome for those who envisaged, for example, that the opening ceremony would be as far removed from anything martial as humanly possible. It would be important to celebrate what really made Britain great, which as it turned out included being brilliant at being ill and getting HM The Queen on the end of a parachute – all accompanied by a lot of swirly dancing and popular beat combo music that pleases a global, youthful ear. Hurrah for all that.

On the other hand, by early 2012 the military enthusiasm for overdoing planning, even worrying about plans that were entirely other people's business, was indicating that the arrangements the Home Office had for mass labour support looked a bit fragile. They needed around 20,000 people to inspect handbags and do unarmed perimeter security – almost none of whom had yet been identified, let alone trained and organized. Not to worry though, this is what manpower support organizations do well: they find large numbers of people with just enough limbs, cognitive life and language at the last minute to stick in luminous jackets with a photograph of themselves hung on their necks. Even the most egregious excuse for a human can rise to the occasion when well led and issued with a whistle. This is, after all, how a lot of British infantry has distinguished itself over the centuries.

As 2012 wore on, 'not to worry' became 'worry a bit', then 'worry a lot more', and finally 'worry with every fibre'. The more it became clear that the plans to find and organize this labour were falling behind the more the nerves in the highest political circles frayed: the London Olympics would be an administrative clusterfuck that no amount of razzamatazz at the opening ceremony could conceal.

The answer – obviously – was to backfill with sailors, soldiers, airmen, and marines. The total went from zero when the first enquiry was scornfully dismissed with a wave of the hand by the rest of Whitehall to around 18,000 when the Games opened. The last 3,000 were agreed in a slightly tetchy Cabinet committee meeting that I briefed only a week before the opening, and the rush to get them in place meant a lot of military folk spent their Olympics dossing on the floor of empty warehouses in London in between their shifts.

My hands-on part in this was actually very small, as my deputy Bob Judson (a famously loquacious Air Vice Marshall who was never going to be defeated by officialdom trying to talk him out) managed the day-to-day Whitehall battle, and the 'Standing Joint Commander UK' in the shape of General Sir Nick Parker led the 'force' from his army headquarters. It was actually quite touching to see the relief on the faces of ministers and officials when Nick Parker and his team imposed themselves on Games security and parts of its administration.

What it meant for thousands of members of the armed forces was that they had several weeks off being martial to be marshals at all the Games venues. None of this was going to challenge their skill or character, after all if you have won your place as a trained member of the armed forces you are going to be a natural at inspecting a handbag. What was really novel was that for very many people in the UK this was their first and indeed only encounter with a living member of their own armed forces.

Some, I think, were nervous at this prospect, perhaps assuming that they would be spread-eagled on the tarmac whilst each and all of their bodily cavities were given a proper rummage with the sharp end of an army pencil. They would then be given half an hour of instruction in marching and saluting before they were allowed to collect their ticket. What they actually found was a very engaging and healthy bunch of mostly young men and women very much enjoying spending some weeks in their capital. For many military folk it was their first visit to London, living as they normally did in various wildernesses in the UK and Europe.

The value in which the military were held during the Olympics extended to free travel on the London transport network. This might have helped some of them to get to work on time, but mostly it helped them enjoy the riches of the capital when not required for duty. We noticed that the buses that were provided to transfer them back from their Games venues to their temporary bedspaces at the end of the shift were increasingly unused. It became clear that many were losing no opportunity to strike up friendships over the briefest of introductions around handbag inspection. Most of the service personnel were male and mostly in their early twenties, therefore equipped with not only an immense amount of testosterone, but also testosterone inflamed by rigorous physical training and now on full alert as a consequence of the tsunami of international femininity (I acknowledge that all other options were also accommodated) that the Olympics had literally queueing to meet them.

A survey of the London birth rate in East London in spring 2013 would surely reveal that many fleeting introductions were converted to successful congress. Consistent with the history of all major military undertakings, not all of this attention to genitals-based community relations was well judged. The maintenance of local air defence missile cover over the Olympic stadium relied on equipment positioned on the top of several tower blocks. The operation of this vital capability might have been occasionally more certain if some of the operators had been less fastidious in enjoying the horizontal hospitality offered by some of the more accommodating residents.

This whole experience illustrated – hardly for the first time – that there really is something in the way that military organizations understand planning and orchestrating complex activities that is widely applicable (when sensibly done) to other parts of government. It also illustrated that many who work in government are strong at understanding their complex problems and in creating policy, but not schooled in converting that wisdom into action – certainly not against the clock in very novel circumstances. Yet despite this, the reluctance to call on the military to help in good time and allowing them to play to their strengths remains palpable today, in the UK anyway.

Sometimes this is the result of people being so caught up in the maelstrom of a major event such as large-scale flooding that just getting to tomorrow without collapsing (either personally or institutionally) is success. Sometimes it's a bit more disreputable: a big drama means a small group of senior people is having its moments in the sun and it's disinclined to share this shot at glory with random military types, who will only start bellowing and demand to take charge. The answer we need is more sophisticated than that.

Even in the context of the Olympics, one of the standing objections to military help was how the cost would be managed. There is also the question of the value of 'contingency': military commanders understand the imperative of holding capability in reserve in order to plug holes or reinforce success. Many politicians and civil servants understand only the imperative of efficiency, where everything is run essentially to the finest of margins and executed just in time. Contingency is just flab. So when people like me argue that the Olympics will be fine *provided everything in the plan works perfectly all the time*, I found that many of my peers in Whitehall thought that was an entirely reasonable proposition by which to proceed.

I freely confess I loved every day (almost) in the role of DCDS(MSO); having my hand on the entire spectrum of UK military strategy and activity was undoubtedly a professional high point. As it entailed a certain amount of jetting about the world to chew things over with my counterparts in the likes of the US, France, Germany, and Italy, there was some decent lunching to be done as well. There was some tinkering with money that came with the job, but nothing like the ass pain of the first water in my quite long enough stint as the army's Assistant Chief.

It also meant getting alongside the UK's National Security agencies, and although it wasn't the first time that I had worked closely with various strands of spy and spook, this job entailed being close to their senior leaders and making common cause, not least in things like cyber. The agencies (SIS, GCHQ, MI5 etc) are each really quite different in culture and organization, and to some degree they compete for attention, resources, and leadership. What they do is also really quite difficult and not just important but to some extent inevitably doomed to fail as they can't cover everything all the time. Nobody should fault their dedication or commitment to doing the best job they can in the circumstances. The defence and security of the UK involves a lot more than the armed forces.

There are fairly few truly standout moments in the life of one career officer in the British Armed Forces, partly because – as I hope this series of letters has affirmed – there is really quite a lot that makes most days quite special compared to the lives of many. *Not dying* as a result of proximity to shot and shell or in the fiery tangle of a helicopter landing badly remain significant moments in the minds of many military people. Nobody forgets the exuberant mix of misery and achievement that leads to successfully passing through initial officer training at Sandhurst. But one of the standouts for me has to be the day that you are told you are to be promoted to the highest rank, in my case general, and given charge of one of the major pillars of the armed forces that you have been part of for three decades. It also meant joining the 'Chiefs of Staff Committee' (the group of six senior officers that oversee all aspects of UK military affairs below ministerial level), command of some 23,000 people around the world, and the requirement to bring in a budget of billions on a sixpence every year. There really was quite a lot to think about and to get right. I became Commander of Joint Forces Command (JFC) in April 2013.

I expected that I would spend some of every day in this appointment explaining to people what the hell JFC was and why it mattered. I was right. No other armed forces in the world have quite the same construct, which is to create a sibling to the Royal Navy, Army, and Royal Air Force that takes charge of all the stuff that is common to them all and connects them up. Like any sibling relationship this is part love, part jealousy, and a lot of simply being stuck with each other. JFC could appear to be a bit of a bucket-of-bits to some, but underlying it was the common thread that each dimension brought something vital to UK defence and it was necessary – both better and cheaper – to corral them around a unifying purpose and accountability rather than have them wander around the defence firmament as stroppy orphans. It is called Strategic Command now.

So I took charge of: the Defence Intelligence Service, the operational command and control machinery focused on the Permanent Joint Headquarters ('PJHQ') located at Northwood; the standing overseas bases (the Falkland Islands, Cyprus, Gibraltar, Diego Garcia and latterly Bahrain); Special Forces 'capability' (its people, kit, training, development); the Defence Academy; operational logistics; the Defence Medical Services; and Defence Information Services (including acquisition). I found myself responsible for buying decisions stretching from satellites and anti-submarine aircraft to mobile phones, at a cost to the taxpayer of about £2.3 billion a year. Anyone ought to be able to do some damage with that, and with all the other things like pay my budget came to around £4.3 billion by 2016. Sounds a lot, but it was at least £500 milion a year short of what was needed to do all this stuff properly, and £1 billion short of being a transformative epic. This job was one of the few times in my life when I really wanted to be an American four star awash with dollars.

The other big part of this job was to join the gang known as the 'Chiefs of Staff', the group of four-star officers sitting at the apex of the UK Armed Forces for both operational and budgetary purposes. There once was a time when the Chiefs broadly decided what wars the UK should fight and how to fight them, announcing this to the Crown and Parliament and later submitting the bill. Indeed for centuries the navy and the army pretty much did their own thing and only came together to squabble over money or when the latter needed the former to give them a ride to wherever needed invading. As noted above, however, the NSC was created in 2010 and since then the Chiefs en masse have been kept at one remove from sitting with the Prime Minister to mull over the war du jour.

Nonetheless, my position as a chief of staff meant I would spend as much time lurking in the corridors of the Ministry of Defence as I would gracing the landscape of my command. Having to make this balance illuminated one of the core dilemmas of very senior leadership, which is that there will always be way, way more that needs to be done than there is the personal capacity to do it. It is very easy to be overcome by the sheer volume of concurrent issues or the weight of multiple decisions, each of which bear major consequences for real people and outcomes. As I have said elsewhere, the capacity to be the master of all the detail for which an officer has responsibility certainly expires on promotion to major general (two star). Anyone who isn't comfortable with a pretty ruthless approach to delegation, empowerment, and holding people to account will fail at that level. By four star it has to become the natural way of doing things, or the leader in question becomes a mental health casualty as well as a major liability to the defence of the nation. I am out of therapy now.

Given the elevated status of a four-star officer and the relatively short time in appointment (typically three years) it is entirely possible to simply sit on top of one's empire and enjoy the view and the ride. There will be plenty of ribbons to cut and plaques to unveil whilst dressed for tea with Queen Victoria. There will also be hordes of gifted subordinates (in my case five three-star officers and about twenty two-star officers) who will be only too willing to crack on without much guidance. Yet management by the accidental consensus of a galloping herd of energetic single-issue fanatics is rarely optimal.

I also found some people who thought that my job really was to tart about the military world, focusing on the martial equivalent of kissing babies and opening fetes. I certainly had the uniform for this, my ceremonial rig involved a massive frockcoat accoutred with all the gold dangly bits and hefty badges that Queen's Regulations endow. This rig has been unchanged for decades, ignoring not just climate change but also the advent of central heating. Wearing it indoors is a very sweaty experience indeed, leavened only by wearing something comfortable and inappropriate underneath – like my 'I'm Batman' T-shirt.

My command of the far-flung bits of the residual British military presence around the world was a licence to travel, albeit not usually to the places that the beautiful people normally choose. Travel meant a fight every time to avoid being crammed with the goats and drug mules right at the back of the plane going from one dusty shithole to another. The British civil service is at its happiest when ensuring senior military officers with the temerity to go further than Ealing arrive broken in body and spirit for a crammed visit programme as a result of ten hours stuck between migrant potato pickers many days away from their last bath.

The Falkland Islands are scenically fabulous, yet located at the other end of one eight-hour flight on a Royal Air Force equivalent of a flying trolley to Ascension Island, followed by another eight hours in the same machine to actually reach the Falklands. Ascension Island, being tropical, means removing as much clothing as possible for the four hours it takes the drivers to change seats, and the Falkland Islands are the global capital of wind, which means putting it all back on again.

The Falklands are the only place I have been to where the requirement is always to park a car with bonnet into the wind, because not doing so means that the door is certain to be ripped off and hurled at Argentina. With barely 3,000 inhabitants and over 500,000 sheep nobody should be surprised that life there feels quite cut off and a bit culturally narrow. I always loved going there. There seem to be only two topics of conversation that mattered: the price of flights to the UK and how the bastard Argentina keeps getting in the way of absolutely everything. Epping Forest in London will vote to be run from Buenos Aires before the Falkland Islanders do. If the oil and gas that are perpetually rumoured to lie within reach of the Falkland Islands are ever actually discovered and extracted, the Falkland Islanders will be able to buy several Epping Forests anyway. And perhaps Argentina too.

There were bigger issues to wrestle with in Cyprus, which once again now has a genuine strategic interest for the UK. There were some smaller issues in Gibraltar, and also an ancient naval fuel depot in Singapore to worry about. However, my runaway winner as a working destination was Diego Garcia in the Indian Ocean, which not only has considerable military import in what is becoming the 'Asian Century', but is also an environmental and ecological treasure. I had never seen a coconut crab before, capable of breaking open a coconut with its claws, and I quickly resolved never to see one within striking range of any of my limbs or appendages. Diego would be a perfect bolt-hole for any apocalypse-avoiding billionaire, were it not for the military exclusion zone that would have even the most oligarchic superyacht torpedoed.

As I was very ill-disposed to the idea of just being some sort of avuncular trophy leader, the greater part of my time at JFC was spent working out how to modernize and transform UK defence and security, based on my considered analysis that it was in most respects completely screwed. This position is the accrual of the twenty years that had elapsed since the end of the Cold War. That removed the sense of existential peril that normally keeps the armed forces match fit and resourced to stay properly competitive, which is today again essential given the onset of a much more challenging strategic environment (rise of China/lumpy Russia/climate change blah blah) and the implications of the Digital Age. I argued then – and argue still – that the Digital Age makes quite a lot of traditional military equipment and ways of operating pretty redundant, and certainly uncompetitive against armed forces that really do grasp what data, AI, robotics, autonomy, hypersonics, quantum, and all the related stuff will do for them.

Here was an interesting leadership conundrum. We were starting from the premise that JFC was there to coordinate the bits and bobs that the navy, army, and air force needed to have in common, but without anyone thinking this should intrude on their primacy when it came to money or preserving cherished and iconic things like the ships and fast jets that people could rush about in filled with proper military earnestness. There was actually quite a lot to do to join up the bits and bobs into something that was cohesive and benefited from some unity of purpose and a firm, single hand on the money. That took about the first year of my tenure.

The second year was about becoming competitive in arguing for what 'defence' in the current time needed and swinging the resources to get it. In the first instance this meant winning the argument for about an extra £1 billion over four years. Framing this argument as the senior leader entailed me convincing a talented inner circle of senior staff to align with something new and different, often undoing plans that had taken many man-years of ass pain to put together. Only they could be master of the process and the detail that would convert new thought into actual plans and budgets. Along the way there would be a dollop of consent and evade to manage, more in the 'frozen middle' of the organization than at the top or the bottom.

Far worse was trying to heave the MoD bureaucracy that owned project scrutiny and money into enabling change rather than conduct an internal ambush of it. This relied on some gifted civil servants smelling the coffee and seeing how things could be done differently, some risks taken, and new stuff managed. For every one of those enlightened ones I could find five more, military and civilian, who had a book of rules that was inviolate, a spreadsheet that was beautifully balanced and cast in iron, and a vital engagement with their navel fluff to keep.

By my third and final year, with the 2015 Security and refence review looming, it was time to advance from being competitive to being transformative. I had had time enough to work out what I thought needed to be done and I knew I would not get many better chances to see if it could fly. Scarred as I was by my previous encounters with defence reviews I applied two important (to me) lessons: first, my team and I got our ideas organized well in advance of the match starting. We knew that once the review kick-off whistle was blown we would be immediately sucked into knife fights in a phone box with the other big chunks of defence. So we took the time to go away (as it happens, only to the Royal School of Artillery not the sun-kissed beach resorts of a decent corporate away-fest) and construct an agenda which became 'Warfare in the Information Age' (WITIA).

I am struck today as I transcend the Afterlife by how few senior leaders make time just for thinking about the big decisions that are actually the most important part of their job, and regard 'away days' as occasions for juggling their spreadsheets or jiggling with the 'strategy' of how to get better numbers by the end of next week. In fact, as Commander JFC, I made a point of heading off at least once a month on my own to somewhere like the library at the Queen's College Oxford (where I am blessed to be an Honorary Fellow, having turned in one of the worst PPE performances in academic history some years ago). This day was just thinking time, devoted entirely to staring at an ornate ceiling and sketching out the bigger aspects of my responsibilities. Needless to say, other than it gave them a quiet day to themselves, the staff learned to fear these days for the wanton destruction that would follow for their carefully laid and now suddenly obsolete plans. But somebody has to take charge of the madness and I figured that was done best by me.

The second lesson I applied was that there was no point having brilliant ideas (and we did) if no one knew of them or they remained unpersuaded. In this particular case, my challenge was to convince the top of the shop in the Ministry of Defence that WITIA was really their conception and needed to form the heart of the instructions that they would impose on the rest of defence in the way that the future of defence was mapped out.

This was never going to be easy because it would undermine faith and investment in some iconic equipment and ways of working, and in which a tonne of money and political capital (some of it dressed up as industrial strategy) had been sunk. So we set about mounting a consistent and powerful argument over and over again in the months leading up to the 2015 review and during it. I recall saying at the outset to my team that this is the sort of argument that we should expect to lose on at least the first three occasions that we mounted it, but by the fourth or fifth outing we would begin to get traction as other people started to make the case for us. If they also wanted to claim it as their own thinking, fine by me. Even then, the forces of darkness assembled against this transformation would remain powerful and total success for us was very unlikely.

In a nutshell, I ended up asking for about £17 billion to be swung to JFC over four years and success was measured by an outcome of about £13 billion. Some of the things I didn't win I am still arguing for now, from the other side of the fence, and winning. Time and timing matter here: the time to make profound changes had clearly arrived, but the time it would take to secure them would have to be judged as a long process rather than a one-off event.

It was not as if we could simply throw away quite a lot of defence inventory and magic up the new stuff overnight. Some of the new stuff only existed in our heads then, but it is now starting to fly, drive, and sail – as well as hum, or whatever noise data in the cloud makes.

In and around all this transformative stuff, I freely confess I was having an absolute ball as Commander JFC. Pretty much wherever I went there would be an audience that felt obliged to listen politely or display some other form of cooperative appreciation. There were vital trips to places like Hawaii to spend a couple of days masquerading as the UK Chief of Defence, at one of those conferences which involve speed dating international peers in twenty-minute bursts of cobblers interposed between giant banquets. Even some of that required the skill and nerve that only comes with senior command, such as holding a conversation at length with a senior general from a small Asian country whose interpreter possibly spoke his own language reasonably well but had no ostensible grasp of any known form of English at all. I know I was talking about missile defence or some such, which I do well, but I also know that the only words that ended up in common understanding during the whole session were 'Manchester United'.

One of the joys of this post was the ability to live within walking distance of the shop, courtesy of a government-owned house that came with the job. In this case it was the fairly massive portals of Admiralty House in Northwood, which had been in uninterrupted military use since the 1950s. Over the intervening sixty years or so it would be fair to say that the enthusiasm of the public purse to sustain housing for senior military leaders had transitioned from reasonably generous, down through judicious parsimony, to grudging minimal sustainment. The house itself was pretty huge, built for a time when there were staff positioned in every corner, but now as much as possible was neglected until it actually fell down or became irredeemably disease ridden. The low point was discovering that the commercial grade kitchen installed some thirty years earlier was a unique combination of steel, gas, and electricity in a timebomb just waiting for me to try and sort some toast out.

Nevertheless, with wife, family, the remaining help, and pretty free access to my less than bottomless wallet, we were able to host some senior overseas visitors and some memorable public events. This included one thoroughly charming visiting senior leader and his wife from Latin America whose baggage train consisted of more than twenty pieces managed by two of his countrymen who were there only to carry it and iron the contents. His wife entered house legend by refusing to step out onto the gravel terrace because of the risk that the terrain would inflict terminal damage on her shoes, which we established were worth more than the terrace anyway. Visiting senior US leaders required armed police patrols in the grounds at night, though if Al Qaeda had found its way there it would be competing with the foxes who regarded it as their own once the sun went down. Even Al Qaeda has no answer to fox shit on their sandals.

Making all this work relied a lot on the small coterie of people who ran my office and my administration, including the house. My ability to focus on what I was really meant to do was significant, enhanced by having bright and highly dedicated people managing the flow of business in all directions. There is something of an art to surrendering one's diary to others, relying on them to fill it intelligently and to make sure the preparations were on the money. Choosing good people to do this was well worth the effort and creating a high-tempo, high-calibre close-knit team was a very significant 'force multiplier'. I thought it was important that this team was directed by me rather than I became its prisoner, but within the bounds of good taste in public service we also became good friends and had quite a laugh (sometimes at ourselves but mostly at other people).

And then everybody needs a Doyle when they do this sort of job. Kevin Doyle had joined me first in Germany at HQ ARRC as a newly appointed sergeant, where he took on the massive task of keeping the official house, the tonne of kit, and driving the staff car. Not having to worry about any of these things, apart from giving him some advance sense of what might be needed to reduce his reliance on clairvoyance or telepathy, liberated several hours a day for more productive output from me. The Doyle stuck with me through the ensuing years in Afghanistan, where he became the driver of my close protection team, two jobs in London – one of which where we were both existed permanently at four hours' notice for a drama, and finally in Northwood where he took on the work that had historically been done by at least three people full time. An old-fashioned idea maybe, but massively efficient and effective.

For all these reasons, when the day came in 2016 that my tenure as commander came to an end there was almost no way to prepare for the shock. On the final morning in post, I woke up responsible for over £4 billion and more than 20,000 people, supported by an excellent private office and administrative team that drove the car and sorted out uniforms. By the afternoon of that day I was standing in the driveway of my own house with only an iPhone to help. Suddenly, there is no position or authority, nobody cramming the diary with interesting things to do, and nobody to conspire with about how to take down the forces of darkness at home or abroad.

This is how the Afterlife starts. A vocation that has lasted forty years is over and suddenly there is the prospect of at least twenty-five years useful life before potentially becoming a bit too crumbly and dribbly. My strong preference is still to avoid going out in a downward spiral of physical and mental collapse, much preferring to be given the opportunity to have a – maybe quite doddery – last charge naked and armed only with a bayonet at the most insidious enemies of the Crown on that day. We'll see.

As I know now, nobody like me ever thinks about what happens when the uniform comes off for the last time. It just hits them in the face. What then happens is always going to be different, personally I doubt that it will ever feel as good, but it need not be without purpose, challenge, or merit – and it might even feel quite liberating. It is certainly different.

Index

Accommodation (place), 39, 45–6, 71, 88, 98, 177
   service families' accommodation, 98
Accommodation/power sharing, see Power sharing
Accommodation services, 33
ACGS, see Assistant Chief General Staff
Admiralty House, 211
Advance Party, see British Army Advance Party
Aeroplanes, 33, 37, 55–7, 65, 67–8, 75, 77, 122, 132, 154, 173, 207
Afghan aristocracy, 78
Afghan army, 78, 87
Afghan government, 64, 69, 187
Afghan jurisdiction, see Jurisdiction
Afghan Northern Alliance, 64
Afghan police, see Police
Afghan president, see Karzai, President-Designate
Afghanistan/Afghan, 22, 31, 56–7, 60–1, 64–88, 103, 106–109, 111, 148, 152–4, 162–3, 178, 182–4, 186–91, 195–9, 212
Africa/African, 23, 29, 60, 111, 200
Afterlife, 89, 96, 129, 137, 153, 156, 159, 165, 171, 210, 213
Agincourt, 26
   Battle of, 26
Agriculture, 2, 7, 10
AI, see Artificial Intelligence
Air defence missiles, see Missiles
Air forces, 6, 12–3, 21, 23, 25, 38, 47–9, 68, 78, 97, 104, 107, 124, 132–3, 151, 156, 160–1, 164, 171, 201, 206, 208–209
Airborne Corps, see United States Army
Aircraft, 10, 23, 36, 38–9, 42, 48, 54–7, 67, 70, 77, 79–80, 124, 133, 149, 151, 154, 193, 200–202, 205–206
Aircraft carriers, 48, 193

Airmen, 22, 60, 160, 162–4, 203
AK-47s (guns), see Guns
Al Muthanna, Iraq, 109–110
Al Qaeda, 56, 62, 65, 74, 176–7, 183, 212
ALARP, see As Low As Reasonably Practical
Aleppo, Syria, 10
Al-Faw Palace, Baghdad, 175, 179
Algorithms, 46, 133, 136, 140
Alliances, 40, 64, 72, 74
Allied forces, 67, 85, 196, 199
Allied Rapid Reaction Corps (ARRC), 181–2, 212
   Headquarters, 181–2, 212
Allied zone, 10
   see also Green Zone
Allies, see Allied forces
Alps, The, 75
Amalfi Coast, Italy, 182
Amazon (online company), 105
Amazonian, 91
America/American, see United States of America
American comrades, see Comrades
American counterparts, see Counterparts
American Embassy, 188–9
American troops, see Troops
Americas, The, 23
Ammunition, 5, 11, 37, 51, 63, 66, 87–8, 105, 128, 165, 191
Amsterdam, The Netherlands, 91
Anglo-German cooperation, 33
Anti-submarine aircraft, 206
Anti-tank mines, 11
Anti-tank missiles, see Missiles
Arabs, 18, 95, 110, 114, 116, 176–9, 183
   Shia, 110, 114, 177
   Sunni, 110, 176–7, 183
Arctic kit, 39, 57, 67

Index

Argentina, 208
Aristocracy, see Afghan aristocracy
Armagh, Northern Ireland, 122, 142–3, 151
   South Armagh, 122, 142–3, 151
Armed forces, 21–4, 40, 48, 51, 59, 66, 91, 96, 98, 104, 116–7, 129, 135, 152, 156, 165, 170–1, 191, 202–203, 205–206, 208–209
Armed Forces Committee, see House of Commons
Armed forces of the Third Reich, see Wehrmacht
Armed police, see Police
Armoured vehicles, 3, 6–7, 11, 32, 40, 61, 106, 125, 179, 188
Arms Plot Move, 3
Army, 2–9, 11–5, 18, 21–5, 32–3, 36–7, 39, 42–4, 46–8, 50, 53–4, 62–4, 66, 70, 73, 78, 82–3, 85–7, 91, 97, 99–100, 103–107, 110–11, 113, 115, 119, 121, 124, 128, 133, 141, 143, 148, 150, 152–6, 158–9, 161, 164, 167–9, 171–3, 175, 177, 181, 188–94, 196, 203, 205–206, 209
Army Cadet Force, 42
Army Manual of Dinner Night Procedure, 8
Army Staff College, 24–5, 31, 39, 42, 50, 70, 96, 104
ARRC, see Allied Rapid Reaction Corps
Artificial Intelligence, 94, 129, 133, 136, 209
Artillery, 5–6, 10–13, 15, 37, 48–9, 64, 68, 106, 113, 125–9, 136, 141, 149, 201
   field, 64
   light, 49
   rocket artillery, 6
      long-range, 6
Artillery guns, see Guns
Artillery shells, 12
As Low As Reasonably Practical (ALARP), 151
Ascension Island, 208
Asia/Asian, 57, 65, 79–80, 208, 211
Assistant Chief General Staff (ACGS), 189–90, 195–6
Asylum, 44
Atlantic, 23, 160
   North Atlantic, 160

ATMs (cash machines), 148
Attaché, 155
Attack helicopters, see Helicopters
Austin, Lieutenant General Lloyd, 175–6, 180
Australasia, 58
Australia/Australian, 75, 110
Austria, 33
Autobahn (Germany), 1
Autonomous guns, see Guns
Autonomous machines, 140
Autonomous weapons, see Weapons
Autonomy, 133–5, 140, 209

BA, see British Airways
Baghdad, Iraq, 18, 54–5, 62, 105, 109, 116–7, 119, 122, 173–5, 178–83, 188
   airport, 62
Bagram, Afghanistan, 67–8, 70, 72
Bahamas, 75
Bahrain, 206
Balkans, The, 24–6, 29, 41, 54, 64, 111, 115, 148–9, 187
Banja Luka, 54
   airstrip, 54
BAOR, see British Army of the Rhine
   garrison, see British Army of the Rhine
Barracks, 2, 6, 9, 21, 32, 46, 73, 175, 197
Barrons, General Sir Richard, *passim*
   becoming major general, 173–195
   leadership, 156–172
   nearly becoming general, 141–155
Basra, Iraq, 54, 107, 109–16, 118–9, 122, 145, 153, 178
   airport, 112
BATES, see Battlefield Artillery Engagement System
Battle groups, 43, 49, 52, 110
Battlefield Artillery Engagement System (BATES), 127–30
Battlefields, 105, 161, 167, 174
Battles, 9–12, 14, 23, 25–6, 28, 38, 48, 54, 75–6, 90, 105, 123, 144, 153, 156, 158, 160, 162–4, 173, 203
Belfast, 122, 142–5, 147–8, 151
   East Belfast, 148
Belgium/Belgian, 11–2, 53, 60–2, 105, 162
Belize, 59

Belsen (Bergen-Belsen) concentration camp, 2
Benghazi, Libya, 199
Bergen-Hohne, Germany, 2, 19, 64–5
Berkshire, England, 86, 158–60, 168, 205
Berlin, Germany, 10, 20–3, 171
   Berlin Wall, 22–3
   fall of, 22–3
Bezos, Jeff, 140
BHC, *see* Bosnia and Herzegovina Command
Big Pharma, 136
bin Faisal, Ghazi, 179
bin Laden, Osama, 65
Bioscience, 135–6, 138
Birmingham, England, 106
Blackadder (television series), 157
Blackhawk helicopters, *see* Helicopters
Blair, Prime Minster Tony, 24
Blogs, 6
Bluetooth, 6
Blyton, Enid, 92
BMWs, 29, 144
Boeing, 56–8, 67, 79
   C-17, 56–8, 67, 79
Bolt, Usain, 82
Bonaparte, Napoleon/Napoléon, 23, 67, 109
Bomb disposal, 99
Bombs/bombers/bombings, 6, 10, 13, 22–3, 56, 62, 67, 78, 94, 99, 108, 119–21, 128, 143, 146–8, 182, 185, 187–8, 199–201
Bosnia/Bosnian, *see* Bosnia and Herzegovina
Bosnia and Herzegovina/Bosnian, 30–52, 54–6, 59, 61, 76, 102, 123, 178, 182
   Eastern Bosnia, 50
Bosnia and Herzegovina Command (BHC), 52
   Headquarters, 52
Bosnian Croats, 36, 47, 49
Bosnian Muslims, *see* Muslims
Bosnian Serb forces, 37, 47, 49, 55
Bosnian Serbs, 35–7, 47, 49, 55
Boston, USA, 132
Botox, 90
Bradley, Omar Nelson, 171
Bravery, 7, 11, 13, 30, 39, 43, 102, 122, 140, 162, 192

Bremer, Paul, 118–9
Bremerhaven, Germany, 65
Brexit, 2
Brigade Headquarters, 33, 100
Britain/British, 2, 4–5, 7, 9–15, 17, 20–4, 30, 36, 38–41, 44–5, 48–54, 58, 60–1, 64, 66, 71, 75–7, 79, 82, 85, 87, 95, 97, 104–105, 107–109, 111–2, 117, 119–20, 124–5, 127, 141, 143, 152–3, 155, 157–9, 162–3, 171, 173, 175, 179, 181, 189, 191, 195, 197, 199, 202–203, 205, 207
   Battle of, 23
BRITFOR, 41
   Headquarters, 41
British Air Force, *see* Royal Air Force
British Airways (BA), 39
British Ambassador, 189
   residence, 189
British armed forces, 21, 23, 40, 51, 66, 202, 205–206
British Army, 2, 4–5, 9–14, 21–2, 25, 39, 43–4, 47–8, 50, 53, 62, 64–6, 73, 79, 81, 83, 86, 99, 105–107, 109–110, 112, 116, 118–9, 122, 124, 141–3, 153, 155, 158–60, 183, 188–9, 191
   1 (UK) Armoured Division, 25, 105–107, 109, 112, 116
   3 (UK) Mechanized Division, 65–6, 81, 105, 107, 112, 183
      Headquarters, 65–6, 81, 105
   19 Mechanized Brigade, 109–110, 118–9
   16 Air Assault Brigade, 73
   38 Engineer Regiment, 110
   39 Infantry Brigade, 122, 141
   Cheshire Regiment, 43, 47
      1 Battalion, 43
   I British Corps, 10–14, 21
   Royal Army Ordnance Corps, 99
   Royal Electrical and Mechanical Engineers, 79, 83, 99
   Royal Horse Artillery, 2, 64, 99
      1 Regiment, 2
      3 Regiment, 64
   Royal Logistic Corps, 99
   Royal Marines, 160
   Royal Military Police, 62, 86, 188
   Territorial Army, 12–3
   see also Royal Military Academy Sandhurst

British Army Advance Party, 39
British Army of the Rhine (BAOR), 2, 5, 12, 20, 98, 125
    garrison, 98
British Embassy, 71, 79, 189
    Kabul, 71
British Empire, 23
British engineering, *see* Engineering
British forces, 51, 66, 202, 205
British government, 4, 12, 22–3, 34, 41, 44, 50–1, 66, 69, 71, 79–81, 88, 91, 95, 102, 109, 117, 130–1, 138–40, 152, 155, 160, 179, 181, 189–98, 202–205, 207, 209–211
    Cabinet, 138, 197–8, 203
        Cabinet Committee, 203
        meetings, 203
    Chancellor of the Exchequer, 41
    Downing Street (No. 10), London, 109, 194, 198
    HM Revenue and Customs (HMRC), 130–1
    Home Office (HO), 44, 202
    Ministry of Defence (MoD), 4, 41, 44, 79, 81, 91, 95, 102, 117, 131, 152, 179, 190–1, 193, 196, 207, 209–210
    Treasury, 23, 192
    Whitehall, 44, 193, 196–8, 202–203, 205
British Headquarters, 54
British military, 7, 20, 24, 41, 49, 60–1, 108, 152, 162, 207
British military history, 7
British navy, *see* Royal Navy
British Parliament, 47, 195, 198, 206
British prime ministers, *see* Blair and Cameron
British soldiers, 11, 107, 120, 162
British special forces, 70
British troops, *see* Troops
Brize Norton, England, 66–7, 183
Brownies, 154
Bryant, Air Chief Marshal/Wing Commander Simon, 73–4
Buckingham Palace, 191
Bulford, England, 64, 66, 74, 109, 168
Bullets, 5, 14–5, 17, 26, 49, 57, 75, 85, 93, 99, 118, 120–1, 142, 144–5, 185

Cabinet, *see* British government
Cabinet Committee, *see* British government
    meetings, *see* British government
Cadbury factory, 196
Calais, France, 13–4
California, USA, 10, 132, 175
    Call of Duty (computer game), 97, 100, 163
Camberley, England, 24
Cameron, Prime Minister David, 196
Camouflage, 6, 9
    face paint, 9
    nets, 6
Camp Victory, 62, 179
Campaigns, 31, 42, 47, 60, 64, 102–3, 109, 112–3, 117, 122, 140, 142, 149, 162, 174, 180, 182, 188, 190, 195, 199, 201
Camping, 38, 40, 43, 46, 55, 57, 77–9, 81, 185, 190
    holidays, *see* Holidays
Canada/Canadian, 35, 59, 75
    Canadian Prairie, 59
Cannons, 10, 132, 145, 147
    water, 145
Canterbury, Archbishop of, 3, 76, 102, 198
Capewell, Lieutenant General David, 197
Carabinieri, 76
Caribbean, 75
Cartridges (for guns), 5, 15
Catterick, England, 110
Cavalry, 6, 58, 99, 116
CCTV, 139
Celle, Germany, 20, 64
Central Intelligence Agency (CIA), 129
Chain of command, 7, 24, 40
Chancellor of the Exchequer, *see* British government
Channel, *see* English Channel
Channel Coast, *see* English Channel
Charlatans, 44
Chemicals, 37, 84
Chemical warfare, 106
Chemical weapons, *see* Weapons
Chemistry, 37, 92, 125, 130
Chicago, USA, 24
Chicken Street, Kabul, 69, 84

218   War and Peace

Chief of Defence, 104, 196, 211
   Deputy, 196
   Vice, 104
   United Kingdom, 211
Chief of Joint Operations, 197
Chiefs of Police, *see* Police
Chiefs of Staff, United Kingdom, 205–206
China/Chinese, 16, 191, 199–200, 209
Chinook helicopters, *see* Helicopters
   CH-47s, *see* Helicopters
Christians, 111, 187
Christmas, 5, 29, 34, 37, 66, 73–5, 79, 102, 116, 135
   Christmas Eve, 79
CIA, *see* Central Intelligence Agency
Civil Service/Civil servants, 69, 89, 95, 130, 165, 192, 198, 205, 207, 209
   Civil Service Code, 95
Civilian aircraft, *see* Non-military aircraft
Civilians, 15, 44, 53, 58, 86, 95, 151, 154, 169, 188, 209
Civvies, 97
Clapham, London, 4
Clarkson, Jeremy, 159
Clausewitzian, 25, 106, 123
Clear and present danger, 4
Climate change, 59, 191, 207, 209
Clinton, President Bill, 96
Clooney, George, 90
Close protection team, 62–3, 188, 212
Code Red Cluster, 65
CODEL, *see* Congressional Delegation
Colchester, England, 75
Cold War, *see* Wars
College, 24–5, 31, 39, 42, 50, 70, 96, 104, 107, 155, 210
Combat, 2, 23, 25, 40, 44, 62, 78, 81, 83, 87, 99, 101, 141, 152–3, 157, 174, 196, 199
Communications, 40–1, 43, 48, 66, 110, 186
   satellite, 40–1, 43, 48
   secure, 66
Computer science, *see* Science
Comrades, 60, 82, 93, 100, 167, 177, 180, 184
   American, 180
   Kurdish, 177

Congress, *see* United States Congress
Congressional Delegation (CODEL), 117–9
Constipation, 43
Corps counter-stroke, 25
Corruption, 69, 117, 177–8, 186
Counter-attacks, 14
Counterparts, 31, 33, 118, 176, 205
   American, 176
   European, 118
   French, 205
   German, 33, 205
   Iraqi, 176
   Italian, 205
   local, 31
Court martial, 94
Covering force brigade, 12–3
Covid-19, 16, 28
Cranfield, England, 136, 160
Crimean War, *see* Wars
Crimes, 2, 20, 45, 56, 67, 72, 94, 96, 111, 114, 120, 167, 179
   see also War crimes
Croatia/Croatian, 33, 35–6, 38–9, 44–7, 49, 123
Croatian troops, *see* Troops
Crown, The, 213
   see also Royals
Cummings, Andrew, 47
Current operations, 112
   Current operations department (J3), *see* Joint departments
Customs (government department), 130–1
   see also British government
Customs (traditions), 3
Cyber attacks, 132
Cyber war/warfare, 10, 131–2, 199, 205
Cyprus/Cypriot, 57–8, 73, 98, 206, 208

Daily Mail, 106
Dalai Lama, 198
Daleks, 157, 169
Dalmatian Coast, Croatia, 38
Dambusters, 23
Danger/dangerous, 4, 11, 25, 44, 58, 62–3, 87, 100–102, 108, 132, 150, 161, 168, 173
Danish battle group, 110

Dari, 69, 73
Dark Ages, 82
Dartmouth, England, 160
Darwin, Charles, 19
D-Day, 105
de Gaulle, President Charles, 171
Defence administration, 190
Defence Board, 193
Defence Information Services, 206
Defence Intelligence Service, 206
Defence Medical Services, 206
Deliveroo, 166
Deputy Chief of Defence, *see* Chief of Defence
Deutsche Marks, 19–20
DFC, *see* Distinguished Flying Cross
Dhi Qar, Iraq, 109–110
Diarrhoea, 110
Diego Garcia, 206, 208
Digital Age, 3, 26, 93, 97, 124, 132–3, 139–40, 209
Dinaric Alps, Bosnia and Herzegovina, 56
Diplomats, 30, 55, 71, 111, 188
Disease, 37, 43, 91, 137, 211
Distinguished Flying Cross (DFC), 162
Divulje barracks, 46
DIY, 46
DNA, 136–40
Doctor Who (television series), 157
Dorset, England, 43
Double Medium Scale Enduring, 153
Downing Street (No. 10), *see* British government
Dress regulations, 58
Drones, 134, 200, 202
Drug dealers, 144
Drug mules, 207
Dubai, 58, 69, 186
Dutch, *see* Netherlands, The
Dutch battle group, 110
Dutch marines, 110

Earth (planet), 3, 68, 70, 125–6
East Belfast, *see* Belfast
East Germany/East German, *see* Germany
East London, *see* London
Eastern Bosnia, *see* Bosnia and Herzegovina

Eastern Europe/Eastern European, *see* Europe/European
Economy, 7–8, 69, 87, 116, 148, 153, 177
Education, 3, 23, 26, 30, 62, 86, 148, 155, 170
Eisenhower, President Dwight D., 171
Elizabeth II, 4–5, 18, 24, 50, 53–4, 59, 61, 66, 71, 80, 88, 90, 97–8, 100, 107–108, 115, 129, 144, 170, 190–2, 202, 207
Enemy Number One, 23
Engineering, 54, 114, 125, 130, 184, 191–2
  British, 54
Engineers, 54, 79, 83, 99, 110, 113, 141
England/English, 6, 14, 37, 40, 44–5, 52, 64–6, 70, 73, 78, 82, 92, 110, 120, 144, 148, 151, 153, 173, 211
English breakfast, 6
English Channel, 3, 10
  coast, 10
English coast, 151
English District, 14
English language, 44
Environmental health, *see* Health
Epping Forest, England, 208
Erbil, Iraq, 177
Erich (Totenkopf Panzer Division), 96
Estonia/Estonian, 105
Eternal Truth One, 33–4
Eternal Truth Two, 34
Ethics, 3, 134
Eton College, 138
Europe/European, 4, 6, 10–14, 21, 24–5, 30–52, 54–6, 59, 61, 64–6, 70, 72–3, 75–8, 82, 86, 92, 102, 105, 107, 110, 115–6, 118, 120, 123, 128, 144, 156, 159, 171, 173–4, 178, 182, 185, 197, 201–203, 205
  Eastern Europe/Eastern European, 30–52, 54–6, 59, 61, 76, 102, 123, 178, 182
  Western Europe/Western European, 6, 10, 12–4, 30, 37, 40, 44–5, 52, 64–6, 70, 73, 75–6, 78, 82, 92, 105, 110, 120, 144, 148, 151, 153, 171, 173, 197, 205, 211
European counterparts, *see* Counterparts
European empires, 4
Evacuations, 76, 78

Exotic holidays, *see* Holidays
Expeditions, 43, 79, 185
Explosives, 6–7, 13, 18, 62, 78, 119, 129, 133, 200

FA Cup, 145
   final, 145
Falkland Islands/Falklands/Falkland Islanders, 23, 35, 67, 206, 208
Falls Road facelift, 58
Farewell, dinners/drinks, 64, 184
Fear of Missing Out (FOMO), 202
Field artillery, *see* Artillery
   computing equipment, 125
Finland/Finnish, 77, 128
Finnish Civil-Military Integration Team, 77
Fire Brigades Union, 109
First Tactical Echelon, 14
First World War, *see* Wars
Flashmans, 3
Flu, 46
FOMO, *see* Fear of Missing Out
Force Reintegration Cell (FRIC), 184, 186–7, 189
Fort Bragg, 174
Four-by-fours, 45
France/French, 12–4, 30, 75–6, 105, 171, 197, 205
Free World, 10, 171
French counterparts, *see* Counterparts
French presidents, *see* de Gaulle, Charles
FRIC, *see* Force Reintegration Cell
Fritz, Frau, 6
Fry, Stephen, 157

G4S, 192
Gaddafi, 199–201
Gates, Bill, 56, 124
GB, *see* Britain
GCHQ, *see* Government Communications Headquarters
General Order Number One, 185
Generalship, 196–213
   see also Senior generalship
Generation Z, 125
Generators, 47, 84, 111, 114, 118, 168, 200

Geneva Conventions, 134
Genocide, 56, 96, 167
German counterparts, *see* Counterparts
Germany/German, 1–16, 19–23, 25, 30, 32–3, 35, 38–40, 50, 61, 64–5, 68, 75–7, 86, 98, 100, 105, 141, 157, 171, 181–3, 205, 212
   East Germany/East German, 7, 14, 19, 21
   Northern Germany, 20
   West Germany/West German, 10–11, 14–5, 19–20, 61, 181
   battle for, 10
Gibraltar, 206, 208
Global Positioning System (GPS), 125, 133
Gloucester, England, 182
Gloucestershire, England, 182
Goebbels, Joseph, 100
Gold Card, 35
Good Friday Agreement, 142
Google, 33, 45, 97, 127, 130, 157
Government, 12, 19, 22, 34, 36, 50–1, 64–6, 68–71, 73, 78, 80, 83–4, 88, 111–2, 116–8, 120, 122, 132, 138–40, 153, 155, 158, 160, 177–8, 181, 186–7, 189–95, 197–8, 201, 204, 211
Government Communications Headquarters (GCHQ), 205
GPS, *see* Global Positioning System
Granville-Chapman, Tim, 104
Great Britain, *see* Britain
Great War, The, *see* First World War
Greece/Greek, 33, 90
Green Zone, 62, 179
   see also Allied zone
Grenades, 5, 25, 63, 85
   hand, 5, 25
   rocket propelled, 85
Ground forces, *see* Troops (ground)
Ground troops, *see* Troops
Guardsman, 9, 99–100, 159
Guides, 154
Gulf, The, 49, 106, 199
Gulf War (First), *see* Wars
Gulf War One, *see* Wars
Gunpowder, 26, 124, 132

Guns, 7, 10, 15, 23, 26, 34, 48, 55, 61, 63, 79, 84–5, 106, 112, 124–9, 135, 144, 151, 161, 167, 201
  30mm, 48
  AK-47s (guns), 85
  artillery, 15, 106, 125–6, 128
  autonomous, 135
  machine/sub-machine, 7, 55, 61, 63, 124, 167
Gurkhas, 100–101

Hamburg, Germany, 20
Hand grenades, *see* Grenades
Hannover, Germany, 4, 9–10, 13
  Hannover Plain, 10
    battle for, 9
Harwich, England, 64–5
Hawker Siddeley 125, 54
HCSC, *see* Higher Command and Staff Course
Headquarters, 33, 38, 40–1, 51–2, 54, 65–6, 74–8, 80–1, 87, 89, 91–4, 97, 100, 103, 105, 112–3, 115, 152–3, 174–6, 181–3, 187–8, 203, 205–206, 212
Health, 23, 84, 87, 114, 122, 135, 148, 179, 207
  environmental, 87
    inspectors, 87
  mental, 207
Health and safety, 84, 87, 114
Heathrow Airport, 1, 183
  Terminal Five, 183
Heavily armoured equipment, 3
Heinz (Totenkopf Panzer Division), 96
Helicopters, 10, 46, 62, 88, 148, 151–2, 163, 179, 189, 202, 205
  attack, 10
  Blackhawks, 62
  Chinooks, 151
    CH-47s, 151
  Sea Kings, 46
Helmand, Afghanistan, 60, 152–3
Hercules, 24
Herzegovina/Bosnian, *see* Bosnia and Herzegovina/Bosnian
High frequency radios, *see* Radios
Higher Command and Staff Course (HCSC), 64, 104–105, 107

Highway Code, 133
Hitler, Adolf, 67, 96, 109
HM Revenue and Customs (HMRC), *see* British government
HMRC, *see* British government
HO, *see* British government
Hohne, Germany, 2–3, 6, 8, 19, 64–5
Holidays, 17, 33–4, 38, 64, 75, 81, 90, 96–7, 177
  camping, 81
  exotic, 97
Holland, *see* Netherlands, The
Hollywood, USA, 27, 164
Home Office (HO), *see* British government
Hospital admissions, 91, 140
Hospitality, 204
Hospitals, 91, 140, 200
Hotel Split, *see* Croatia
House of Commons, 117
  Armed Forces Committee, 117
Howitzer, 65
  AS-90 (155mm), 65
  self-propelled, 65
HQ, *see* Headquarters
HR department (J1), *see* Joint departments
HS-125 (aircraft), 54–5, 73
Human resources (HR) department (J1), *see* Joint departments
Humanitarian agencies, 115
Humanitarian aid/support, 34–5, 39, 49–52
Hussein, Saddam, 106–107, 110–11, 114, 116, 118, 176–7, 179
Hypersonic missiles, *see* Missiles
Hypersonics, 133, 209

IGB, *see* Inner German Border
Immigration, 131
Immunity, 9, 31, 72
India/Indian, 2, 23, 145, 208
Indian Ocean, 208
Indian police, *see* Police
Infantry, 7, 11–2, 22, 47–8, 50, 58, 77, 122, 141, 150, 163, 192, 203
Information age, 210
Information system, 131
Information Technology (IT), 48, 130–1

Injuries, 8, 34, 102, 128, 147, 161, 169
Inner German Border (IGB), 4–5, 10–11, 19, 21
Intelligence, 40, 77, 112–3, 121, 131, 187, 206
   intelligence department (J2), *see* Joint departments
International community, 29, 31, 69, 84, 86, 186
International forces, 31, 64, 68, 79, 122
International military, 68, 72, 83, 85–6, 122, 188
International Security Assistance Force (ISAF), 74–5, 77, 79, 81–2, 86–8, 183, 185, 187–8
   Headquarters, 75, 77, 183, 187–8
   XI, 88
Internet, 58, 104, 127, 133–4, 139
Interpreters, 44, 78–9, 128, 211
Invasion, 2, 5, 21, 23, 100, 105, 107–108, 111, 119, 158, 173
   military, 105
   Soviet, 100
   threat of, 2, 21
IRA, *see* Irish Republican Army
Iraq/Iraqi, 18, 22, 31, 54–5, 61–3, 104–122, 145, 148, 153–4, 162, 173, 175–83, 187, 190, 195, 199
   Southern Iraq, 54–5, 107–119, 122, 145, 153, 178
Iraqi army, 107, 119, 175, 177
Iraqi counterparts, *see* Counterparts
Iraqi ground forces, 176
   Command, 176
   Headquarters, 176
Iraqi Kurds, *see* Kurds
Iraqi police, *see* Police
Irish Republican Army (IRA), 182
Irish Sea, 151
ISAF, *see* International Security Assistance Force
   Headquarters, *see* International Security Assistance Force
   XI, *see* International Security Assistance Force
Islam, *see* Muslims
Israel/Israeli, 129
Israeli armed forces, 129

IT, *see* Information Technology
Italian armed forces, 110
   Italian Mechanized Brigade, 110
Italian counterparts, *see* Counterparts
Italian security forces, 82
Italian special forces, 76
Italy/Italian, 30, 33, 48, 76–7, 82–3, 110, 141, 182, 205
   Southern Italy, 83

Japan/Japanese, 118, 184, 189
Japanese Embassy, 189
JCBs, 148
Jedi, 24, 43, 64–5
JFC, *see* Joint Forces Command
Jihadis, 108
Jim (Deputy Chief of Staff), 40
Joint departments, 112
   J1 (HR department), 112
   J2 (intelligence department), 112
   J3 (current operations department), 112
   J4 (logistics department), 112
   J5 (planning department), 112
Joint Forces Command (JFC), 206, 208–211
Joint Operations, 197
Jurisdiction, 72
   Afghan, 72

Kabul, Afghanistan, 56–9, 64–5, 67–75, 77–88, 153, 182–3, 185–6, 188–9
   airport, 67, 78–9
Karzai, President-Designate, 65, 71, 83
Kevlar, 57
King of Iraq, *see* bin Faisal, Ghazi
Kosovo/Kosovan, 145, 178, 182
Kremlin (Russia), 5
Kurdish comrades, *see* Comrades
Kurds/Kurdish, 110, 177–8
   Iraqi, 177–8
Kuwait, 106

Lamb, Major General Graeme, 107, 115–7, 119, 183
Land Rovers, 39, 43, 76, 88, 125–6, 152
   Land Rover Discovery, 88
   Land Rover Freelander, 152
Las Vegas, USA, 90

Last Big Tumble, 2
Latin, 197
Latin America/Latin American, 29, 211
Lawyers, 120–1, 169
    military, 120–1
Leadership, 70, 88, 94, 109, 117, 122, 130, 142, 144, 148–50, 156–172, 175, 185–89, 199, 205, 207, 209
    United States, 109, 199
Legal/legally, 73, 108, 169
    institutions, 169
Libya/Libyan, 199–202
Light artillery, *see* Artillery
Light vehicles, 43
Limousines/limos, 90
Lithuania/Lithuanian, 110
Litvinenko, Alexander, 152
Lloyd Austin, Lieutenant General, *see* Austin, Lieutenant General Lloyd
Local counterparts, *see* Counterparts
Local police, *see* Police
Lockheed Hercules, 38–9, 42, 55–7, 67, 73, 79, 84
    C-130, 38–9, 42, 55–7, 67, 73, 79, 84
Logistics, 40, 43, 74, 79, 112–3, 141, 193, 206
    Logistics department (J4), *see* Joint departments
London, England, 1–2, 40, 50–3, 58, 61, 73, 81, 89–90, 98, 116–7, 119–20, 157, 189–90, 196, 202–204, 208, 212
    City of, 89–90
    East London, 157, 204
    transport network, 204
Long-range rocket artillery, *see* Artillery
Lords (cricket ground), 98
Loya Jirga, 83, 88
Lüneberg Heath, Germany, 33

M3 (motorway), 109
M25 (motorway), 1
MacArthur, Douglas, 118
MacBook, 89
Machine/Sub-machine guns, *see* Guns
Main Defensive Area, 13
Majid, Lieutenant General Ali Ghaidan, 176
Maldives, 17

Malevolence, 121, 137
Mall, The, 190, 192
Manchester United, 173, 211
Marines, 22, 39, 60, 110, 160, 162–4, 181, 188, 197, 203
Marriot, Patrick, 116
Mars (planet), 96
Mars Bars (confectionary), 38, 77
Maths, 1, 130, 190
Maysan, Iraq, 109–110
MC, *see* Military Cross
MCC, 88
McCain, Senator John, 119
McChrystal, General Stan, 183–4, 187, 189
McColl, Major General John, 64–5, 71, 87–8, 107
McDonalds (fast-food restaurant), 19
Medals, 7, 12, 17, 25, 43, 61, 75, 102, 109, 162
Medical evacuation, 76
Medical science, *see* Science
Medical services, 108, 206
Medical supplies, 87
Mediterranean, 38, 57
Melchett, General Sir Anthony Cecil Hogmanay, 157–8
Members of Parliament (MPs), 117
Memsahibs, 8
Mental health, *see* Health
Mention in Dispatches, 162
Mercedes, 33, 186
Metal box factory, 54
MI5, *see* Military Intelligence 5
Microsoft, 128
Middle East, 79, 105
Middle England, 37
Military aircraft, *see* Aircraft
Military Cross (MC), 162
Military equipment, *passim*
Military forces, 33–4, 75, 83, 135, 142
Military history, 7, 10, 14, 158, 161, 171, 199
Military inadequacy, 99
Military intelligence, 205
Military Intelligence 5 (MI5), 205
Military intervention, 35, 105, 109, 111, 173, 196

Military invasion, *see* Invasion
Military lawyers, *see* Lawyers
Military medals, *see* Medals
Military police, 62, 86, 110, 113, 120, 142, 188
    see also Royal Military Police
Military secretary, 157, 182
Military ships, *see* Ships
Military Sports Club, 78–80
Military training, *see* Training
Military uniform, *see* Uniform
Military vehicles, *see* Vehicles
Military weapons, *see* Weapons
Minden, Germany, 32
Mines, 11, 13, 49, 97, 163
Ministers, 30, 70, 73, 79, 150, 186, 191, 197–8, 207
    Minister of Defence, 79, 191
    Prime Minister, 73, 150, 197–8, 207
Ministry of Defence (MoD), *see* British government
Missiles, 10, 55, 57, 106, 132–4, 145, 151, 154, 200, 204, 211
    air defence, 200, 204
    anti-tank missiles, 10
    hypersonic, 133
    Scud, 106
Missions, 9, 33–4, 50, 52, 65, 68, 70, 81, 89, 162–3, 168, 181
Mission Command, 162–3
MNCI/MNC(I), *see* Multi-National Corps Iraq
Mönchengladbach, Germany, 181
MoD, *see* British government
Montgomery, Field Marshal Bernard, 171
Moore, Brigadier Bill, 118
Mortars, 185
Mostar, Bosnia and Herzegovina, 52
Mount Igman, 56
MPs, *see* Members of Parliament
Multi-National Corps Iraq, 173
Multi-National Division (MND), 109–110, 117–8
    South East (MND-SE), 117–8
MND, *see* Multi-National Division
MND-SE, *see* Multi-National Division – South East
Murder, 2, 20, 179

Musk, Elon, 133
Muslims, 36, 47, 49–50, 68–9
    Bosnian, 36, 47, 49

NAAFI, *see* Navy, Army, Air Force Institutes
Napoleon/Napoléon, *see* Bonaparte, Napoleon/Napoléon
Narcotics, 69, 78
    trade, 69, 78
National security, *see* Security
National security agencies, 205
National Security Council (NSC), 198, 206
National Support Elements (NSE), 76–7, 185
Native speakers, 44
NATO, *see* North Atlantic Treaty Organization
Naval Air Squadron, 46
Naval ships, *see* Ships
Navy, 21, 23, 25, 46–7, 97, 104, 133, 156, 160–1, 164, 171, 206, 208–209
Navy, Army, Air Force Institutes (NAAFI), 181–2
Nazis, 156
Nelson, Horatio, 23
Netflix, 30, 124, 157
Netherlands, The/Dutch, 12, 91, 110
New York, USA, 52
New Zealand/New Zealander, 76, 110
Nights Out of Bed (NOOBs), 154
Non-Government Organizations, 36
Non-military aircraft, 39, 79, 151
NOOBs, *see* Nights Out of Bed
North America, 72
North Atlantic, *see* Atlantic
North Atlantic Treaty Organization (NATO), 7, 13, 21, 23, 40, 42, 75, 88, 105, 141, 153, 174, 181–5, 188, 199–201
North Pole, 37
North Yorkshire, England, 110
Northern Alliance, 64, 72
    see also Afghan Northern Alliance
Northern Germany/Northern German, *see* Germany
Northern Ireland/Northern Irish, 22, 26, 32, 58, 102, 122, 141–5, 147–9, 151, 187

Northolt, England, 73–4
Northwood, 74, 78, 206, 211–2
  Headquarters, 74
Norway/Norwegian, 110, 128
NSC, *see* National Security Council
NSE, *see* National Support Elements
Nuclear weapons, *see* Weapons

Obama, President Barack, 180
OBE, *see* Order of the British Empire
Obsessive Compulsive Disorder, 59
OCD, *see* Obsessive Compulsive Disorder
Officers' mess, 7, 19, 62, 98, 179
O-Levels, 136, 190
Olympics, 87, 106, 157, 202–205
  London 2012, 157, 202–205
Omaha Beach, 105
Oman, 57, 67, 73, 84
Operating bases, 47
Operation Certain Death, 164
Operation Secure Something, 176
Opium, 69, 78, 186–7
  trade, 78
Order of the Bath, 102
Order of the British Empire (OBE), 43
Ostend, Belgium, 14
Overseas bases, 206
Oxford, 137
Oxford English Dictionary, 92
Oxford Street, London 84
Oxford University, *see* University of Oxford
Oxfordshire, 137

P45s, 103
Paddington, London, 1
PADS, *see* Position Azimuth and Direction System
Pakistan/Pakistani, 67, 71, 184, 187
Pandemic, 2, 16, 32, 53, 93, 97
Panzers, *see* Tanks
Paratroopers, 60, 75
Paris, France, 171
Parker, General Sir Nick, 203
Parliaments, 47, 72–3, 117, 195, 198, 206
Pashto, 69
Pashtuns, 69
Passats, 9

Patton, George S., 171
Peace, 22, 28–30, 50, 68–9, 86, 106, 116, 122, 129, 142, 149, 184, 187, 200
Pentagon, The, 130
Penthouses, 103
Permanent Joint Headquarters (PJHQ), *see* United Kingdom Permanent Joint Headquarters
Phases:
  Phase One, 10
  Phase Two, 10–11
  Phase Three, 11
  Phase Four, 11–12
  Phase Five, 12–4
    Part One, 12–3
    Part Two, 13–4
  Phase Six, 14
  Phase Six (Alternative), 14–5
Phycologists, 123
Physics, 25, 54, 125, 130
Physiology, 174
Pichai, Mr, 133
Pillage, 20
Pin-table battle, 14
PJHQ, *see* United Kingdom Permanent Joint Headquarters
Planes, *see* Aeroplanes
Planet Start-Up, 89–91, 93–4
Planets, 2, 15, 18, 55, 69, 89, 109, 125, 133–4, 191
Planning, 40, 48, 96, 112–3, 155, 165, 186–7, 196, 202, 204
  Planning department (J5), *see* Joint departments
Poland/Polish, 61, 64
Police, 30, 62, 72, 84–6, 88, 92, 110–11, 113, 116, 119–20, 130, 142–8, 175, 178, 188, 191, 212
  Afghan, 85
  armed, 212
  chiefs of, 30
  German, 86
  Indian, 145
  Iraqi, 119
  local, 72, 86
  Royal Air Force police, 88
  see also Police Service of Northern Ireland and Royal Military Police

Police Service of Northern Ireland, 142, 144
Politicians, 12, 29, 105–106, 119, 130, 192, 201, 205
   Iraqi, 119
Politics, 4, 12–3, 24, 26, 29, 31, 36, 55, 69–70, 85, 105–106, 111–2, 117, 119, 130, 160–1, 168, 178, 186, 191–2, 194–5, 199–201, 203, 205, 210
Polyglots, 107
Porsches, 103
Portugal/Portuguese, 110
Portuguese National Guard, 110
Position Azimuth and Direction System, 126
Post-Cold War, 32, 195
Pot, Pol, 96
Power sharing, 187
PowerPoint, 23, 73, 105, 175–6
PoWs see Prisoners of War
PPE, 210
Practice Survival Area, see Survival
Premier Inn, 98
Premier League, 143, 201
Presidents, see Clinton, de Gaulle, Eisenhower, Karzai, Obama and Putin
Prime Minister, see Ministers
Prime ministers, see Blair and Cameron
Prisoners, 7, 25, 121, 212
Prisoners of War (PoW), 7
Prisons, 121
   staff, 121
Promotion, 95, 141, 166, 170, 207
Protagonists, 29, 35, 51–2, 58, 146, 148
Putin, President Vladimir, 131, 190

Quantum, 22, 96, 209
Queen Elizabeth II, see Elizabeth II
Queen Victoria, see Victoria I
Queen's College, The, see University of Oxford
Queens of England, see Elizabeth I and Victoria I

Rachaels, 158
Radios, 6, 9, 20, 48, 125, 127, 133, 169
   high frequency, 48
   radiogram, 6
   transmission, 9

RAF, see Royal Air Force
RAF Big Book of Rules, 54
RAF Brize Norton, 66–7, 183
RAF Cranfield, 136, 160
RAF Northolt, 73–4
RAF Royal flight jets, see Royal flight jets
Rape, 20
Reading, England, 22
Reconnaissance, 11, 50, 200–201
   aircraft, 200–201
Regent Street, London, 19
Religion, 99
Rheindahlen Camp, 182
Rhine River, 2, 5
Richard, Cliff, 102
RN, see Royal Navy
Roberts, Julia, 96
Robocop, 147
Robots/Robotics, 135, 140, 148, 209
Rocket artillery, see Artillery
Rocket propelled grenades, see Grenades
Rocket scientists, see Scientists
Rockets, 6, 66, 85, 112, 136, 138, 185
RoE, see Rules of Engagement
Romania/Romanian, 110
Romanian mechanized battalion, 110
Route Irish, 62–3
Royal Air Force, 13, 15, 21, 23, 49, 78, 53–5, 57–8, 66–8, 73–4, 79, 88, 104, 151, 154, 160, 183, 206, 208
Royal Air Force police, see Police
Royal College of Defence Studies, 155
Royal Electrical and Mechanical Engineers, see British Army
Royal flight jets, 53
Royal Military Academy Sandhurst, 158–60, 168, 205
Royal Navy, 21, 23, 104, 160, 206
Royal palaces, 159, 190–1
   see also Buckingham Palace and St James's Palace
Royal School of Artillery, 128, 210
Royals, 4–5, 18, 22, 24, 50, 53–4, 59, 61, 66, 71, 80, 88, 90, 97–8, 100, 107–108, 115, 129, 144, 159, 170, 190–2, 202, 207, 213
   see also Crown, The
RPGs, see Grenades
Rules of Engagement (RoE), 11, 50, 120

Rumsfeld, Secretary of Defense Donald, 118
Ruperts, 158
Russia/Russian, 5, 14–6, 20–1, 23–4, 67, 88, 96, 109, 131, 152, 171, 182, 190, 194, 200, 209
Russian army, 5
  tank division, 5
Russian submarines, *see* Submarines
Russian presidents, *see* Putin, Vladimir
Ryanair, 79

Sailors, 22, 60, 160, 162–4, 203
Saint James's Palace, *see* St James Palace
Saint Paul's Cathedral, *see* St Paul's Cathedral
Salaries, 12, 51, 71
Salisbury, England, 39, 64, 108, 125, 152
  Salisbury Plain, 64, 108, 125
Saloth (Pol Pot), 96
Saluting game, 9
Sandhurst, England, 158–60, 168, 205
Sarajevo, Bosnia and Herzegovina, 35, 39, 49–50, 55–6
Satellite communications, *see* Communications
Saville Row, London, 158
Schmidt, Herr, 9
Schützenfest (German beer festival), 77
Science, 26, 37, 62, 64, 79, 91, 127, 136–7, 190
  computer, 127
  medical, 91
Scientists, 136–8
  rocket, 136, 138
Scotland/Scottish, 28, 107–108, 110, 114, 151
  battalion, 107
  mountains, 114
Scouts, 154
Screen Force, 11
  battle, 11
Scud missiles, *see* Missiles
Sea King helicopters, *see* Helicopters
Second Operational Echelon, 14
Second Tactical Echelon, 14
Second World War, *see* Wars
Secret Intelligence Service (SIS), 205

Secure communications, *see* Communications
Security, 1, 3, 50, 64–5, 67–8, 74, 81–9, 92, 108, 110, 116–8, 122, 129, 140, 143, 152–3, 175, 178, 184, 188, 191, 193, 195, 197–8, 202–203, 205, 208–209
Seeb, Oman, 73
Self-defence, 50–1, 72, 144
Senior generalship, 196–213
  see also Generalship
September, 11 (9/11), 64
Serb air force, 48
Serb aircraft, 36
Serbo-Croat (language), 44
Service families' accommodation, *see* Accommodation
Sexually transmitted disease, 91
Shells/shelling, 5, 12, 15, 35, 49, 78, 88, 103, 113, 125, 128, 154, 185, 205
Shia Arabs, *see* Arabs
Shipcraft, *see* Ships
Ships, 38, 40, 43, 134, 209
Silicon Valley, 130, 133
Singapore, 208
SIS, *see* Secret Intelligence Service
Situation reports, 42
Sky News, 48
Slovenia/Slovenian, 35
Small machine gun range, 55
Small missile range, 55
Smith, Gunner, 59
Snipers, 9, 35, 64, 68, 70
SOFA, *see* Status of Forces Agreement
Soldiers, *passim*
  British soldiers, *see* British soldiers
Solomon, 95
South Armagh, *see* Armagh
Southern Iraq, *see* Iraq
Southern Italy, *see* Italy
Soviet advance, 13–4
Soviet air force, 12
Soviet aircraft, 23
Soviet invasion, *see* Invasion
Soviet Union/Soviets, 4–6, 9–14, 19, 21–3, 25, 32, 62, 68, 100, 126–8, 158, 176
Spartans, 24, 154
Special forces, 7, 70, 76, 107, 129, 184, 199, 206

Spetsnaz cheese, 7, 9
Split, Croatia, 36, 38–9, 43, 45–6, 49
　airport, 39
　docks, 49
　Hotel Split, 45–6
Spies/Spying, 44, 131, 205
St Helena, 23
St James's Palace, 190
St James's Park, 190
St Paul's Cathedral, 19
Staff College, *see* Army Staff College
Stalingrad, 11
　battle for, 11
Stanekzai, Mohammed Masoom, 186, 189
Status of Forces Agreement (SOFA), 72–3
Stealth aircraft, 133
Stealth technology, 133
Stewart, Lieutenant Colonel Bob, 47
Stone Age, 24
Stop the Killer Robots campaign, 140
Strategic Command, 206
Subaltern, 4, 8
Sub-machine guns, *see* Guns
Submariners, 60
Submarines, 10, 23, 60
　Russian, 23
Suicide bombers, 22, 78
Sunni Arabs, *see* Arabs
Surprise, 13, 15, 17–31, 42, 62, 64, 102–103, 137, 140, 146, 152, 177–8
Surveillance, 138–9, 148, 199
Survival, 6, 10–11, 36, 89, 134, 152, 161, 198
　Practice Survival Area, 6
Swindon, England, 54, 104, 106
Syria/Syrian, 10, 26, 54

T-72 tanks, *see* Tanks
Taliban/Talibs, 56, 60, 64–5, 67, 69–72, 74, 183–4, 186–8
Tanks, 3, 5–6, 9–15, 37, 48–9, 61, 68, 75, 85, 94, 96, 105–106, 108, 149, 152, 168, 194, 200–201
　Panzers, 9, 61, 96
　T-72s, 5–6
Taxpayers, 13, 18, 23, 39, 45, 51, 81, 85, 104, 131, 135, 164, 176–7, 184, 206
Technology, 1, 15, 25–6, 41, 48, 56, 123–140, 192

Territorial Army, *see* British Army
Terrorism/terrorists, 22, 116, 119, 134–5, 138, 198, 202
Tesco (supermarket), 104
Theft, 44, 184
Third Reich, 32
Third Shock Army, 4, 11, 13
Third World War, 25
Thomas the Tank Engine, 75
Thunberg, Greta, 190
Time (magazine), 74
Tinder, 12
Tito, 32
Totenkopf Panzer Division, 96
Tower of Babel, 112
Toyota Land Cruisers, 62
Toyota, Mr, 63, 179
Trabants, 19–20
Trafalgar, Battle of, 23
Training, 2, 12, 15, 21, 23, 29–30, 33, 87, 95, 97, 102, 107, 109, 128, 152, 154, 158, 161, 164, 166, 168, 170, 182, 184, 191, 201, 204–206
Transmissions, 9, 42, 47
Transport, 39, 49, 55, 58, 65, 78–9, 178, 204
Travel, 5, 19, 49, 53–63, 67, 102, 118, 139, 186, 204, 207
Treasury, *see* British government
Troops, 11, 14, 20, 31, 46, 72–5, 83, 99, 105, 176, 185, 200
　American, 176
　British, 20
　Croatian, 46
　ground, 176
Troubles, The, 22, 147–9
True believers, 58
Tuzla, *see* Bosnia and Herzegovina, 35–6
Turkey/Turkish, 66, 68, 81, 87–8
Twentieth century, 3, 7, 33
Twenty-first century, 3, 28
Twickenham (rugby stadium), 98
Twitter, 3
Typhoons jets, 151–2

UK, *see* United Kingdom
UKLO, *see* United Kingdom Liaison Officers
Ukraine/Ukrainian, 80, 158

Index

UN, *see* United Nations
   Headquarters, *see* United Nations
UNHCR, *see* United Nations High Commissioner for Refugees
Uniform, 18, 39, 44, 47, 52, 57–8, 91, 98, 102, 115, 130, 133
United Kingdom, 4, 12, 15, 21–3, 34–5, 38, 40–4, 48, 50, 63–5, 70–5, 78–9, 81, 87, 90, 98, 102, 104–105, 107, 109, 112, 117–8, 120, 125, 130–1, 138, 141, 152–3, 155–6, 173, 177, 181–3, 185, 189, 193, 195–6, 198, 203–206, 208, 211
United Kingdom armed forces, *see* British armed forces
United Kingdom, Chief of Defence, *see* Chief of Defence
United Kingdom government, *see* British government
United Kingdom Land Command, 152
United Kingdom Liaison Officers (UKLO), 48
United Kingdom military, 35, 42, 79, 102, 105, 152, 196, 205
United Kingdom national security, 152, 198, 205
United Kingdom Permanent Joint Headquarters (PJHQ), 152, 206
United Kingdom special forces, *see* Special forces
United Nations, 33, 35–6, 49–52, 55, 134, 186, 200
   Headquarters, 52
   High Commissioner for Refugees (UNHCR), 35–6, 49
United States, *see* United States of America
United States Air Force, 68
United States Army, 174, 180–1
   Airborne Corps, 174, 180
      18 (XVIII) Airborne Corps, 174, 180
      Headquarters, 174
   Marine Corps, 181
United States Congress, 117
United States Embassy, *see* American Embassy
United States House of Representatives, 117
United States leadership, *see* Leadership
United States liaison officers, 83
United States of America, 10, 18, 30, 35, 37, 55, 62, 64–5, 67–8, 70–2, 81, 83–5, 90, 105, 107, 110–11, 117–9, 130, 132–4, 141, 161, 173–7, 179–81, 183–5, 187–8, 199–201, 205, 212
United States presidents, *see* Clinton, Eisenhower and Obama
United States Secretary of Defense, *see* Rumsfeld, Donald
United States Senate, 117
United States special forces, 70
Universal Defence and Security Solutions Ltd, 89
University of Oxford, 137, 210
   Queen's College, The, 210
Urchfont, England, 125
US, *see* United States of America
USA, *see* United States of America

Vauxhall Cavalier, 99, 101
VC, *see* Victoria Cross
VD, 91
Vehicles, 3, 5–7, 9, 11, 19, 32, 40, 43, 45, 48–50, 61–3, 79, 88, 106, 125, 133, 179, 188
Veterans, 58, 180
Viagra, 131
Vice Chief of Defence, *see* Chief of Defence
Victims, 34, 36, 51, 95, 100
Victoria Cross (VC), 17
Victoria I, 207
Victorian Era, 8, 22
Victory parades, 97, 106
Victory Services Club, 1
Vietcong, 161
Vietnam/Vietnamese, 35, 161
Violence, 3, 25, 33–4, 43, 53, 56, 117–8, 122–3, 135, 144, 148–9, 198, 202
Vitez, Bosnia and Herzegovina 43, 49
Volkswagen, 86

Wages, *see* Salaries
Waitrose (supermarket), 139, 168
Wales/Welsh, 108, 129
Wall, Brigadier Peter, 73
War/Warfare, *passim*

War crimes, 67, 94
  see also Crimes
Warfare in the Information Age (WITIA), 210
Warlords, 29, 87
Wars, 1–16, 18–20, 22, 24, 31–2, 34–5, 48–9, 54–7, 60–1, 63–88, 91, 102–22, 133, 141, 145, 148, 152–4, 162–3, 168, 171, 173, 175–84, 186–91, 195–9, 208, 212
  Afghanistan, 22, 31, 56–7, 60–1, 64–88, 103, 106–109, 111, 148, 152–4, 162–3, 178, 182–4, 186–91, 195–9, 212
  Cold War, 1–16, 19, 24, 32, 48, 61, 102, 105, 168, 181, 195, 208
  Crimean War, 80
  First World War, 91, 141, 162
  Gulf War (First), 49
  Iraq, 18, 22, 31, 54–5, 63, 104–22, 145, 148, 153–4, 162, 173, 175–83, 187, 190, 195, 199
  Second World War, 2, 6, 20, 34–5, 74, 80, 133, 171, 182
Washington DC, USA, 117
Water cannons, see Cannons
Waterloo, Belgium, 11, 53, 60–2, 105, 162
  Battle of, 11, 105, 162
Weapons, 10, 12, 14–5, 19, 23, 41, 57, 63, 76, 87, 106, 128, 131, 133–4, 140, 170, 184
  autonomous, 134–5
  chemical, 106
  of mass destruction, 140
  nuclear, 10, 12, 14–5, 19, 23, 76, 128, 133
Weather, 26, 56, 65, 76, 82, 107, 125, 151, 163
Wegberg, Germany, 182
Wehrmacht (armed forces of the Third Reich), 2
Wembley (football stadium), 98
West Germany/West German, see Germany

West, The/ Western World, The, 2, 10, 19–22, 32, 112, 158
West Wing (television series), 30
Western Europe/Western European, see Europe/European
Westminster, London, 117
WhatsApp, 97
White House, 188
Whitehall, *see* British government
Wikipedia, 105, 127
Wilton, England, 39, 42, 152
Wiltshire, England, 104
Wimbledon (tennis courts), 98
Wired (magazine), 59
WITIA, *see* Warfare in the Information Age
Work/Workers, 4–5, 7, 10, 24, 30, 33, 35–6, 40, 42, 45–6, 48–50, 59–61, 64, 75–7, 80–1, 83–4, 86, 88–103, 108–109, 113–5, 118, 124, 129–31, 133, 136, 140, 147, 150–1, 153–4, 159, 161, 164–5, 168, 174, 176, 178, 181, 183, 186, 190, 192, 194, 196–7, 204, 212
World Headquarters, 89, 91–3, 97, 103
World leaders, 69
  see also Blair, Cameron, Clinton, de Gaulle, Eisenhower, Karzai, Obama and Putin
World War II, *see* Wars
World War III, *see* Wars
Wotsits (crisps), 36
Wright brothers, 124

Yorkshire, 2, 24, 110, 197
Yugoslav army, 46
Yugoslavia, 32–3, 37, 44

Zagreb, Croatia, 55
Zeppelins, 58
Zoom (online website), 19, 97
Zulu, 17
Zulu (film), 17

Dear Reader,

We hope you have enjoyed this book, but why not share your views on social media? You can also follow our pages to see more about our other products: facebook.com/penandswordbooks or follow us on Twitter @penswordbooks

You can also view our products at www.pen-and-sword.co.uk (UK and ROW) or www.penandswordbooks.com (North America).

To keep up to date with our latest releases and online catalogues, please sign up to our newsletter at: www.pen-and-sword.co.uk/newsletter

If you would like a printed catalogue with our latest books, then please email: enquiries@pen-and-sword.co.uk or telephone: 01226 734555 (UK and ROW) or email: uspen-and-sword@casematepublishers.com or telephone: (610) 853-9131 (North America).

We respect your privacy and we will only use personal information to send you information about our products.

Thank you!